THE COMPLETE WOOD PELLET BARBEQUE COOKBOOK

THE ULTIMATE GUIDE & RECIPE BOOK FOR WOOD PELLET GRILLS

BOB DEVON

SQUAREONE
PUBLISHERS

Cover Designer: Jeannie Tudor
Typesetter: Gary A. Rosenberg
Editor: Joanne Abrams

Square One Publishers
115 Herricks Road • Garden City Park, NY 11040
(866) 900-BOOK • (516) 535-2010 • www.squareonepublishers.com

Library of Congress Cataloging-in-Publication Data

Devon, Bob.
  The complete wood pellet barbeque cookbook : the ultimate guide and recipe
book for wood pellet grills / Bob Devon.
     pages cm
  Includes index.
  ISBN 978-0-7570-0337-0 (pbk.)
  1. Barbecuing. I. Title.
  TX840.B3D48 2012
  641.7'6--dc23
                                        2011050430

Printed in the United States of America

10   9   8   7

Contents

Acknowledgments

For my wife, Cheryl, and me, wood pellet grilling is a passion and a joy. We love working together to produce delicious foods and serve them to friends and family. But when we had the idea of creating a book of all our pellet grill recipes, we knew that we couldn't do it alone. In the next few pages, I will endeavor to thank just some of the people who helped us along the way.

Once we made the decision to put our recipes into book form, we realized the need to "test" the recipes not just at our dinner table, but wherever barbeque-loving folks gather. For this reason, we solicited the support of the organizations and people listed below to conduct what we referred to as "the acid test." Based on their reactions, we adjusted ingredients and techniques as needed. The following businesses, their staffs, and their clientele have been especially helpful in providing feedback and support:

Pellet Grill Outlet Management and Staff, West Linn, Oregon.
We owe a tremendous amount of thanks to Rich Lightowler and Anna Maria Wyllie for their continuous encouragement, "critical reviews," and unwavering support. An extra special thank-you goes to the late John Lightowler and to Gloria Lightowler, who kept us focused, evaluated our cooking techniques, and willingly shared their own extensive experience in pellet grilling. www.pellet grilloutlet.com

Falkner Winery and Pinnacle Restaurant of Temecula, California.
A tremendous amount of gratitude goes out to Ray and Loretta Falkner, Tricket Heald and the talented staff of the Falkner Winery Tasting Room, winemakers Steve Hagata and George Myers, and Pinnacle Restaurant chefs Gianni Ciciliot and Jason Volkov. These wonderful people made themselves available any time we needed advice, and especially when food samples were involved. They also brought a variety of wines under many different labels to try with our "taste test" offerings. No one left unhappy with either the food or the wine. www.falknerwinery.com

Joannie's Cantina, Murrieta, California
We owe a huge thank-you to Joannie's owner Annie Borel and "Nurse Karen" for allowing us to bring in pellet grill samples for the Monday Night Football patrons. We also want to

thank all of the patrons—especially Wayne, Walt, Byron, Luann, Suzie, Vic, Wendell, Maria, Maxine, and Jeff— for their comments, praise, and criticisms. The only shortage we had here was providing enough food. By the way, the reviews were all positive.

Once our dishes had been tasted, tested, and "tweaked," Cheryl and I set about finding a way to make our recipes available to everyone with a wood pellet grill. In this regard, we were tremendously lucky to find Lisa Messinger. An author of seven food books, a long-time newspaper food editor, and the winner of many writing awards, Lisa offered us encouragement and guided us in putting the finishing touches on our manuscript before sending it out to meet its fate in the world of publishing. Most important, she introduced us to Rudy Shur, president of Square One Publishers in New York. Cheryl and I are grateful to Lisa, Rudy, and editor Joanne Abrams for their help, praise, and practical assistance in turning a towering pile of recipes into a finished book. To them—and to everyone else who helped us perfect our recipes and make them accessible to our readers—we offer our deepest thanks.

Introduction

A number of years ago, my wife Cheryl and I discovered wood pellet grilling, a new way of cooking outdoors that goes beyond charcoal grills, gas grills, and smokers. We had created many enjoyable meals on our earlier grills, but learned that this new cooker offers not only an astonishing array of gourmet options but also a healthier way of preparing food. Because the juices from the meat don't fall onto hot coals or heated surfaces when using a wood pellet grill, our foods aren't exposed to the potentially harmful substances that form when food is cooked on most other grills. So this cooker pleases not just our taste buds but also our desire for more wholesome food.

Although the health benefits of wood pellet cooking are very real, what has intrigued us most of all is that the wood pellet grill can function as a smoker, a grill, a barbeque, and a convection oven. Since this device is so versatile—and can be fueled by a variety of wood pellets, each of which imparts distinct flavors and aromas—the backyard chef can cook the exact same ingredients in different ways and enjoy deliciously different results. Adjust the temperature (and, therefore, the cooking method), and you'll have a dish that is subtly different. Use another type of pellet—hickory instead of apple, for instance—and you will again transform the dish. Of course, there is also a tremendous range of flavors and aromas that can be introduced by adding rubs, seasoning blends, marinades, and barbeque sauces. The possibilities are truly endless. And because the pellet grill is capable of so many different types of cooking, you can prepare foods that you never dreamed of making outside the confines of your kitchen. My wife and I have been amazed to find that nearly everything we make in our kitchen oven and stovetop—as well as many foods that we wouldn't attempt to prepare in a conventional oven—can be cooked easily (and better) on our grill.

When we began using the wood pellet grill, we didn't realize that this wonderful piece of equipment would become our favorite way to prepare foods, and that over the years, we would develop dozens of pellet grill recipes. The cookbook you are holding in your hands is the result of our "love affair" with wood pellet cooking. It was designed as a comprehensive guide to using this outdoor cooker to create delicious foods, from burgers, steaks, and poultry to savory vegetables and sweet desserts.

Because this type of grill may be new to you, Chapter 1 presents all the basics of wood pellet cooking. In this chapter, you'll learn how the grill works and how you can use and maintain it for best results. You will also learn about the different types of cooking made possible by the grill, and you'll find a guide to the many varieties of wood pellets that are available to fuel your cooker and add flavor and aroma to your food. A handy table tells you how to use the internal temperature of meat to gauge doneness so that meats, poultry, and seafood are always cooked to perfection.

Once you're familiar with the basics, you'll want to start cooking. Chapter 2 begins this recipe collection by offering tried-and-true barbeque rubs, seasoning blends, marinades, and sauces. In the chapters that follow, you'll find tantalizing recipes for beef; burgers, hot dogs, and sausages; pork; chicken; turkey; seafood; vegetables; breads, pizzas, and grilled sandwiches; and even desserts—including cakes and cookies. All in all, there are over one hundred and thirty recipes, each of which has been carefully developed, tested, and re-tested so that it works superbly on your wood pellet grill.

Wood pellet cooking fits beautifully into our busy schedules. We use our grill practically every day. However, in flipping through the recipes, you will notice that in some cases, meats should be left to absorb a marinade or seasoning blend for several hours, and that some cuts, like briskets and ribs, require longer cooking times so that the meat has a chance to absorb the aromatic smoke and become tender and flavorful. In other words, some dishes take longer to prepare than others. For that reason, every recipe begins by providing the times required for marinating or seasoning and cooking. This will help you choose the best recipe not only for your tastes, but also for your day. I think you'll find that although some recipes require long cooking times, it is the grill that does most of the work. Once you place the meat on the grate to smoke or to cook "low and slow," the grill will prepare your food to perfection while you tend to other matters. Because the wood pellet grill cooks through *indirect heat,* you don't even have to turn the food over to ensure even cooking. When a recipe directs you to turn the food, it is usually done to create appealing grill marks or to enable you to baste both sides of the meat.

In some cases, you'll find that a recipe is accompanied by Quick Grilling instructions that guide you in cooking the food more quickly by increasing the level of heat. Although it is not always possible to speed cooking time, in some cases, you can shave off minutes or even hours and still enjoy a delicious dish. (For more information on Quick Grilling times, see page 12.)

Besides listing the times required for marination and cooking, each recipe also clearly states the wood pellets that I have found to best complement that dish. Just keep in mind that although this may be *my* favorite choice, you may prefer to use another wood pellet when preparing that dish, and you may even want to blend several different woods. That's one of the beauties of wood pellet cooking: It gives you so many opportunities to be creative and to tailor each dish according to your personal preferences.

So fire up the grill and get ready to enjoy a new and unique culinary experience. A world of delicious outdoor cooking awaits you just a few pages away.

1.
The Basics of Wood Pellet Grill Cooking

Your wood pellet grill will enable you to produce mouth-watering dishes of all types, from steaks and burgers to poultry and seafood—even breads, pizzas, and cakes. But to get the very best results, it's important to learn how the grill works and how it is different from traditional charcoal and gas barbeques. That's why I urge you to take the time to read this chapter and to also familiarize yourself with the owner's manual that came with your grill. Once you get the hang of cooking with this wonderful device, you are sure to find that every meal is a new "best" and that "same old" is a thing of the past. Because of the amazing versatility of the wood pellet grill, a single food can be prepared in a variety of ways—using different cooking techniques and different aromatic hardwood pellets—with deliciously different results.

This chapter begins by explaining what wood pellet grilling is and why it is so unique. You'll learn how to use your grill and how to maintain it so that it will continue to serve you throughout the years, producing one delicious meal after another. I then briefly explain the different types of cooking that your wood pellet grill can handle to perfection, including smoking, barbequing, grilling, roasting, braising, and baking. You'll learn about some of the different types of wood pellets that are available to fuel your grill and flavor your food, and finally, you'll discover how to determine when every food you prepare is done to perfection.

HOW DOES A PELLET GRILL WORK?

Cooking with wood pellets is not new, but if this is your first wood pellet grill, you may be wondering how this cooker works and why it produces such superior results. To understand this, it's helpful to first take a look at conventional grills.

Conventional barbeques typically make use of *direct* heat that's produced by burning charcoal or gas directly beneath the food and cooking it from the bottom up. Owners of gas and charcoal grills sometimes attempt to imitate an indirect method of cooking by moving the heat source over to one side of the grill and the food to the opposite side, where the heat is more gentle. Nevertheless, there are inherent hot spots in these grills, and this tends to make cooking uneven and fairly difficult to control.

Like a charcoal or gas grill, your pellet grill has a heat source—in this case, wood pellets, which are burned in a fire pot that's located in the center of the grill. But that's pretty much where the similarity between pellet grills and other outdoor cookers ends. When you start your wood pellet grill, the electrically charged heater rod becomes red hot for only a few minutes, just long enough to ignite the pellets. The grill then turns the rod off, leaving the pellets smoldering. An electronic circuit and auger feed the pellets into the fire box at a rate that is determined by the selected temperature. This circuit constantly compares the desired temperature to the actual temperature of the cooking chamber, and modifies the rate at which the pellets are fed into the box accordingly. If the temperature is too low, the pellets are fed into the box at a faster rate; if it is too high, the pellets are fed more slowly. At the same time, a fan located under the pellet reservoir circulates the air inside the cooking chamber, which is above the fire box. Just like the fan in a convection oven, this creates an even temperature throughout the grill, preventing hot spots from forming. In fact, the temperature is so consistent that you don't have to turn your food to ensure even cooking. When the recipes in this book direct you to flip meat or vegetables over, it is done only to create appealing grill marks on the surface or to make it possible to baste the second side.

But wood pellet grills are far more than outdoor convection ovens. By selecting the desired temperature, which can range from very low and "Smoke" to well over 475°F, you will be able to smoke a variety of foods; grill hot dogs, steaks, vegetables, and other fast-cooking dishes; barbeque briskets and other large cuts of meat; make wood-fired pizzas; and even bake cakes, breads, and cookies. This makes the wood pellet grills far more versatile and exciting than your standard charcoal or gas grill.

Wood pellet grills also have another distinct advantage over conventional grills. As meats cook on a charcoal or gas grill, fats and juices drip onto the heat source, causing carcinogens (cancer-causing substances) to form. When the juices evaporate, carcinogen-laden smoke rises, and the harmful substances are deposited on your food. When meat is cooked on a wood pellet grill, however, the story is very different. In this case, the juices and fats drip into a tray that directs them away from the heat source so that carcinogens don't form on your food.

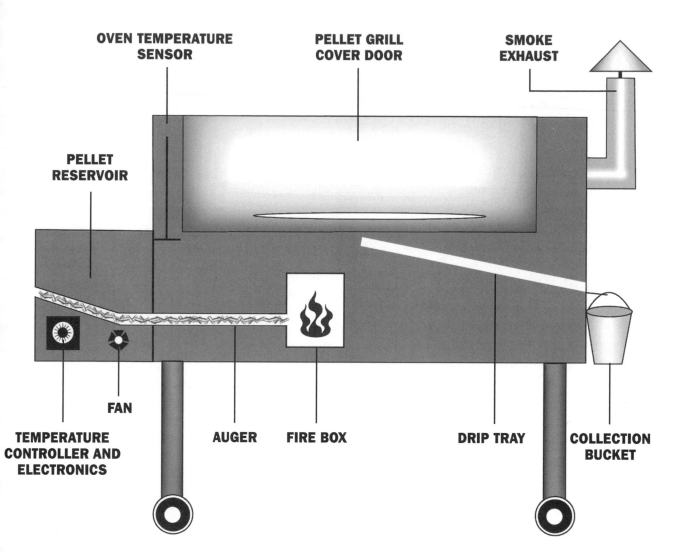

OVEN TEMPERATURE SENSOR

PELLET GRILL COVER DOOR

SMOKE EXHAUST

PELLET RESERVOIR

FAN

TEMPERATURE CONTROLLER AND ELECTRONICS

AUGER

FIRE BOX

DRIP TRAY

COLLECTION BUCKET

The Wood Pellet Grill. Although every wood pellet grill has a slightly different design, all of these grills have certain key components in common. If you look at the diagram above, you'll see that the wood pellets are loaded into a *pellet reservoir.* From there, an *auger*—which is a rotating screw-type blade—conveys the pellets to the *fire box,* which is located under the cooking chamber. When more heat is desired, the auger delivers the pellets at a faster rate. When the temperature is too high, the auger feeds the pellets to the box more slowly. At the same time, the *fan* found under the pellet reservoir circulates the heated air through the cooking chamber so that an even temperature is maintained throughout the grill. Any fat that drips from the meat falls into the *drip tray,* which leads to a container for disposal. The smoke is vented through a *smoke exhaust.* The *grill door* must be kept closed during cooking so that the proper level of heat can be maintained at all times.

Wood Pellet Grill Safety Tips

Wood pellet grills were designed with safety in mind. Nevertheless, whenever you are dealing with hot surfaces and any type of food, it is wise to take certain commonsense precautions, both to prevent burns and to avoid contaminating your meal. The following tips will help ensure that your grilling experiences are as safe and trouble-free as they are rewarding.

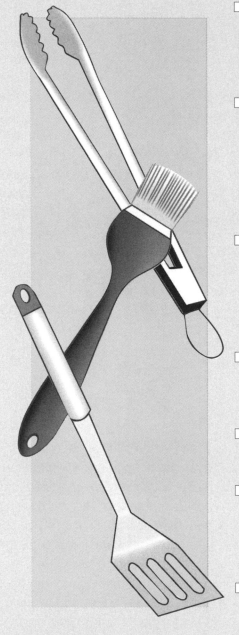

☐ If you want to prevent foods from sticking to the grill, brush, rub, or spray cooking oil on the grate *before* you start the grill up. *Never* spray the grill while there is a fire in the pot as this can cause a flare-up.

☐ Invest in a pair of long-handled tongs for turning meats and long-handled spatulas to turn burgers and fish. The longer handles will keep you a safe distance from the heat source, preventing possible burns. Don't use forks for turning, as they will pierce the meat and cause flavorful juices to run off.

☐ To prevent cross-contamination, use one platter for uncooked meats and a different platter for cooked meats. Another option is to wash the "raw food" platter in hot soapy water before using it to serve the cooked dish.

☐ To avoid cross-contamination, use a different utensil to spoon or brush each basting sauce and marinade on your food.

☐ Keep hot foods hot (above 140°F) and cold foods cold (below 37°F).

☐ Once you have turned on the grill and it begins heating up, do not leave it unattended. There are too many opportunities for guests—especially "small grillers"—to come into contact with hot surfaces.

☐ Wear closed shoes, not sandals, to protect your feet from hot grease and any hot foods that may fall from the grill.

THE COMPLETE WOOD PELLET BARBEQUE COOKBOOK

OPERATION AND MAINTENANCE BASICS

Be sure to follow your owner's manual when assembling your grill so that it operates properly. Because every grill is a little different, your best course of action is to pay close attention to the manufacturer's instructions. However, I do suggest that during assembly, you cover the drip tray with heavy-duty aluminum foil so that it can be more easily cleaned after meal preparation.

When you use your grill, you should, once again, *carefully* follow the step-by-step instructions that came with the appliance. Basically, you will fill the pellet reservoir with your wood pellet selection and then use the temperature control to start the grill. Some manufacturer's recommend starting the grill in the "Smoke" mode so that the pellets feed slowly into the fire box at first. If the pellets are fed too quickly, the fire box will fill to capacity and may waste fuel and cause an unnecessary amount of smoke. When you're ready to cook, you will reset the temperature control according to the directions in your recipe, and wait until the grill reaches the desired temperature, a process that may take from twenty to thirty minutes, depending on the weather conditions. Now you can start cooking. Remember that after you place your food on the grill grate, you must close the door of the grill in order to maintain the correct temperature. Never use your wood pellet grill with the door open.

After you have used the grill a few times, you may want to clean it so that it will remain in good working order and the flavor of your foods will not be affected by the remnants of previous meals. Following the start-up of the grill, use a wire brush to remove any burned food particles and grease from the grate, and allow the heat from the burning pellets to sterilize the grate. Most of the time, this will be all that is required to get the grill ready for food preparation.

If deeper cleaning is required, remove the grill grate, the drip collection tray, and the fire pot diffuser found beneath the tray. Discard the used aluminum foil from the drip tray, and remove any caked-on grease, foil, or ash debris. Next, take the leftover pellets out of the reservoir, being sure to also remove the sawdust that has accumulated at the bottom. If you have a shop vacuum on hand, you'll find that it works well to eliminate the sawdust and ash residue from the fire box and the cooking cavity of the grill. If you don't have a shop vacuum, you can use a number of other simple tools—a whisk broom and small shovel, a garden trowel, or a dust pan—to remove the ash and dirt. Smoke and grease removal from the inside of the grill requires a little more work, but this usually needs to be done only three or four times per year, depending on how often your grill is used. I have to thoroughly clean mine at least every month, if not more often, since we use the grill nearly every day of the week.

To reassemble your wood pellet grill, start by reinstalling the fire pot diffuser. Then wrap the drip tray in heavy-duty aluminum foil and install the tray over the diffuser. After the drip tray has been installed, replace the grate in the cooking chamber. Thoroughly wipe down the door and the exterior of the grill with some warm soapy water and a little elbow grease. Make it look good because it's almost "show time"!

Important Facts About Wood Pellet Cooking

If you are new to wood pellet grilling, you're in for a treat, as this is one of the most versatile cooking tools you'll ever use. In addition to grilling, it smokes, roasts, braises, barbeques, and more, and it does it all beautifully. For best results, though, you'll want to understand a few important facts about outdoor cooking in general and wood pellet cooking in particular.

☐ **Unlike a standard charcoal or gas grill, your wood pellet grill does *not* use direct heat.** If you think of your grill as a convection oven that runs on wood, you will have a much better sense of how it works. The fact that this wonderful appliance uses even, indirect heat makes it able to handle a wide range of jobs, from grilling chicken wings to baking cakes and slow-cooking beef briskets and ribs. However, it also explains why tasks like toasting rolls are better accomplished in the broiler of your conventional indoor oven.

☐ **Every time you open the door of the grill, heat escapes and the temperature in the grill falls.** Since it takes time for the grill to again reach the desired temp, this can have a very real effect on your cooking time. For that reason, you'll want to keep the grill closed whenever possible, and, when it is necessary to open the grill door, you'll want to close it again as quickly as you can.

☐ **Environmental conditions can have a real effect on outdoor grilling.** When you use your grill on a cold, windy day, the grill may have a little more trouble reaching the desired temperature. The final results will still be spectacular, but the cooking time may be longer than it is on a day that is warm and calm.

☐ **Sweet marinades and barbeque sauces can burn at high temperatures.** Therefore, when using them in your cooking, you'll want to follow the recipe directions regarding both the level of heat used and the time at which the sauces are added to the meat.

☐ **The lower the temperature, the more smoke will come in contact with your food.** If you love the complex flavors and aromas of smoke, choose those recipes at which the food is cooked—at least for a while—at 180°F to 225°F. Higher temperatures produce less smoke.

THE MANY USES OF YOUR WOOD PELLET GRILL

Some people purchase separate smokers, outdoor grills, and outdoor ovens so they can prepare a range of foods in different ways. But with a pellet grill, you can smoke, grill, roast, slow-cook, and bake with one beautifully designed device. What's the difference between these cooking methods? In the following pages, you'll learn about each type of cooking and how you can accomplish it—easily and deliciously—with your wood pellet grill.

SMOKING

In smoking, wood is burned so that its aromatics are deposited on and penetrate the food, enhancing its flavor—including any spices or marinades that were used—and adding a distinctive and delicious aroma. To smoke food in your grill, the temperature control is set to "Smoke" or a low temperature (180°F to 225°F) so that the pellets are fed into the fire box at a slow rate. This causes the wood to burn slowly and produce smoke, which is released into the cooking chamber. Usually, food is smoked for a long period of time, often many hours, depending on the cut, size, and type of food being prepared. For example, a beef brisket is generally a tough piece of meat. When exposed to low heat (180°F) for twelve to fourteen hours—first uncovered, so that it comes in contact with the smoke, and then covered, to finish the cooking process—the fats melt into the muscle fibers, developing the flavors and tenderizing the meat; and the aromatics from the smoke penetrate as far as possible, further enhancing flavor and aroma.

There are at least two types of smoking: cold and hot. Because cold smoking should be used only by trained professionals, this book focuses on hot smoking, which takes place between 180°F and 225°F. It is generally used to flavor and cook raw meat, poultry, and fish, but it can also be used to add a smoky flavor to cooked seafoods and meats, as well as breads and even vegetables. The choice of specific wood pellets is especially important when smoking foods, as it will greatly influence the flavor and aroma of the finished dish. (See page 11 for information on the different pellets that are available.)

Whenever you use your wood pellet grill, but especially when you're using it to smoke food, keep in mind that opening the grill access cover can lower the temperature inside the grill. The wider the crack, the cooler the temperature. Since this will create more smoke but a smaller temperature increase in the meat, you should not allow the temperature of the grill to fall below 160°F.

BARBEQUING

Barbequing is similar to smoking in that the temperature is low—between 180°F to 300°F, in this case—and the meat cooks for hours. This "low and slow" method of cooking is used for large pieces of tough, high-fat cuts of meat, such as beef brisket, beef and pork ribs, and pork shoulder. The process slowly breaks down the fibers, melts the fat away, and evenly cooks even large roasts, creating meat that is moist and tender. Because the food is exposed to smoke as it is barbequed, it is also very flavorful and has the celebrated "smoke ring" inside the meat, often to a depth of about a quarter of an inch. Sometimes meat is barbequed directly on the grate, and sometimes it is wrapped in aluminum foil for a portion of the cooking time.

GRILLING

In grilling, food is cooked at a higher temperature, from 300°F to as high as 450°F, for a relatively short period of time—usually only minutes. (Although some grills are capable of reaching temperatures near 600°F, I do not recommend grilling above 450°F.) Grilling sears the surface of the meat, sealing in the juices; encourages a caramelized crust to form; and also creates appetizing "grill marks" on the surface of the meat or poultry.

Grilling is used for relatively tender, fast-cooking types of meat, such as steaks, burgers, frankfurters, and boneless, skinless chicken breasts. It is also appropriate for searing roasts prior to lowering the heat for barbequing, and for quickly cooking some vegetables, such as asparagus.

ROASTING AND BRAISING

Roasting is generally defined as a way of cooking food in a moderate oven with very little or no moisture. Braising involves first browning the meat and then simmering it in liquid within a covered container. Unlike most conventional grills, the wood pellet grill actually allows you to either roast or braise your food without heating up your kitchen.

To roast food in your pellet grill, set it to a temperature from 275°F (for a slow oven) to 350°F. Both the food you are cook-

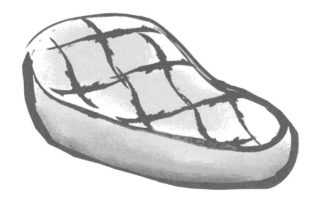

ing and your own preferences will help determine the temperature that you choose. Place the food in a roasting pan, leaving it uncovered. This is a long, slow process, and is generally used for large, tender cuts of meat, such as roast beef and roast pork, as well as for root vegetables and corn on the cob.

Braising is similar to roasting except that the meat is first browned and then cooked in liquid with the grill set at a low temperature, usually between 250°F and 275°F, depending on the meat. Because the covered cooking vessel allows the meat to "steam" and become tender, braising is used for tougher cuts of beef, pork, or veal. To enhance the flavor, the meat can be both seasoned and smoked prior to the addition of a liquid such as the meat's natural juices, condensed stock, or wine.

BAKING

The wood pellet grill is unique in that it can bake cookies, cakes, breads, and pizzas just as successfully as an indoor oven. In fact, it works very much like the wood-burning stoves of the past. For baked goods, I set my grill at 350°F or 375°F, depending on what I'm making. At these relatively hot temperatures, cakes and cookies do not develop a "smoked" flavor because the higher the heat, the less smoke the grill produces.

CHOOSING THE WOOD PELLETS

One of the many extraordinary features of the wood pellet grill is that your fuel source actually imparts wonderful flavor to your food and allows you to vary taste and aroma simply by choosing a different hardwood. When buying pellets, remember that they must be specifically manufactured for use in your wood pellet grill (not a wood-burning stove) and should be made only of natural woods, with no fillers or additives such as wax, glue, or artificial flavorings. Unnatural additives may adversely affect flavor and even create carcinogens in your food. Obtaining high-quality wood pellets should not be a problem as they are now manufactured by several companies. When you get your pellets home, make sure to store them in a container that will keep them bone-dry. All-natural pellets are made from compressed hardwood sawdust; no binders are used. If the wood gets damp or wet, it will disintegrate into sawdust mush and will clog the auger in the grill, preventing the wood from reaching the fire box.

Every recipe in this book recommends the pellets that I've found to be particularly noteworthy with that dish, but you should feel free to experiment with different flavors to find the combinations that you like best. The most common pellet woods, their characteristics, and their recommended uses are listed at right. When choosing wood pellets, remember that the lower the temperature, the more important the pellet choice, because the grill produces more smoke at lower temperatures like 180°F to 225°F, thereby having a more noticeable influence on food flavor and aroma. At higher temperatures, such as those used to grill and bake, the wood choice is less important.

Alder. This wood has a mild flavor with some sweetness. Use it with seafood and poultry.

Apple. Apple pellets have a fruity flavor and are best used in the preparation of poultry, beef, ham, lamb, pork, and sausages.

Black Walnut. These pellets produce a very strong, intense smoke that can be bitter. Use them with pork, beef, and game.

Cherry. Slightly sweet and a little tart, these pellets are appropriate for beef, pork, turkey, and chicken, as well as for highly spiced seafood dishes such as Cajun shrimp.

Hickory. Hickory pellets impart a rich, smoky, bacon-like flavor to all meats, including chicken and poultry.

Maple. With a sweet aroma and gentle flavor, these pellets work well with white meats such as pork, chicken, and turkey, but are also wonderful when preparing beef.

Mesquite. The strong, smoky "campfire" flavor of mesquite makes it perfect for use with red meats. Highly seasoned poultry, such as chicken that's been rubbed with Southwestern or Jamaican jerk blends, also benefits from mesquite smoke.

Oak. Oak has a mild flavor and is great for high-temperature cooking. Use it when you are preparing beef and seafood.

Orange. The mild, tangy citrus smoke from this wood imparts a golden color to food. Use it for meat and seafood.

Pecan. This wood has sweet aromatics and a gentle smoke, a little stronger than oak. It is great with beef, pork, and fish.

QUICK GRILLING TIMES

The recipes in this book have been designed to make the best use of the wood pellet grill's ability to add tantalizing smoked flavor and aroma to a wide range of foods, from beef and poultry to seafood and vegetables. Often, I have chosen to cook foods at temperatures that may be lower than those found in other grilling cookbooks. Lower temperatures give the aromatic smoke a chance to permeate the food, and also help avoid the blackened exterior and uneven cooking that is the hallmark of poorly barbequed food.

Nevertheless, there are days when time is in short supply and you want to get your meal on the table as quickly as possible. That's why, whenever possible, I have included Quick Grilling tips, (see page 53 for an example), which guide you in modifying the cooking temperature so that your dish can be prepared with greater speed.

Why don't all the recipes include instructions for Quick Grilling? Not all dishes can be prepared at higher tem-

peratures. For instance, some cuts of meat, such as the pork butt used in Pulled Pork, have to be cooked low and slow so that heat and smoke have time to break down tough connective tissue. Those dishes that include

sweet marinades and basting sauces also don't lend themselves to Quick Grilling times, as the higher heat causes the sugar in the sauces to burn. Any recipe that principally relies on wood smoke for its flavor and aroma should not be cooked quickly, as the higher temperature will do away with most of the smoke. Finally, those recipes that involve opening the grill door a number of times—to either baste or turn the meat, for instance—cannot be cooked superfast simply because every time you open the grill door, you lose a lot of heat, and it can take some time for the temperature to "recover" after the door is once again closed. When grilling meat at 400°F, for instance, the temperature can drop as much as 100 degrees when the door is opened, and once the door is again shut, it can take as long as fifteen minutes for the oven to regain the lost heat.

You can feel confident that any of the recipes in this book which include Quick Grilling information can be successfully prepared either the standard or the Quick Grilling way. Keep in mind, though, that whenever you use a higher level of heat, you lose some smoky flavor and aroma.

THE COMPLETE WOOD PELLET BARBEQUE COOKBOOK

JUDGING COOKING TEMPERATURES AND DONENESS

When cooking steaks and beef roasts, you probably favor a specific degree of doneness—medium rare or well done, for instance. When you cook chicken, ground beef, and certain other foods, though, you want to make sure that the food is fully cooked, yet still moist and juicy. How do you determine the degree of doneness? The appearance of the food when cut with a knife is an excellent clue, but the internal temperature as shown by a meat thermometer is more accurate.

The table on pages 14 and 15 lists the internal temperature—as well as typical appearance and texture—for several different types of meat, poultry, and fish. In some cases, several degrees of doneness are included so that you can cook the food as you and your family prefer. Remember that these are the *internal* temperatures taken at the center of the meat when it has finished cooking; they are not the cooking temperatures, which are far higher. Also be aware that the United States Department of Agriculture (USDA) recommends a safe cooking temperature for each type of beef and pork, as well as for fish and poultry. This is included in the following table as a "USDA Recommendation" so that you can easily identify it. If you like your steak or roast pink and juicy, though, you're probably going to opt for a lower temperature.

Choosing and Using a Meat Thermometer

I would never consider cooking on my wood pellet grill without the help of a meat thermometer. Thermometers take the guesswork out of barbequing and ensure that your food is both safe and cooked to the desired state of doneness.

My favorite thermometer is an instant-read digital device. You simply insert the probe in the meat, poultry, or fish when you think that the food is nearing the preferred level of doneness, and within a few seconds, you get a readout of the food's internal temperature. If you prefer, you can opt for an analog thermometer, in which a hand moves around a dial. I have found these thermometers to be more accurate than the devices that remain in the meat during the cooking process, and most kitchen stores have several reasonably priced models.

To use an instant-read device effectively, follow these easy steps:

1. Open the grill door to gain access to the food.

2. Insert the thermometer probe about 2 inches into the thickest part of the food, without touching any fat or bone. If you're preparing meat patties, insert the thermometer in the patties sideways.

3. Wait for several seconds—it may take up to 15 seconds, depending on the model—and read the dial or digital readout. If the food is not done, remove the thermometer, close the grill door, and test again after a few minutes.

4. After each use, wash the probe of the thermometer in hot, soapy water.

RECOMMENDED INTERNAL TEMPERATURES OF COOKED MEATS, POULTRY, AND SEAFOOD

Cut or Type	Desired Level of Doneness	Appearance and/or Texture	Internal Temperature
BEEF AND VEAL			
Brisket*	Medium	Dark pink in center; slightly juicy; crust on exterior.	135°F to 145°F
	USDA Recommendation	Dark pink in center; slightly juicy; crust on exterior.	145°F
	Medium Well	Tan with pink center; some juice present.	145°F to 155°F
	Well Done	Tan to brown center.	180°F to 190°F
Ground‡	Medium Well to Well Done	Brown with no pink visible; juice on surface.	160°F
	USDA Recommendation	Brown with no pink visible; juice on surface.	160°F
Ribs*	Well Done	Deep tan to brown in color; tender meat falling off bones; bones protruding from meat; juicy.	180°F to 190°F
Roasts & Steaks	Rare	Purple exterior with deep red color at center; very juicy.	120°F to 130°F
	Medium Rare	Red to dark pink in center; juicy; slight crust on exterior.	130°F to 135°F
	Medium	Pink center; less juicy; heavier crust on exterior.	135°F to 145°F
	USDA Recommendation	Pink center; less juicy; heavier crust on exterior.	145°F
	Medium Well	Slightly pink center; less moist meat.	145°F to 155°F
	Well Done	Pink to gray; dry meat.	155°F and greater

* Meat cuts in this category are best when cooked at lower temperatures for a longer period of time. The meat should remain on the grill until it reaches the internal temperature indicated in the chart.

‡ Ground beef and pork must be cooked thoroughly—to the USDA-recommended temperature—to be safe for consumption.

Cut or Type	Desired Level of Doneness	Appearance and/or Texture	Internal Temperature
CHICKEN AND TURKEY			
All Cuts	Well Done	No pink visible; clear juices.	165°F and greater
	USDA Recommendation	No pink visible; clear juices.	165°F and greater
FISH			
All Cuts & Types	Rare	Interior appears raw.	110°F to 120°F
	Medium Rare	Similar to rare, but lighter in color.	120°F to 130°F
	Medium	Slightly translucent; flaky.	140°F to 145°F
	USDA Recommendation	Slightly translucent; flaky.	145°F
	Medium Well	Firm; opaque.	145°F to 155°F
	Well Done	Flakes easily; opaque.	155°F and greater
PORK			
Ground‡	Well Done	Brown, with no pink visible.	160°F
	USDA Recommendation	Brown, with no pink visible.	160°F
Ribs	Well Done	Pale to white interior; meat falling off bones; bones protruding from meat; juicy.	180°F to 190°F
Roasts & Chops	Rare	Pink to pale at center; juicy.	120°F to 130°F
	Medium Rare	Slightly pink to tan; juicy.	130°F TO 135°F
	Medium	Tan; clear juices.	135°F to 145°F
	USDA Recommendation	Tan; clear juices.	145°F
	Medium Well	Tan; firm texture; clear juices.	145°F to 155°F
	Well Done	Dry; tough meat; clear juices.	155°F and greater
Shoulder	Well Done	Falling off the bone; brown; juicy.	180°F

CONCLUSION

The versatility of the wood pellet grill makes it like no other cooker you've ever owned. If you've been using a conventional outdoor appliance until now, you'll find ways to make old standbys new and interesting. You'll also start preparing gourmet meals you may never have thought possible outside of a restaurant. As you experiment, I encourage you to keep a notebook of your cooking experiences. Write down each recipe, as well as all of your variations and the final results. Your notes will make it all the easier to develop creative versions of other dishes.

The next chapter gets you closer to your first cooking adventure by presenting a range of recipes for spice blends, rubs, marinades, and sauces. Like your pellet grill, these recipes will help you perfect your favorite dishes and create new ones that are delicious, exciting, and well above the ordinary.

2.

Basic Barbeque Rubs, Spice Blends, Marinades, and Sauces

Preparing meat for cooking can be as easy as adding a little salt and freshly ground pepper. But those of us who seek the most delicious results possible every time we use our pellet grill know that a good rub, marinade, or sauce can enhance the flavor of smoke-infused meat, elevating both taste and aroma to new levels. This chapter presents my favorite recipes for zesty barbeque rubs, seasoning blends, marinades, and sauces. All are wonderful, and all can be created in your kitchen with ingredients that, for the most part, may already be found on your pantry shelves or spice rack.

While the rubs and other flavor enhancers offered in this chapter are easy to put together, before starting out, you'll want to make sure that your spices and dried herbs—

key ingredients in these recipes—are fresh and vibrant. Fresh spices bring a mouthwatering array of aromas and flavors to the party. Older spices, on the other hand, may have lost their pungency and unique character. It is worth the effort to check the seasonings you have in your pantry for freshness. Just open each spice or herb container and take a whiff. If the aroma of that particular seasoning is not vibrant and distinctive, or if you know that the jar has been on your shelf forever, it could be time to replace it. My recipes usually yield an amount sufficient to prepare an individual recipe. If any rub or seasoning is left over after you prepare your meat, store it in a clean airtight container, such as a previously used spice jar. Try to use the remainder up within six months so that the flavors remain full and bright. To avoid bacterial contamination, do not save any rub that has been exposed to raw meat or its juices. On the other hand, you may find that you love a particular seasoning blend and want to make it in larger quantities so that a supply is always within reach. In that case, you can simply double (or triple) the recipe, use what you need, and store the rest for later use.

As you follow the recipes found in this chapter, don't be afraid to use more or less herbs and spices—or to play with different ones—to suit your tastes. There's plenty of room for creativity. Also don't hesitate to add more of the chosen rub, spice blend, or sauce to your food just before you remove it from the grill. I have learned that "less is more" during the cooking process; you want to highlight, not obliterate, the flavors of the meat, poultry, seafood, or vegetables you're preparing. But if you want to place greater emphasis on the spices, by all means, add more seasoning or sauce shortly before the food is cooked to the desired degree of doneness. When seasoning is added near the end of the cooking process, it packs more of a punch.

In addition to rubs, spice blends, marinades, and sauces, this chapter includes basic recipes and directions for brining. (See the inset on page 38.) Designed to improve the flavor, texture, and moisture content of lean meats, brining can be used when preparing turkey, chicken, and pork. Feel free to vary the herbs in these recipes to suit the meat you're using. For example, a chicken or turkey is marvelous when brined with tarragon or sage. Pork can be enhanced with the addition of thyme or basil and a little brown sugar. Keep a record of what you use and whether you like the results, as this will help enhance your skills as a chef. Remember that the only rule in wood pellet cooking is that you should enjoy every moment of the experience!

BASIC BARBEQUE RUBS

Rubs are so basic to barbequing that every region of the country has its own versions of these spicy concoctions. Most rubs are a simple mixture of salt, sugar, herbs, and spices, but each blend imparts unique flavors and levels of heat through the specific spices it uses as well as the proportions of the ingredients.

When making certain rubs, it may be necessary to grind the spices and herbs in a spice mill or to use a mortar and pestle. I prefer the spice mill, although if I am making a large amount of meat, I sometimes have to work in batches to obtain the necessary quantity.

Apply rub blends to the meat several hours before cooking. (You can gauge the approximate amount to use by looking at each recipe's yield information, which indicates how many pounds of meat can be covered by that rub. As you will see, some rubs go farther than others.) Simply sprinkle the mixture over the food and then gently rub it in by hand, ideally wearing food-grade disposable gloves so that the rub doesn't remain stuck to your fingers. Wrap the meat tightly in plastic wrap and refrigerate it for several hours. If you have time, leave the rub on the meat overnight so that the food will become infused with the flavors. When you cook the meat, you'll find that the rub has added flavor and color, and in many cases, has also formed a tantalizing crust. To maximize crust formation, don't move the meat around during cooking, but let it sit on the grill grate undisturbed until it reaches the desired degree of doneness.

The following rub recipes feature flavor combinations favored in different areas of the country, as well as blends I've developed for specific cuts of meat. The vast array of herbs and spices available in the markets allows for more experimentation, so you can develop your own blends that are suited to your tastes and desires. The opportunities and combinations are endless.

Kansas City-Style Rub

Kansas City loves the sweeter side of barbeque, and the amount of sugar in their rubs can range from $1/2$ cup to over 2 cups per recipe. Usually, the spices are a combination of paprika, black pepper, salt or smoked salt, chili powder, garlic powder, and crushed red pepper flakes. Sometimes, dry mustard and herbs are added, depending on the meat and the desired result. For example, rosemary or sweet basil may be added when making lamb, sage is good on beef, and oregano can lend an Italian note. For a true Kansas City-style dish, you'll want to add a sweet tomato-based sauce at the end of the cooking time. (For my Basic Kansas City-Style Barbeque Sauce, see page 43.)

YIELD: ABOUT 2¹/₄ CUPS (ENOUGH FOR 8 POUNDS OF MEAT)

³/₄ cup packed brown sugar	¹/₄ cup coarse sea salt
¹/₂ cup smoked paprika	1 tablespoon garlic powder
¹/₂ cup chili powder	1 tablespoon onion powder
¹/₄ cup coarsely ground black pepper	1 tablespoon crushed red pepper flakes

---

1. Place all the ingredients in a medium-size bowl, and use a whisk to blend well.

2. Sprinkle the mixture over one side of the meat and rub into the meat. Turn the meat over and repeat on other side.

3. Wrap the meat tightly in plastic wrap and place in the refrigerator for at least 4 hours or as long as overnight. Store any remaining rub in an airtight container for up to 6 months.

4. Cook the meat as directed in the recipe of your choice.

Memphis-Style Rub

The Memphis, Tennessee barbeque region places paramount importance on the quality and flavor of the meat. That's why Memphis-style rubs are designed to enhance the taste of the meat but not overpower it. The spices most often found in these mixtures are cumin, garlic, paprika, and onion, and the meat is cooked at a low temperature with lots of smoke until it's nearly falling off the bone. If a barbeque sauce is used, it is generally applied or "mopped" onto the food at the last minute, and is also served on the plate for dipping. Use this rub on beef or pork.

YIELD: ABOUT 1 CUP (ENOUGH FOR 4 POUNDS OF MEAT)

¼ cup sweet paprika	1 tablespoon garlic powder
2 tablespoons tomato powder* (optional)	2 teaspoons ground cumin
	2 teaspoons ground black pepper
2 tablespoons crushed red pepper flakes	1 teaspoon onion powder
1 tablespoon plus 1 teaspoon mustard seed	1 teaspoon dried oregano
	1 teaspoon dried thyme
1 tablespoon plus 1 teaspoon coarse sea salt	
1 tablespoon plus 1 teaspoon brown sugar	* This dehydrated flavoring can be obtained from Internet stores and some specialty shops. See the inset on page 28 for more information.

---

1. Place all the ingredients in a small bowl, and use a whisk to blend well.

2. Sprinkle the mixture over one side of the meat and rub the mixture into the meat. Turn the meat over and repeat on the other side.

3. Wrap the meat tightly in plastic wrap and place in the refrigerator for at least 4 hours or as long as overnight. Store any remaining rub in an airtight container for up to 6 months.

4. Cook the meat as directed in the recipe of your choice.

THE COMPLETE WOOD PELLET BARBEQUE COOKBOOK

Competition-Style Barbeque Rub

Contestants in barbeque competitions have their own special blends of herbs and spices that they use as rubs. The mixtures are applied to the meat approximately twelve hours before beginning the cooking process, and sauces are added later to enhance the spices so that the flavors, aromas, and colors please the judging staffs. In this rub, we provide the basic element of sweetness along with the pungent barbeque smells of onion and garlic, chili powder, celery seed, and a bit of cayenne pepper. You can use this rub as the sole seasoning for beef brisket, beef and pork roasts and ribs, and chicken, or you can add a sauce such as the Spicy Rum Barbeque Sauce (page 48).

YIELD: About 1 cup (enough for 4 pounds of meat)

¹/₄ cup plus 2 tablespoons packed brown sugar	1 tablespoon plus 1 teaspoon onion powder
¹/₄ cup paprika	2 teaspoons chili powder
¹/₄ cup coarsely ground black pepper	2 teaspoons celery seed
¹/₄ cup coarse sea salt	2 teaspoons tomato powder* (optional)
1 tablespoon plus 1 teaspoon garlic powder	1 teaspoon cayenne pepper

* This dehydrated flavoring can be obtained from Internet stores and some specialty shops. See the inset on page 28 for more information.

1. Place all the ingredients in a small bowl, and use a whisk to blend well.

2. Sprinkle the mixture over one side of the meat and rub into the meat. Turn the meat over and repeat on other side.

3. Wrap the meat tightly in plastic wrap and place in the refrigerator for at least 4 hours or as long as overnight. Store any remaining rub in an airtight container for up to 6 months.

4. Cook the meat as directed in the recipe of your choice.

Texas-Style Rub

Texans love their beef, and it's not uncommon to find a fully rubbed side of beef slowly turning on a spit, filling the air with aromatic smoke. Texans make a lot of pork, too, and this rub can be used with success on either meat. The biggest difference between the Texas- and Memphis-style rubs is the use of chili peppers. Influenced by their neighbors in Mexico, Texans include a large proportion of dried chilies and chili powders in their rubs as well as other traditional South of the Border herbs and spices.

YIELD: About 1 cup (enough for 4 pounds of meat)

1–2 dried chipotle chili peppers, sliced lengthwise and seeded, or 1¹/₂ tablespoons ground chipotle chili*

1¹/₂ tablespoons black peppercorns

1 tablespoon cumin seeds

1 tablespoon coriander seeds

1 tablespoon mustard seeds

¹/₄ cup chili powder

2¹/₂ tablespoons coarse sea salt

2 tablespoons smoked paprika

2 tablespoons brown sugar

1 tablespoon dried minced garlic

1 tablespoon dried flaked onion

1 tablespoon dried oregano

* If you use ground chipotle chili instead of whole chili peppers, add the pre-ground powder to the bowl in Step 4, after the toasted seeds have been crushed or milled. Do not roast or grind the chili powder.

---

1. Preheat a small cast-iron or stainless steel skillet over medium heat. Add the chipotle chilies first (if using), followed by the peppercorns, cumin seeds, coriander seeds, and mustard seeds. Toast, stirring occasionally, for 2 to 4 minutes, or just until fragrant. Do not overheat the seeds or they will become bitter.

2. Remove the chili and seeds from the heat and transfer to a heatproof bowl to cool.

3. Using a mortar and pestle or a spice mill, grind the spices to a fine powder.

4. Return the spice mixture to the bowl and mix in the remaining ingredients using a whisk. If you are using pre-ground chipotle chili instead of whole peppers, add the chipotle chili powder now and blend thoroughly.

5. Sprinkle the mixture over one side of the meat and rub into the meat. Turn the meat over and repeat on other side.

6. Wrap the meat tightly in plastic wrap and place in the refrigerator for at least 4 hours or as long as overnight. Store any remaining rub in an airtight container for up to 6 months.

7. Cook the meat as directed in the recipe of your choice.

Pulled Pork Rub

Originating in the Carolinas, pulled pork is made from pork butt that's slow-roasted over apple, mesquite, or hickory smoke until the meat is so tender that it can be literally pulled off the bone with your fingers. The spices combine with the smoke, permeating the meat with flavors and aromas that tantalize the palate. You will detect a light sweetness followed by the spicy blend of the chili powder and cumin, and finally, a combination of salt and the heat of the peppers.

YIELD: ABOUT I CUP (ENOUGH FOR 7–8 POUNDS OF PORK BUTT)

1/2 cup packed light brown or dark brown sugar	2 tablespoons ground cumin
1/3 cup sea salt	1 tablespoon coarsely ground black pepper
1/4 cup smoked paprika	2 teaspoons dry mustard
1/4 cup chili powder	2 teaspoons crushed red pepper flakes

1. Place all the ingredients in a small bowl, and use a whisk to blend well.

2. Sprinkle the mixture over one side of the meat and rub into the meat. Turn the meat over and repeat on other side.

3. Wrap the meat tightly in plastic wrap and place in the refrigerator for at least 4 hours or overnight. Store any remaining rub in an airtight container for up to 6 months.

4. Cook the pork as directed in the recipe of your choice.

The Skinny on Pork Butt

When making pulled pork, the preferred cut of meat is the *pork butt*—a name that confuses many people. Strangely, it is not the rear end of a pig, but the upper part of the pig's shoulder. This cut, which is inexpensive, contains tough connective tissue and lots of fat. After many hours of slow cooking over low heat, though, the meat becomes moist, tender, and easy to shred.

Most supermarkets carry individually wrapped pork butts with much of the external fat removed. Warehouse stores sell them in Cryovac packs with much of the fat still intact. Both types are fine. Be aware, however, that many pork butts have been "enhanced," which means that the meat has been injected with a solution of water, salt, and other ingredients to make the pork moister (and saltier). It also means that you are paying for water instead of meat. Check the fine print on labels, which must let you know if a solution has been added. Marketing terms like "guaranteed tender" and "always moist and juicy" are also indications that the meat is enhanced.

Prime Rib Rub

This rub is a "must" whenever prime rib is prepared for a special occasion. It may seem like a relatively small amount of spice for such a big roast, but it's all that's needed to enhance this extraordinary cut of beef.

YIELD: ABOUT 1 CUP (ENOUGH FOR A 15-POUND RIB ROAST)

¹/₂ cup coarse sea salt	1 tablespoon plus 1 teaspoon dried thyme
2 tablespoons coarsely ground black pepper	1 tablespoon plus 1 teaspoon dried parsley
2 tablespoons plus 1 teaspoon sugar	1 teaspoon cayenne pepper
1 tablespoon plus 1 teaspoon ground dried sage	1 teaspoon ground coriander

1. Place all the ingredients in a medium-size bowl, and use a whisk to blend well.

2. Sprinkle the mixture all over the roast and rub into the meat. Wrap the meat tightly in plastic wrap and place in the refrigerator for at least 4 hours or as long as overnight. Store any remaining rub in an airtight container for up to 6 months.

3. Cook the meat as directed in the recipe of your choice.

Savory Spice Rub and Seasoning Blend

This blend is a favorite of mine. It's versatile, too—just as delicious when used as a rub on chicken and pork as it is when sprinkled on asparagus and broccoli. Although the herbs and spices may not seem to belong together, they "marry" quite well and add a unique spin to a variety of entrées and side dishes. You'll find that a little goes a long way.

YIELD: ABOUT ³/₄ CUP (ENOUGH FOR ABOUT 6 POUNDS OF MEAT)

3 tablespoons dried oregano	1 tablespoon ground ginger
2 tablespoons ground cinnamon	1 tablespoon sea salt
2 tablespoons garlic powder	1 tablespoon ground black pepper
2 tablespoons paprika	2 teaspoons ground cumin

1. Place all the ingredients in a small bowl, and use a whisk to blend well.

2. If using as a seasoning blend, use as directed in the recipe of your choice. If using as a rub, sprinkle the mixture over one side of the meat and rub into the meat. Turn the meat over and repeat on the other side.

3. Wrap the meat tightly in plastic wrap and place in the refrigerator for at least 4 hours or as long as overnight. Store any remaining rub in an airtight container for up to 6 months.

4. Cook the meat as directed in the recipe of your choice.

Jamaican Jerk Rub

Hot and spicy, this rub is flavored with lemon zest; regional seasonings like allspice, ginger, cinnamon, and nutmeg; and a little bit of cayenne for heat. I especially love this blend on chicken. As the smoke and spice aromas are wafting through the air, my thoughts drift back to the first time I visited that magical isle. Mix yourself a piña colada, put on some Bob Marley reggae music, and take a backyard trip to the island of Jamaica.

YIELD: About $^1/_2$ cup (enough for about 2 pounds of meat)

$^1/_4$ cup grated lemon zest	1 teaspoon ground allspice
2 teaspoons sea salt	1 teaspoon cayenne pepper
2 teaspoons sugar	1 teaspoon ground ginger
2 teaspoons ground cinnamon	1 teaspoon dried thyme
2 teaspoons ground black pepper	$^1/_2$ teaspoon freshly grated nutmeg

1. Place all the ingredients in a small bowl, and use a whisk to blend well.

2. Sprinkle the mixture over one side of the meat and rub into the meat. Turn the meat over and repeat on the other side.

3. Wrap the meat tightly in plastic wrap and place in the refrigerator for at least 4 hours or as long as overnight. Store any remaining rub in an airtight container for up to 6 months.

4. Cook the meat as directed in the recipe of your choice.

SPICE AND HERB BLENDS

The following spice and herb blends are used throughout this cookbook. I created these blends to magically meld with and enhance the natural flavors and aromas of the foods with which they're cooked. When these blends are used on meat, they are sprinkled on prior to cooking rather than being rubbed on, or are incorporated in a sauce or a quick marinade. While rubs are often applied to meat that will be slow-cooked, such as a brisket, the following blends are usually used on quick-cooking cuts, such as steaks or chops. Many of the blends are equally delicious on vegetables, where just a small amount quickly turns the dish into an extraordinary experience.

Each of the following recipes makes enough seasoning for an average recipe—two to four pounds of meat. If you are preparing a larger quantity of meat, simply multiply the amounts as necessary. As when making dry rubs, you may have to use a mortar and pestle or a spice mill, which is my preference. To obtain the best results, always use quality herbs and spices that have maintained their distinctive aromas.

Home-Style Seasoning Mix

This unique blend of spices and herbs is accented by a light hickory smoke flavor and a bit of heat from crushed red pepper flakes. It makes a great addition to anything you prepare on the grill.

YIELD: About ¹/₄ cup (enough for 4 pounds of meat)

1 tablespoon sugar	¹/₂ teaspoon hickory smoke powder*
1 tablespoon brown sugar	¹/₄ teaspoon crushed red pepper flakes
1 teaspoon sea salt	¹/₄ teaspoon onion powder
1 teaspoon paprika	¹/₄ teaspoon garlic powder
1 teaspoon dried oregano	¹/₄ teaspoon chili powder
1 teaspoon dried basil	¹/₈ teaspoon ground turmeric
¹/₂ teaspoon ground black pepper	
¹/₂ teaspoon dried thyme	

* This dehydrated flavoring can be obtained from Internet sources and some specialty shops. See the inset on page 28 for more information.

1. Place all the ingredients in a small bowl, and use a whisk to blend well.

2. Use the seasoning blend as directed in the recipe of your choice, and store any remaining blend in an airtight container for up to 6 months.

Southwestern Seasoning Blend and Rub

Combining salt, spice, and a little smoke, this blend brings Southwestern cuisine to the table. It spices up beef, pork, poultry, and any other food it touches, and can be used as either a seasoning or a rub.

YIELD: ABOUT ¹/₂ CUP (ENOUGH FOR 6 POUNDS OF MEAT)

2 tablespoons paprika	1 teaspoon hickory smoke powder*
1 tablespoon plus 1 teaspoon coarse sea salt	1 teaspoon garlic powder
2 teaspoons sugar	1 teaspoon onion powder
2 teaspoons rice vinegar powder* (optional)	¹/₂ teaspoon ground cinnamon
1¹/₂ teaspoons chili powder	¹/₂ teaspoon celery seeds
1 teaspoon ground cumin	¹/₂ teaspoon cayenne pepper
1 teaspoon ground black pepper	
1 teaspoon tomato powder* (optional)	

* This dehydrated flavoring can be obtained from Internet stores and some specialty shops. See the inset on page 28 for more information.

1. Place all the ingredients in a small bowl, and use a whisk to blend well.

2. Use the seasoning blend as directed in the recipe of your choice, and store any remaining blend in an airtight container for up to 6 months.

Barbeque Seasoning Blend

This unique blend of spices and herbs reflects the Memphis, Tennessee and Texas styles of barbeque cooking. More spicy than sweet, this mix is so well balanced that no particular flavor is dominant, although a hint of citrus can be detected in the finish. Use this blend on beef, pork, or poultry.

YIELD: ABOUT ¹/₂ CUP (ENOUGH FOR 4 POUNDS OF MEAT)

2 tablespoons chili powder

2 tablespoons paprika

1 tablespoon plus 1 teaspoon coarse sea salt

2 teaspoons tomato powder* (optional)

2 teaspoons hickory smoke powder*

1 teaspoon sugar

1 teaspoon garlic powder

1 teaspoon onion powder

1 teaspoon dried thyme

1 teaspoon dried lemon peel

* This dehydrated flavoring can be obtained from Internet stores and some specialty shops. See the inset below for more information.

1. Place all the ingredients in a small bowl, and use a whisk to blend well.

2. Use the seasoning blend as directed in the recipe of your choice, and store any remaining blend in an airtight container for up to 6 months.

Special Rub and Barbeque Sauce Flavorings

Most of the herbs, spices, and other ingredients used in this chapter are easy to find in your local supermarket. In some cases a spice blend or sauce includes a flavoring that is a little more unusual. Each of the ingredients listed on page 29—as well as many more common herbs and spices—can be obtained through Internet stores and in some specialty shops, as well. (To learn more about these sources, see the Resource List on page 193.) These ingredients have unique properties that can round out a blend or add a unique flavor. In some cases—noted in the individual recipes—these ingredients are optional; the finished product will still be wonderful without them. In other cases, the flavor is essential to achieve the desired result.

Cajun Spice

Like all Cajun cuisine, this blend has its origins in a section of Louisiana where the food has been influenced by French and Spanish culinary traditions. Slightly spicy, slightly earthy, with a hint of citrus, it can be sprinkled generously on beef, pork, chicken, turkey, or seafood, and is great on shrimp.

YIELD: ABOUT 1/4 CUP (ENOUGH FOR 4 POUNDS OF MEAT OR SEAFOOD)

1 tablespoon sea salt	1/2 teaspoon dried lemon peel
2 teaspoons sugar	1/2 teaspoon vinegar powder* (optional)
1 teaspoon chili powder	1/2 teaspoon cayenne pepper
1 teaspoon onion or garlic powder	1/2 teaspoon Worcestershire powder*
1 teaspoon dry mustard	
1 teaspoon smoked paprika	* This dehydrated flavoring can be obtained from Internet stores and some specialty shops. See the inset below for more information.
1/2 teaspoon ground cumin	

1. Place all the ingredients in a small bowl, and use a whisk to blend well.

2. Use the seasoning blend as directed in the recipe of your choice, and store any remaining blend in an airtight container for up to 6 months.

Hickory smoke powder. Containing natural smoke flavor, this dry seasoning is very concentrated and is used to give a "campfire" flavor to foods.

Lemon powder. Sometimes called lemon juice powder, this dehydrated product is made from lemon juice, and sometimes also includes the oils from lemon peel. It is useful in adding lemon flavor to rubs and seasoning blends.

Lime powder. This product is made from dehydrated lime juice and oils. It adds an acidic lime tang to rubs, seasoning blends, and sauces.

Tomato powder. Containing dehydrated tomatoes, tomato powder imparts intense tomato flavor to dry rubs and sauces.

Vinegar powder. Made of dehydrated red, white, or rice wine vinegar, this handy powder lends a characteristic vinegar flavor and aroma to rubs, sauces, and dressings.

Worcestershire powder. A powdered form of Worcestershire sauce, this seasoning adds the flavor of the well-known sauce to rubs, seasoning blends, and other foods.

Mediterranean Spice Seasoning

Blending salt, citrus, Mediterranean herbs, and spices—with just a hint of sweetness—this seasoning brings out the best in beef, pork, and veal; is perfect on stronger-flavored green vegetables such as Brussels sprouts; and adds interest to grilled buttered asparagus.

YIELD: 1/4 CUP (ENOUGH FOR 4 POUNDS OF FOOD)

2 1/2 teaspoons dried lemon peel	1/2 teaspoon ground coriander
2 teaspoons coarse sea salt	1/2 teaspoon brown sugar
1 1/2 teaspoons ground fennel seed	1/2 teaspoon tomato powder* (optional)
1 teaspoon garlic powder	1/2 teaspoon cayenne pepper
1 teaspoon onion powder	* This dehydrated flavoring can be obtained from Internet stores and some specialty shops. See the inset on page 28 for more information.
1 teaspoon dried basil	
1 teaspoon dried thyme	

1. Place all the ingredients in a small bowl, and use a whisk to blend well.

2. Use the seasoning blend as directed in the recipe of your choice, and store any remaining blend in an airtight container for up to 6 months.

Lemon and Herb Spice Blend

Uniting citrus fruits, herbs, and spices, this is an exciting blend that awakens the flavors of any food, from vegetables to chicken, beef, pork, and seafood.

YIELD: ABOUT 1/4 CUP (ENOUGH FOR 4 POUNDS OF FOOD)

1 1/2 tablespoons brown sugar	1/2 teaspoon dried parsley
1 1/2 tablespoons dried lemon peel	1/2 teaspoon dried oregano
1 teaspoon coarse sea salt	1/4 teaspoon ground dried sage
1 teaspoon dried orange peel	1/4 teaspoon ground coriander
1/2 teaspoon ground black pepper	1/4 teaspoon garlic powder

1. Place all the ingredients in a small bowl, and use a whisk to blend well.

2. Use the seasoning blend as directed in the recipe of your choice, and store any remaining blend in an airtight container for up to 6 months.

Classic French Spice

This is a fascinating blend of aromas and flavors that are uniquely French. Mustard is in the forefront, supported by a sweet combination of spices. When used on beef, pork, or fish, it is best to allow it to "season" for at least 20 minutes before cooking. Set the grill on a low temperature so that the smoke permeates the food, enhancing flavors and aromas. Then increase the grill temperature to finish cooking the food.

YIELD: ABOUT ¹/₄ CUP (ENOUGH FOR 2 POUNDS OF MEAT OR SEAFOOD)

2 tablespoons dry mustard

1 teaspoon sea salt

1 teaspoon sugar

1 teaspoon paprika

1 teaspoon tomato powder* (optional)

¹/₂ teaspoon onion powder

¹/₂ teaspoon garlic powder

¹/₂ teaspoon vinegar powder*

¹/₂ teaspoon hickory smoke powder*

¹/₄ teaspoon ground black pepper

¹/₄ teaspoon chili powder

¹/₄ teaspoon lemon powder,* or ¹/₄ teaspoon each powdered sugar and ground dried lemon peel

¹/₄ teaspoon ground cinnamon

¹/₄ teaspoon celery seed

¹/₄ teaspoon cayenne pepper

* This dehydrated flavoring can be obtained from Internet stores and some specialty shops. See the inset on page 28 for more information.

1. Place all the ingredients in a small bowl, and use a whisk to blend well.

2. Use the seasoning blend as directed in the recipe of your choice, and store any remaining blend in an airtight container for up to 6 months.

Herb and Garlic Seasoning Blend

This blend is perfect on all meats, including poultry. When making poultry, apply the blend liberally inside as well as out to enjoy uniform flavor. When preparing chops and other fast-cooking cuts, again, apply a liberal amount. This will create a delicious crust and a juicy interior.

YIELD: ABOUT 1/4 CUP (ENOUGH FOR 4 POUNDS OF MEAT)

2 tablespoons sugar	1/2 teaspoon dried rosemary
2 teaspoons sea salt	1/2 teaspoon ground dried sage
2 teaspoons dried minced onion	1/2 teaspoon dried basil
1 teaspoon garlic powder	1/2 teaspoon dried thyme
1 teaspoon ground black pepper	1/2 teaspoon dried lemon peel
1 teaspoon dried parsley	1/4 teaspoon dried orange peel

1. Place all the ingredients in a small bowl, and use a whisk to blend well.

2. Use the seasoning blend as directed in the recipe of your choice, and store any remaining blend in an airtight container for up to 6 months.

Sweet Lemon Spice

With its blend of lemon, orange, herbs, and spices, Sweet Lemon Spice is an unusual seasoning that's great on chicken, pork chops, and grilled salmon.

YIELD: ABOUT 2 1/4 TABLESPOONS (ENOUGH FOR 2 POUNDS OF FOOD)

1 1/2 teaspoons lemon powder* (optional)	1/4 teaspoon ground dried sage
1 1/2 teaspoons brown sugar	1/4 teaspoon dried oregano
1/2 teaspoon sea salt	1/4 teaspoon celery seed
1/2 teaspoon dried lemon peel	1/4 teaspoon garlic powder
1/2 teaspoon dried orange peel	1/4 teaspoon ground black pepper
1/2 teaspoon dried parsley	
1/2 teaspoon vinegar powder* (optional)	* This dehydrated flavoring can be obtained from Internet stores and some specialty shops. See the inset on page 28 for more information.
1/4 teaspoon ground coriander	

1. Place all the ingredients in a small bowl, and use a whisk to blend well.

2. Use the seasoning blend as directed in the recipe of your choice, and store any remaining blend in an airtight container for up to 6 months.

Dijon Spice Blend

The Dijon Spice Blend works magic with shrimp and other seafood, complementing the flavor of the dish. It is slightly salty but spicy, with the cayenne pepper providing just a little heat. This blend is fantastic when added to melted butter and brushed liberally on grilled lobster tails or shrimp. For an exciting change of pace, sprinkle it on halibut, catfish, or tilapia before grilling.

YIELD: ABOUT 2 TABLESPOONS (ENOUGH FOR 2 POUNDS OF SEAFOOD)

$1\frac{1}{2}$ teaspoons dry mustard	$\frac{1}{4}$ teaspoon tomato powder* (optional)
1 teaspoon coarse sea salt	$\frac{1}{4}$ teaspoon celery seed
1 teaspoon sugar	$\frac{1}{4}$ teaspoon dried dill
$\frac{1}{2}$ teaspoon vinegar powder*	$\frac{1}{8}$ teaspoon ground cinnamon
$\frac{1}{2}$ teaspoon ground black pepper	$\frac{1}{8}$ teaspoon cayenne pepper
$\frac{1}{2}$ teaspoon paprika	
$\frac{1}{4}$ teaspoon garlic powder	* This dehydrated flavoring can be obtained from Internet stores and some specialty shops. See the inset on page 28 for more information.
$\frac{1}{4}$ teaspoon onion powder	

1. Place all the ingredients in a small bowl, and use a whisk to blend well.

2. Use the seasoning blend as directed in the recipe of your choice, and store any remaining blend in an airtight container for up to 6 months.

MARINADES

Marinades are liquids that are used to boost flavor, enhance tenderness, and, through moisture, protect meat, fish, or fowl during cooking. Some type of acid, such as vinegar or citrus juice, is a common component of marinades, as it serves to break down the fibers of the meat. Spices and herbs are carefully chosen to complement the liquids and create a distinctive taste—perhaps tropical flair or a Tennessee tang.

Always be sure to dry your food well before placing it in a marinade, as the liquid better penetrates food that doesn't have a wet surface. Usually, meat and poultry are steeped in a marinade for several hours before cooking, and sometimes, they are left in the marinade for up to a day. Seafood, however, should not be placed in a marinade for more than an hour. Longer exposure can actually "cook" the fish, which is not what you want. Be sure to refrigerate the meat, poultry, or seafood during this process to prevent the growth of bacteria.

If, after removing the food from the marinade, you want to use the liquid as a basting or table sauce, be aware that you first have to destroy any bacteria it may have picked up from the uncooked food. Simply transfer the liquid to a saucepan and bring it to a rolling boil over high heat. Allow it to remain at a boil for at least three minutes before continuing with your recipe.

The following marinades can be used to enhance the flavor and aroma of all the foods you cook on your wood pellet grill. As always, feel free to adjust the seasonings or otherwise change the recipe to suit your tastes. Be adventurous, and you will be rewarded with new and exciting dishes every time you fire up the grill.

Asian Ginger Marinade

This marinade adds excitement and oriental flair to beef, pork, and chicken. The saltiness of the soy sauce combined with the sweetness of the marmalade and the complexity of the ginger and garlic take your food to a whole new level.

YIELD: About ³/₄ cups (enough for 3–4 pounds of food)

¹/₂ cup soy sauce	2 garlic cloves, minced
2 tablespoons orange marmalade	1 shallot, chopped
2 teaspoons minced fresh ginger root	¹/₄ teaspoon crushed red pepper flakes
	¹/₂ teaspoon curry powder

1. Place all of the ingredients in a small bowl, and stir to blend.

2. Place the food in a resealable plastic bag or a covered glass dish, and add the marinade, turning the food to coat. Place in the refrigerator and marinate for at least 3 hours or as long as overnight, turning occasionally to ensure even coating.

3. Remove the food from the marinade, discarding the marinade or boiling it for reuse as a basting sauce. (See the directions on page 34.) Cook the meat as directed in the recipe of your choice.

Basic Memphis-Style Vinegar Marinade

This marinade is spectacular when used to tenderize and flavor tougher cuts like beef brisket. The apple cider vinegar and barbeque sauce provide sweetness and smokiness, and the mustard and garlic add bite. This marinade can also be used as a basting sauce on pork ribs or pork baby back ribs.

YIELD: ABOUT 3 CUPS (ENOUGH FOR 8–10 POUNDS OF MEAT)

2 cups apple cider vinegar	2 tablespoons lemon juice
1 cup Uncle Bob's Basic Barbeque Sauce (page 47) or commercial spicy barbeque sauce	2 tablespoons dry mustard
	1 tablespoon sea salt
	1 tablespoon garlic powder

1. Place all the ingredients in a medium-size saucepan, and bring to a simmer over low heat, stirring to blend. Simmer for 15 minutes, stirring frequently. Remove from the heat and allow the marinade to cool to room temperature.

2. Place the food in a resealable plastic bag or a covered glass dish, and add the cooled marinade, turning the food to coat. Place in the refrigerator and marinate for at least 3 hours or as long as overnight, turning occasionally to ensure even coating.

3. Remove the food from the marinade, discarding the marinade or boiling it for reuse as a basting sauce. (See the directions on page 34.) Cook the meat as directed in the recipe of your choice.

Greek-Style Lemon Marinade

The Greeks have a passion for lemon in their foods. This marinade is very similar to one that I enjoyed on the island of Rhodes. Aromatic and flavorful, it is excellent on lamb and chicken.

YIELD: ABOUT ³/₄ CUP (ENOUGH FOR ABOUT 3 POUNDS OF MEAT)

¹/₃ cup extra virgin olive oil

¹/₄ cup fresh lemon juice (about 2 small lemons)

1 tablespoon minced garlic

1 tablespoon Greek seasoning, or any blend of salt, pepper, garlic, lemon, and oregano

1¹/₂ teaspoons sea salt

1¹/₂ teaspoons ground black pepper

1 teaspoon dried oregano

1 teaspoon poultry seasoning

1 tablespoon grated lemon zest

1. Place all of the ingredients in a small bowl, and stir to blend.

2. Place the food in a resealable plastic bag or a covered glass dish, and add the marinade, turning the food to coat. Place in the refrigerator and marinate for at least 8 hours or as long as overnight, turning occasionally to ensure even coating.

3. Remove the food from the marinade, discarding the marinade or boiling it for reuse as a basting sauce. (See the directions on page 34.) Cook the meat as directed in the recipe of your choice.

Citrus Marinade

With its blend of tangy lemon, lime, and orange juices; a touch of honey to balance the citrus; and savory herbs and spices, this marinade is a perfect complement to poultry, pork, and even beef.

YIELD: ABOUT ¹/₄ CUP (ENOUGH FOR 2 POUNDS OF MEAT)

2 tablespoons fresh lemon juice

2 tablespoons fresh lime juice

2 tablespoons fresh orange juice

2 tablespoons extra virgin olive oil

1 tablespoon honey

1 tablespoon chopped cilantro

¹/₂ teaspoon salt

¹/₂ teaspoon chili powder

¹/₄ teaspoon ground cumin

1. Place all of the ingredients in a small bowl, and stir to blend.

2. Place the food in a resealable plastic bag or a covered glass dish, and add the marinade, turning the food to coat. Place in the refrigerator and marinate for at least 2 hours or as long as overnight, turning occasionally to ensure even coating.

3. Remove the food from the marinade, discarding the marinade or boiling it for reuse as a basting sauce. (See the directions on page 34.) Cook the meat as directed in the recipe of your choice.

Hawaiian Marinade

This marinade—a combination of teriyaki sauce, soy sauce, scallions, and a citrusy lemon spice blend, along with a little heat—is characteristic of Hawaiian cuisine. I first made it after returning from a trip to the islands, and every time I use it, I am reminded of my time in paradise.

YIELD: ABOUT I CUP (ENOUGH FOR 4 POUNDS OF MEAT)

$^1/_2$ cup teriyaki sauce	1 teaspoon hot pepper sauce
$^1/_4$ cup soy sauce	1 teaspoon Sweet Lemon Spice (page 32)
$^1/_4$ cup chopped scallions	

1. Place all of the ingredients in a small bowl, and stir to blend.

2. Place the food in a resealable plastic bag or a covered glass dish, and add the marinade, turning the food to coat. Place in the refrigerator and marinate for at least 8 hours or as long as overnight, turning occasionally to ensure even coating.

3. Remove the food from the marinade, discarding the marinade or boiling it for reuse as a basting sauce. (See the directions on page 34.) Cook the meat as directed in the recipe of your choice.

Brining Turkey, Chicken, and Pork

Brining fowl and pork before smoking and roasting ensures that the meat will be moist and flavorful. These meats tend to dry out when cooked, but brining saturates the fibers with liquids that remain throughout the cooking process. Although brines contain both salt and sugar, these ingredients don't make the food overly salty or sweet. On the other hand, any herbs you include will enhance both the flavor and the aroma of the cooked meat. Be aware that if the meat of choice is labeled "enhanced" or "self-basting," it is not suitable for brining as it has already been injected with salty fluids.

Below, you will find two great recipes for brines. The first is perfect for whole turkeys, whole chickens, and pork roasts. The second was specially created for turkey wings and drumsticks.

Brine for Whole Turkey, Whole Chicken, and Pork Roasts

This amount of brine is perfect for a 12-pound bird or a large pork roast. Vary the herbs according to the meat you're preparing. Tarragon and sage are great when preparing chicken or turkey, and thyme is a wonderful complement to pork.

YIELD: About 1 gallon

1 gallon room-temperature or warm filtered water

1½ cups kosher salt or any coarse salt

1 cup sugar (for chicken or turkey) or brown sugar (for pork)

5 fresh tarragon leaves, chopped, or ⅓ cup dried tarragon (substitute thyme, basil, or sage as desired)

1 tablespoon coarsely ground black pepper

---

1. Place the water in a large container. Add the remaining ingredients and mix thoroughly to dissolve the salt and sugar.

2. Place the meat in a food-grade plastic bucket and cover completely with brine, adding additional water if necessary. Put a weighted plate on top of the meat to keep it submerged in the brine.

3. Place the container in the refrigerator, and allow the meat to remain in the brine overnight.

4. Remove the food from the brine and discard the liquid. Cook the chicken, turkey, or pork as directed in the recipe of your choice.

Brine for Turkey Legs and Wings

This brine will allow you to prepare about 4 turkey legs or 6 turkey wings if using a roasting pan as a brining container, or up to 6 turkey legs or 8 turkey wings if using a food-grade plastic bucket. (See the "For a Change" variations at the end of the recipe for more drumstick and wing brining ideas.)

YIELD: About 1 gallon

1 gallon filtered water	1 bay leaf
1 cup kosher salt or any coarse salt	1 tablespoon black peppercorns
¹/₂ cup brown sugar (light or dark)	1 teaspoon allspice berries

---

1. In a large stockpot, combine all ingredients. Bring the water to a boil, stirring to dissolve the salt and sugar. Reduce the heat and simmer for 15 minutes. Remove from the heat and allow the brine to cool to room temperature.

2. Place the meat in a roasting pan or food-grade plastic bucket, depending on the amount of turkey legs or wings that you're preparing. Cover the meat completely with brine, adding additional water if necessary. Put a weighted plate on top of the meat to keep it submerged in the brine.

3. Place the container in the refrigerator, and allow the meat to remain in the brine overnight.

4. Remove the food from the brine and discard the liquid. Grill the turkey legs or wings as directed in the recipe of your choice.

For a Change

■ For a festive holiday theme, brine turkey legs or wings in Spicy Apple Brine. Combine 1 quart each of apple and orange juice with ¹/₂ gallon of water, 1 cup kosher salt, 1 cup brown sugar, 5 whole cloves, and 1 teaspoon of ground nutmeg.

■ For Asian flair, mix 1 gallon of water with 1 cup brown sugar, 1 cup kosher salt, 1 cup soy sauce, and 1 tablespoon each of garlic powder, black pepper, and cayenne pepper.

Onion and Garlic Marinade

This marinade blends the pungency of garlic and onions with the tang of lemon juice and the complex flavors of Worcestershire Sauce. Use it to marinate beef, pork, or chicken.

YIELD: ABOUT ³/₄ CUP (ENOUGH FOR 2–3 POUNDS OF MEAT)

¹/₄ cup Worcestershire sauce	2 tablespoons fresh lemon juice
¹/₄ cup minced onion	2 tablespoons extra virgin olive oil
2 garlic cloves, minced	³/₄ teaspoon sea salt

1. Place all of the ingredients in a small bowl, and stir to blend.

2. Place the food in a resealable plastic bag or a covered glass dish, and add the marinade, turning the food to coat. Place in the refrigerator and marinate for at least 3 hours or as long as overnight, turning occasionally to ensure even coating.

3. Remove the food from the marinade, discarding the marinade or boiling it for reuse as a basting sauce. (See the directions on page 34.) Cook the meat as directed in the recipe of your choice.

Barbeque Trivia

Like most people, you probably love good barbeque. But are you truly knowledgeable about common BBQ terms and facts? This short quiz will give you a better idea of your grilling IQ.

1. After meat has been barbequed for hours, what is its rub-flavored coating called?

a. Bark.
b. Peel.
c. Crust.

2. What cut of meat is generally referred to as a "pork butt"?

a. The shoulder of the pig.
b. The rear end of the pig.
c. A full, untrimmed pork loin.

3. What is the barbeque delicacy known as "finger meat"?

a. Any tidbit so small you can pick it up with two fingers.
b. Any bit of meat that falls off a slow-cooked side of beef.
c. The meat found between baby back ribs.

4. What is served when you order "burnt ends" at a Kansas City eatery?

a. Crisp sticks of Kansas City cornbread.
b. Charred bits of beef brisket.
c. Spare ribs made with a dry rub.

5. What is the most commonly barbequed item in the United States?

a. Chicken wings
b. Hot dogs
c. Hamburgers

6. What are you doing when you eat "high on the hog"?

a. You're eating only meat found above the pig's legs.
b. You're eating while intoxicated.
c. You're eating only the choicest pieces of the pig.

Answers

1.a 2.c 3.c 4.b 5.c 6.a

SAUCES FOR MEATS AND SEAFOOD

The remainder of this chapter offers a selection of barbeque sauces that can be used to deliciously flavor the meats you prepare on your wood pellet grill. Many of these sauces were influenced by specific areas of the country, each of which has its own view of what makes a barbeque sauce great. My Kansas City sauce is a sweet tomato-based creation, while my vinegar-based Memphis-style sauce is more acidic. In Texas, they start with a tomato base and spice it up with both hot pepper sauce and crushed red pepper flakes. Each of these sauces can be paired with rubs and specific woods to produce a unique taste.

In the Midwest, grill masters like to use a thick tomato-based sauce that is both spicy and sweet. I have included two of my absolute favorites in this section. Uncle Bob's Basic Barbeque Sauce is deep red in color, thick, and rich, with a little spiciness on the finish. The Spicy Rum Barbeque Sauce has a chocolaty color and is full-bodied with many layers of flavor and a touch of spice.

It is usually best to brush a barbeque sauce over the cooked meat just before removing it from the grill. The sugar in the sauce will cause it to burn if it's applied too early in the cooking process. The exceptions to this rule are the Basic Buffalo Wing Sauce and the Basic Memphis-Style Mop Sauce, which must be brushed on the food several times during cooking, as directed in the recipe. Remember that if you choose to serve any leftover sauce on the side or to refrigerate it for future use, you must not let it come into contact with the raw meat or the basting brush.

Among these recipes, you'll find two sauces that are different from the rest. French Lobster Sauce and Fiesta Lime Spice Butter were designed to add a luxurious touch to grilled seafood, and they do their job beautifully.

The following recipes are simple to make but complex in flavor. Most yield a generous amount, so you'll probably have some left over when you're finished cooking. I highly recommend that you make the barbeque sauces in advance and store them in the refrigerator until ready for use. This allows the ingredients to meld and develop the many layers of flavor that make barbeque so enticing. As long as you transfer them to clean covered jars and store them in the refrigerator, they will keep well for over a month—in some cases, for several months. Of course, in my house, they never last that long!

Basic Memphis-Style Mop Sauce

This simple sauce features the wonderful flavor of apple cider vinegar enhanced by mustard and garlic. When "mopped" over beef or pork, the sauce tenderizes and flavors the meat.

YIELD: ABOUT 2¼ CUPS (ENOUGH FOR 6–8 POUNDS OF MEAT)

2 cups apple cider vinegar	1 teaspoon sea salt
3 tablespoons dry mustard	1 teaspoon garlic powder
2 tablespoons lemon juice	

1. Combine all of the ingredients in a medium-sized saucepan and bring to a simmer over low heat, stirring occasionally. Continue to simmer until the ingredients are well blended.

2. Remove the sauce from the heat and allow it to cool to room temperature. Use the sauce as directed in the recipe of your choice, or brush it on the meat every 30 minutes or so during cooking. Reserve some of the mop sauce to serve with the meat.

3. Transfer any leftover sauce to a clean jar and store in the refrigerator for up to 2 months.

Basic Buffalo Wing Sauce

Buffalo wings originated in Buffalo, New York, but have made a name for themselves all over the world. This sauce—which is more heat than sweet—makes wings a hit at our house when we watch sports events like the Super Bowl, or any time there are three or more of us in front of the TV.

YIELD: ABOUT 1 CUP (ENOUGH FOR 12–15 WINGS)

⅓ cup melted butter	⅓ cup ketchup
⅓ cup hot pepper sauce	2 tablespoons honey

1. Combine all of the ingredients in a small saucepan and bring to a boil. Reduce the heat to a simmer and cook over low heat, stirring occasionally, for 15 minutes.

2. Remove the sauce from the heat and allow it to cool to room temperature.

3. Use the sauce as directed in the recipe of your choice, or brush it on after the wings have been on the grill for 15 minutes or so. Cook for another 15 minutes, turn the wings again, and brush on more sauce. Before removing the wings from the grill, turn and baste one more time.

4. Transfer any leftover sauce to a clean jar and store in the refrigerator for up to 2 weeks.

Basic Kansas City-Style Barbeque Sauce

Rich and thick, this Kansas City-style sauce clings beautifully to meat. Brush it on after the food is fully cooked, just before removing it from the grill. Then allow the sauce to set for a few minutes before serving. Your dish will look and taste spectacular!

YIELD: About 2 cups (enough for 6–8 pounds of meat)

1 cup ketchup	2 tablespoons hickory liquid smoke
$^1/_4$ cup plus 1 tablespoon Worcestershire sauce	$1^1/_2$ tablespoons prepared mustard
$^1/_4$ cup firmly packed brown sugar	$1^1/_2$ tablespoons Kansas City-Style Rub (page 19) or commercial sweet Kansas City-style seasoning
$^1/_4$ cup apple cider vinegar	
3 tablespoons minced yellow onion	1 teaspoon sea salt
3 tablespoons molasses	$^1/_4$ teaspoon hot pepper sauce

1. Combine all of the ingredients in a medium-sized saucepan and bring to a boil, stirring occasionally.

2. Reduce the heat to a simmer and cook over low heat, stirring occasionally, for 20 minutes, or until the sauce is dark red, thick, and rich in flavor.

3. Use the sauce as directed in the recipe of your choice, or brush it on fully cooked food just before removing it from the grill. Allow the meat to sit for a few minutes before serving.

4. Transfer any leftover sauce to a clean jar and store in the refrigerator for up to 2 months.

French Lobster Sauce

This sauce is extraordinary and an absolute must when serving grilled or baked lobster tails. The flavors and aromas of the wine and shallots meld with the butter and lemon to highlight the magnificence of the lobster. For an extra special treat, pair the lobster tails with a brut (very dry) champagne. Bon appétit!

YIELD: About 1$^{1}/_{2}$ cups (enough for 6 tails)	
$^{1}/_{2}$ cup dry white wine	1$^{1}/_{4}$ cups whole milk
2 shallots, minced	Sea salt and pepper to taste
$^{1}/_{4}$ cup butter, divided	1 tablespoon fresh lemon juice
3 tablespoons all-purpose flour	

1. Place the wine in a small saucepan. Add the shallots and slowly simmer over low heat, stirring occasionally, for about 25 minutes, or until the wine is reduced to 2 to 3 tablespoons. Set aside.

Choosing a Dry Wine for Cooking

Whenever a recipe calls for a "dry wine," it's referring to a wine that has no residual sugar. Typically, wines are dry unless the winemaker has stopped fermentation during the winemaking process, leaving the wine (either white or red) a little sweet. This is customary for White Zinfandel and for some Rieslings, which are traditionally sweet. However, there are Rieslings that are fully fermented, meaning that there is virtually no residual sugar remaining, making the wine dry.

One way to determine if a wine is sweet or dry is to check the alcohol content, which is listed on the label. If the content is 10 to 11 percent, the wine is generally sweet. As the alcohol level goes up, the overall sweetness of the wine decreases.

When the alcohol level rises above 15 percent, the wine is considered dry and may actually be "hot," meaning that the alcohol can be sensed as a slight burning in the mouth and throat, similar to the feel of bourbon or vodka, but less extreme. Exceptions to this rule are Port and dessert wines, which are usually made from sweet, late harvest grapes and fortified with additional alcohol. In the case of these products, the alcohol content is usually high (as high as 21 percent), but the wine is sweet.

If you have questions about the best wine to use for a particular purpose, do not hesitate to ask the staff at your local liquor store. They are there to help you make the right choice.

THE COMPLETE WOOD PELLET BARBEQUE COOKBOOK

2. Melt 3 tablespoons of the butter in a medium-size skillet over low heat. Stir in the flour to make a roux.

3. Slowly add the milk to the roux in a constant stream, whisking continuously until the mixture has thickened. Season with salt and pepper to taste.

4. Add the reduced wine and shallots to the milk mixture, and whisk to blend well.

5. Add the remaining tablespoon of butter and the lemon juice to the sauce, and stir continuously to melt the butter.

6. Pour some of the sauce over prepared lobster tails, and serve the remainder on the side. Store any leftover sauce in the refrigerator for up to 2 days.

Fiesta Lime Spice Butter

This seasoned butter is a party looking for a place to happen. The blend of citrus, salt, garlic, herbs, and spices added to melted butter makes a perfect sauce to brush on grilled shrimp or lobster. This is one of my personal favorites.

YIELD: ABOUT $^1/_2$ CUP (ENOUGH FOR UP TO 1$^1/_2$ POUNDS OF SHELLFISH)

$^1/_2$ cup melted butter

1 teaspoon dried lime peel, or chopped zest from 1 fresh lime

1 teaspoon lime powder,* or juice from 1–2 fresh limes

1 teaspoon coarse sea salt

1 teaspoon minced fresh garlic

$^1/_2$ teaspoon onion powder

$^1/_4$ teaspoon sugar

$^1/_4$ teaspoon paprika

$^1/_8$ teaspoon cayenne pepper

$^1/_8$ teaspoon chili powder

$^1/_8$ teaspoon dried basil

* This dehydrated flavoring can be obtained from Internet stores and some specialty shops. See the inset on page 28 for more information.

---

1. Place all the ingredients in a small bowl, and use a spoon to blend well.

2. Brush this seasoned butter on seafood before placing the food on the grill. Then brush each side once more during the grilling process. Store any leftover butter in the refrigerator for up to 2 days.

Spicy Texas-Style Barbeque Sauce

This simple but memorable sauce features the heat that is characteristic of Texas-style barbeque. When tasting this sauce, note the little bit of sweet up front followed by the acidic smoky tang in the middle and a big bite of hot on the back of the palate. This is such a favorite in my house that I often double the recipe to make sure that I have enough on hand. Use it on beef ribs, roasts, and brisket; pork ribs, roasts, and shoulder; and chicken.

YIELD: ABOUT 1³/₄ CUPS (ENOUGH FOR 5–6 POUNDS OF MEAT)

---

1 cup ketchup

¹/₂ cup packed brown sugar

¹/₄ cup plus 1 tablespoon Worcestershire sauce

3 tablespoons finely minced yellow onion (fresh or dried)

1 tablespoon cider vinegar

1 tablespoon plus 1 teaspoon hickory liquid smoke

1 tablespoon prepared mustard

1 teaspoon salt

¹/₂ teaspoon hot pepper sauce

¹/₂ teaspoon crushed red pepper flakes

---

1. Combine all of the ingredients in a medium-sized saucepan and bring to a boil, stirring to mix well.

2. Reduce the heat to a simmer and cook over low heat, stirring occasionally, for 20 minutes, or until the sauce is dark red, thick, and rich in flavor.

3. Use the sauce as directed in the recipe of your choice, or brush it on fully cooked food just before removing it from the grill. Allow the meat to sit for a few minutes before serving.

4. Transfer any leftover sauce to a clean jar and store in the refrigerator for up to 2 months.

Uncle Bob's Basic Barbeque Sauce

This sauce is rich in color, sweet with a spicy finish, and so thick that it instantly clings when it comes in contact with hot food. Use it on beef, pork, chicken, turkey, and even seafood.

YIELD: About 3 1/2 cups (enough for 10–12 pounds of meat)

2 cups ketchup

3/4 cup molasses

1/4 cup Worcestershire sauce

3 tablespoons red wine vinegar

3 tablespoons prepared mustard

2 tablespoons chili powder

1 tablespoon plus 1 teaspoon hickory liquid smoke

3 tablespoons dried minced onion

2 teaspoons dried minced garlic

1–2 teaspoons crushed red pepper flakes or hot pepper sauce (optional)

2 teaspoons sea salt

---

1. Combine all of the ingredients in a medium-size saucepan and bring to a boil, stirring occasionally.

2. Reduce the heat to a simmer and cook over low heat, stirring occasionally, for 20 minutes, or until the sauce is dark red, thick, and rich in flavor.

3. Use the sauce as directed in the recipe of your choice, or brush it on fully cooked food just before removing it from the grill. Allow the meat to sit for a few minutes before serving.

4. Transfer any leftover sauce to a clean jar and store in the refrigerator for up to 6 weeks.

For a Change

■ To make Spicy Wing Sauce, follow the recipe as directed above, but in Step 1, also add 1 teaspoon cayenne pepper, 1 teaspoon smoked paprika, 1/2 teaspoon ground cumin, and 1/4 teaspoon lemon peel granules. If a hotter sauce is desired, increase the cayenne pepper or hot sauce. This is great on turkey wings. (See the Saucy Smoked Turkey Wings recipe on page 124.)

Spicy Rum Barbeque Sauce

When you bite into meat that's been brushed with this sauce, you experience the sweetness of molasses; a mid-palate kick from the vinegar; and some heat from the rum, cayenne, and crushed red pepper. The sauce pairs extremely well with beef, any cut of pork, and chicken. You and your guests will not be disappointed.

YIELD: About 5 cups (enough for 12–14 pounds of meat)

2 cups ketchup	1/4 cup chili powder
1 cup molasses	2 tablespoons dried minced onion
1/2 cup good-quality dark rum	2 tablespoons dried minced garlic
1/2 cup Worcestershire sauce	2 teaspoons crushed red pepper flakes
1/2 cup red wine vinegar	
1/2 cup prepared mustard	2 teaspoons sea salt
2 tablespoons liquid smoke	1 teaspoon cayenne pepper

1. Combine the ketchup, molasses, rum, Worcestershire sauce, vinegar, mustard, and liquid smoke in a 2-quart saucepan, stirring to mix.

2. Combine all of the remaining ingredients in a small bowl. Add to the saucepan, whisking to blend well with the wet ingredients.

3. Bring the mixture to a simmer over low heat, and cook, stirring occasionally, for 30 to 35 minutes, or until thickened.

4. Use the sauce as directed in the recipe of your choice, or brush it on fully cooked food just before removing it from the grill. Let the meat sit for 10 minutes, allowing the sauce to caramelize before serving.

5. Transfer any leftover sauce to a clean jar and store in the refrigerator for up to 6 weeks.

3.

Beautiful Barbecued Beef

Beef is not only the King of Texas-Style Barbeque, but also one of the most popular meats in the barbeque world, and the wood pellet grill is the perfect way to cook this truly sublime food. When the proper spices are combined with smoke from carefully chosen wood, the resulting dish is melt-in-your-mouth tender and full of flavor, with an aroma that will beckon everyone to the dinner table long before it's time to serve your masterpiece.

This chapter guides you in creating a variety of beef dishes using different cuts of meat and a wide range of flavorings and wood pellets. It begins with nearly everyone's favorite, the steak, presenting dishes as beautifully simple as a seasoned filet and as complex and sophisticated as a Stuffed London Broil with

Mushroom Sauce. In each case, you'll learn how to use the grill to flavor and cook the meat to perfection.

In the mood for a little luxury? This chapter instructs you in preparing one of the most sumptuous cuts of beef—the tenderloin. And whether you desire a simple herb-seasoned roast or one that's enhanced with flavorful marinades and sauces, there's a dish that's right for you.

Although the brisket is generally seen as a challenging cut of beef, the wood pellet grill—with its ability to infuse meat with aromatic smoke while providing low, even heat—makes preparation a breeze. In fact, brisket may soon become your family's favorite dish.

If you have a yen for still more beef dishes, don't worry: This chapter serves up several more options in style. The following pages offer recipes for prime rib roasts, roast beef, and two kinds of ribs. And every single one will result in a memorable meal. (For burger recipes, see Chapter 4.)

Although each recipe in this chapter recommends specific spice mixes, marinades, and/or barbeque sauces that perfectly complement that cut of beef, I encourage you to be bold and mix and match different spices and sauces. (See Chapter 2 for a wide assortment of rubs and sauces.) And if you don't have the time to make your own blends, simply look for a commercial spice mixture, marinade, or sauce that contains similar ingredients.

So whether you want to grill up a sensationally flavorful steak or enjoy a steaming plate of slow-cooked Texas-style brisket, you have definitely come to the right place. You'll be amazed by how beautiful beef can be when prepared on a wood pellet grill.

Stuffed London Broil with Mushroom Sauce

This recipe is simple to assemble but elegant in presentation. The combination of the Prime Rib Rub, bread stuffing, and creamy mushroom sauce makes this a winner in the comfort food category, and perfect for special occasions as well. The recommended pellets for this recipe are cherry or maple. Both are a good match with the prime rib seasoning. Enjoy!

YIELD: 6–8 SERVINGS
RECOMMENDED PELLETS: CHERRY OR MAPLE
MARINATION/SEASONING TIME: NONE
COOKING TIME: ABOUT 1 HOUR AND 15 MINUTES

3- to 4-pound London broil, 1½ to 2 inches thick, trimmed of excess fat

3 cups prepared seasoned bread stuffing mix or homemade stuffing

2 tablespoons Prime Rib Rub (page 24) or commercial spice blend for beef

CREAMY BUTTON MUSHROOM SAUCE

2 tablespoons butter, divided

12 ounces button mushrooms, sliced

1½ tablespoons all-purpose flour

½ cup milk or half-and-half

Sea salt and ground black pepper to taste

1. Rinse the London broil in cold water and dry with paper towels. Using a sharp knife, butterfly the London broil in half, but do not cut completely through. Set aside.

2. Start the pellet grill and set the temperature control to 180°F or "Smoke."

3. Open the London broil and arrange the stuffing over one half. Cover the stuffing with the other half of the steak and insert toothpicks through the edges to keep the 2 halves together. Rub 1 tablespoon of the Prime Rib Spice on each side of the London broil.

4. When the grill reaches the desired temperature, place the steak on the grate, close the grill door, and smoke the meat for 30 minutes. Increase the temperature to 350°F and cook for 45 to 50 minutes, or until done as desired. An instant-read thermometer should read 120°F to 130°F for rare, 135°F to 145°F for medium, or 155°F or greater for well done.

5. Transfer the steak to a cutting board, cover with foil, and allow to rest for 5 to 10 minutes.

6. While the meat is resting, make the mushroom sauce by melting 1 tablespoon of the butter in a medium saucepan over medium heat. Add the mushrooms and sauté, stirring occasionally, for 5 to 7 minutes, or until the mushrooms are tender. Remove the mushrooms from the pan. Add the remaining butter to the pan and stir in the flour to make a roux. Add the milk or half-and-half in a slow stream, whisking constantly until the cream begins to thicken. Add salt and pepper to taste and return the mushrooms to the pan, heating just until warm.

7. Slice the London broil into 1-inch-thick serving pieces, and serve immediately with a dish of the mushroom sauce on the side.

Prime, Choice, Select, or Standard?

The United States Department of Agriculture grades beef for quality, which is based on fat marbling and the age of the cattle. In general, the greater the marbling, the more tender and flavorful the meat. As for age, cattle between eighteen and twenty-four months old has the best flavor. Butchers are likely to carry the top four grades:

Prime grade beef is the best. Often coming from younger cattle, the meat is rich with marbling. Less than 3 percent of beef is graded Prime, making it more expensive and usually reserved for fine restaurants.

Choice grade beef is also high quality but has less marbling than Prime. This is the most popular grade because it contains sufficient marbling for taste and tenderness, but is less expensive than Prime. About half the beef is graded Choice.

Select grade beef has less marbling than the other grades. Although it is leaner, it is not as tender, juicy, or flavorful. About a third of graded beef falls into this category.

Standard grade beef has virtually no marbling and little flavor. If the package does not state a grade, the beef is likely to be Standard.

Most supermarkets carry a selection of Choice and Select beef, while a few high-end gourmet markets and butcher shops offer Prime. If they don't have what you want, they may be able to special order it for you.

Filet Mignon

This recipe infuses filet mignon with the flavors and aromas of ginger, garlic, and soy sauce. Wrapped with bacon and grilled over high heat for a short time, this steak literally melts in your mouth. One of life's simple pleasures is an ultra-expensive dish when dining out, but you can enjoy the magnificence of filet mignon at home for a fraction of the cost.

YIELD: 6 SERVINGS
RECOMMENDED PELLETS: OAK OR MESQUITE
MARINATION/SEASONING TIME: 2 TO 4 HOURS
COOKING TIME: ABOUT 30 MINUTES

6 filet mignon steaks, about 6 ounces each	6 strips bacon
$^1/_2$ cup Asian Ginger Marinade (page 34) or commercial soy-ginger marinade	$^1/_2$ teaspoon coarsely ground sea salt
	$^1/_2$ teaspoon coarsely ground black pepper

1. Rinse the steaks in cold water and dry with paper towels. Place the steaks in a resealable plastic bag or a shallow covered glass dish and add the marinade, turning the meat to coat. Transfer to the refrigerator and allow the meat to marinate for 2 to 4 hours, turning once or twice.

2. Remove the meat from the marinade, draining well, and discard the marinade. Allow the steaks to sit at room temperature for 30 minutes. While the steaks are warming, start the pellet grill and set the temperature control to 375°F.

3. Wrap a strip of bacon around the edge of each steak and secure with kitchen twine or a toothpick. Season the steaks generously with salt and pepper.

4. When the grill has reached the desired temperature, transfer the steaks to the grill grate. Close the grill door and cook for 12 to 15 minutes on each side, or until done as desired. An instant-read thermometer should read 120°F to 130° F for rare, 135°F to 145°F for medium, or 155°F or greater for well done.

5. Transfer the steaks to a platter, cover with aluminum foil, and allow to rest for 5 minutes. Remove and discard the strings or toothpicks and serve immediately.

For a Change

■ To enjoy the wonderful flavor of filet mignon without any distractions, omit the marinade and bacon. Simply brush the steak with a very light coating of olive oil, sprinkle with salt and pepper, and grill according to the recipe directions.

QUICK GRILLING FOR FILET MIGNON

For those occasions when you want to cook Filet Mignon more quickly, increase the grill temperature to 400°F and decrease the cooking time to about 10 minutes per side. Just remember that whenever you turn up the temperature of the grill, you reduce the food's smoky flavor and aroma. (For more information on Quick Grilling, see page 12.)

Hawaiian Island Steaks

When you're ready for a getaway, why not choose Hawaii? If you don't have time for an actual trip, the sensual aroma of these steaks will transport you to the islands in no time flat. The recommended pellets for this recipe are a blend of cherry and mesquite. Aloha and Mahalo.

YIELD: 4 SERVINGS
RECOMMENDED PELLETS: CHERRY AND MESQUITE
MARINATION/SEASONING TIME: 4 HOURS
COOKING TIME: ABOUT 30 MINUTES

---

4 New York strip steaks (8 ounces each), about 1 inch thick, trimmed of excess fat

$^1/_2$ cup Asian Ginger Marinade (page 34) or commercial soy-ginger marinade

4 pineapple slices, fresh or canned (unsweetened)

---

1. Rinse the steaks in cold water and dry with paper towels. Place the steaks in a resealable plastic bag or a shallow covered glass dish, and add the marinade, turning the steaks to coat. Transfer to the refrigerator and allow the meat to marinate for 4 hours, turning once or twice.

2. Start the pellet grill and set the temperature control to 350°F.

3. Remove the steaks from the marinade, reserving the marinade. Transfer the marinade to a saucepan and bring to a rolling boil over high heat. Allow it to remain at a boil for at least 3 minutes before continuing with the recipe.

4. When the grill has reached the desired temperature, arrange the steaks on the grill grate. Close the grill door and cook for 12 to 15 minutes on each side, brushing the steaks occasionally with the marinade. When the steaks are almost done, place the pineapple slices on the grill. Brush with the marinade and cook until the pineapple is heated through.

5. Use an instant-read thermometer to check the internal temperature of the steaks. It should read 120°F to 130°F for rare, 135°F to 145°F for medium, or 155°F or greater for well done.

6. Transfer the steaks to a serving platter and place 1 pineapple slice on each steak. Cover with aluminum foil and allow to rest for 5 to 10 minutes before serving.

Porterhouse Steak Italiano

Porterhouse is a marvelous cut of beef that provides two separate options—the top strip on one side of the bone, and the tenderloin on the other. When cooked over oak or mesquite and bathed in a blend of extra virgin olive oil, herbs, and garlic, the results are simply fabulous.

YIELD: 4 SERVINGS
RECOMMENDED PELLETS: OAK OR MESQUITE
MARINATION/SEASONING TIME: NONE
COOKING TIME: ABOUT 30 MINUTES

1³/₄-pound porterhouse steak, 1¹/₂ to 2 inches thick, trimmed of excess fat

1 tablespoon coarsely ground sea salt

1 tablespoon coarsely ground black pepper

1 tablespoon chopped fresh rosemary

6 leaves fresh basil, roughly chopped

1 teaspoon chopped fresh oregano

2 garlic cloves, finely minced

¹/₂ cup extra virgin olive oil

1. Start the pellet grill and set the temperature control to 375°F.

2. Rinse the steak in cold water and dry with paper towels. Generously season the steak with salt and pepper.

3. When the grill reaches the desired temperature, place the steak on the grate, close the grill door, and cook for 12 to 15 minutes per side. After the first 6 to 7 minutes of cooking each side, rotate the steak a few degrees to create crosshatch grill marks on the meat. An instant-read thermometer will read 120°F to 130°F for rare, 135°F to 145°F for medium, or 155°F or greater for well done.

4. Transfer the steak from the grill to a platter, cover with foil, and allow it to rest for 5 minutes. While the steak is resting, scatter the rosemary, basil, oregano, and garlic on the bottom of a wide, deep dish. Place the steak in the dish and pour the olive oil over the top. Turn the meat over several times to coat, and let it sit in the herb and oil mixture for 10 to 15 minutes.

5. Transfer the steak to a cutting board and remove the tenderloin and top loin strip from the bone. Carve the meat across the grain into ¹/₄-inch slices, and transfer to a serving platter. Spoon the oil mixture over the steak and serve.

QUICK GRILLING FOR PORTERHOUSE STEAK

For those occasions when you want to cook Porterhouse Steak Italiano more quickly, increase the grill temperature to 400°F and decrease the cooking time to about 10 minutes per side. Just remember that whenever you turn up the temperature, you reduce the food's smoky flavor and aroma. (For more information on Quick Grilling, see page 12.)

Grilled Sirloin Steak with Mushroom Sauce

This wonderful recipe probably originated in an old American steak house. Updated to eliminate the lard in which the steak used to be cooked, it has emerged healthier but just as flavorful and aromatic. I recommend using mesquite or maple pellets for this recipe.

YIELD: 4 SERVINGS
RECOMMENDED PELLETS: MESQUITE OR MAPLE
MARINATION/SEASONING TIME: 2 HOURS
COOKING TIME: ABOUT 30 MINUTES

1½-pound sirloin steak, 1½ inches thick, trimmed of excess fat

¾ cup Onion and Garlic Marinade (page 40) or commercial onion- or garlic-flavored marinade

MUSHROOM SAUCE

2 tablespoons butter

8 ounces button mushrooms, sliced

1 tablespoon chopped fresh parsley

1 teaspoon Worcestershire sauce

1. Rinse the steak in cold water and dry with paper towels. Place the steak in a resealable plastic bag or a shallow covered glass dish, and add the marinade, turning the steak to coat. Transfer to the refrigerator and allow the meat to marinate for 2 hours, turning once or twice.

2. Start the pellet grill and set the temperature control to 350°F.

3. Remove the steak from the marinade, reserving the marinade. Transfer the marinade to a saucepan and bring to a rolling boil over high heat. Allow it to remain at a boil for at least 3 minutes before continuing with your recipe.

4. When the grill has reached the desired temperature, transfer the steak to the grill grate. Close the grill door and cook for 12 to15 minutes on each side, or until done as desired, occasionally brushing it with the marinade. An instant-read thermometer should read 120°F to 130°F for rare, 135°F to 145°F for medium, or 155°F or greater for well done. Transfer the steak to a cutting board, cover with aluminum foil, and allow to rest for at least 5 minutes.

5. While the steak is resting, make the sauce by heating the butter in a large skillet. Add the mushrooms, turn the heat to high, and sauté, stirring often, for about 5 minutes, or until the mushrooms are tender. Reduce the heat to low and stir in the parsley and Worcestershire sauce. Remove the sauce from the heat just before serving.

6. Slice the steak thinly, arrange it on a serving platter, and top with the sauce. Serve immediately.

Herb and Garlic Fillet of Beef

In this recipe, the aromatics of the rosemary, thyme, and oregano blend with the pungency of the garlic and the light smoke of the grill, creating a wonderful concert of aromas and flavors. For best results, use cherry pellets.

YIELD: 4–6 SERVINGS
RECOMMENDED PELLETS: CHERRY
MARINATION/SEASONING TIME: NONE
COOKING TIME: 50 MINUTES

4-pound beef tenderloin, trimmed of excess fat

2 garlic cloves, cut into thin slivers

2 tablespoons chopped fresh rosemary, or 1¹/₂ tablespoons dried rosemary

1 tablespoon chopped fresh thyme, or 2 teaspoons dried thyme

1 tablespoon chopped fresh oregano, or 2 teaspoons dried oregano

2 teaspoons coarse sea salt

2 teaspoons coarsely ground black pepper

3 tablespoons chopped fresh parsley for garnish

1. Start the pellet grill and set the temperature control to 350°F.

2. Rinse the tenderloin in cold water and dry with paper towels. If the tenderloin is in 2 pieces, tie them together using kitchen twine. Use a sharp knife to cut slits in the surface of the beef; then insert the slivers of garlic.

3. Lay out a sheet of waxed paper large enough to hold the meat. Bruise the fresh rosemary, thyme, and oregano, or rub the dried herbs to release the oils. Evenly spread the herbs and sea salt on the paper.

4. Rub the black pepper evenly over the beef so that the pepper remains in place. Roll the beef fillet in the salt and herb mixture to coat evenly. Then press the herb mixture into the meat by hand.

5. When the grill reaches the desired temperature, transfer the meat to the grate, close the grill door, and roast until it reaches the desired level of doneness, about 50 minutes. An instant-read thermometer will read 120°F to 130°F for rare, 135°F to 145°F for medium, or 155°F or greater for well done.

6. Transfer the meat to the cutting board, cover with aluminum foil, and allow to rest for 10 minutes before thinly slicing. Sprinkle with the parsley and serve.

QUICK GRILLING FOR HERB AND GARLIC FILLET

For those occasions when you want to cook Herb and Garlic Fillet of Beef more quickly, increase the grill temperature to 400°F and decrease the cooking time to about 35 minutes. Just remember that whenever you turn up the temperature of the grill, you reduce the food's smoky flavor and aroma. (For more information on Quick Grilling, see page 12.)

Cherry Smoke Prime Rib Roast

The thought of a rib roast conjures up images of an elegant dinner served to the elite. But with your pellet grill, you can easily make a rib roast that rivals that of any gourmet restaurant. Rib roasts can be prepared in a variety of ways. This particular version uses a simple spice mixture and the pellet grill to achieve perfection. I recommend cherry wood to complement the spices.

YIELD: 4 SERVINGS
RECOMMENDED PELLETS: CHERRY
MARINATION/SEASONING TIME: 4 HOURS TO OVERNIGHT
COOKING TIME: 2 TO 2$^1/_2$ HOURS

5$^1/_2$-pound prime rib roast (2–3 bones) $^1/_2$ cup Prime Rib Rub (page 24)
                                                or commercial spice blend for beef

1. Rinse the rib roast in cold water and dry with paper towels.

2. Rub the spice mix liberally over all sides of the roast. Wrap the meat securely in plastic wrap and refrigerate for at least 4 hours or as long as overnight.

3. Start the pellet grill and set the temperature control to 180°F or "Smoke."

4. When the grill reaches the desired temperature, remove the roast from the refrigerator and discard the plastic wrap. Place the meat in an appropriate size aluminum pan, bone side down, and transfer to the grill. Close the grill door and allow the meat to smoke uncovered for 1$^1/_2$ to 2 hours.

5. Increase the temperature of the grill to 300°F and continue to cook for 35 to 45 minutes, or until the meat reaches the desired degree of doneness. An instant-read thermometer should read 120°F to 130°F for rare, 135°F to 145°F for medium, or 155°F or greater for well done.

6. Remove the pan from the grill and cover it with aluminum foil. Allow the meat to rest for about 15 minutes.

7. Transfer the meat to a cutting board and cut the bones away from the meat. Carve the meat into $^1/_2$-inch slices and serve.

Barbequed Beef Tenderloin

Beef tenderloin is a luxurious cut of meat and a pleasure to present at the dinner table. It is flavorful when coated with salt and pepper, but when seasoned more creatively, it takes on a new and exciting persona. In this recipe, the soft smokiness of the spice augmented with the sesame oil and garlic contributes to the glory of the tenderloin. Mesquite pellets further enhance the dish, resulting in a little piece of heaven.

YIELD: 7–8 SERVINGS
RECOMMENDED PELLETS: MESQUITE
MARINATION/SEASONING TIME: 8 HOURS TO OVERNIGHT
COOKING TIME: ABOUT 2 HOURS

6- to 7-pound beef tenderloin, trimmed of excess fat

MARINADE*

$^{1}/_{2}$ cup Home-Style Seasoning Mix (page 26) or commercial hickory smoke-and-spice blend

$^{3}/_{4}$ cup sesame oil

3 garlic cloves, minced

SAUCE

$2^{1}/_{2}$ cups Spicy Rum Barbeque Sauce (page 48) or commercial rum-based or honey-bourbon barbeque sauce

* Instead of this homemade marinade, you can use $1^{1}/_{4}$ cups of a commercial steakhouse-style marinade.

---

1. Blend the marinade ingredients in a small bowl.

2. Rinse the tenderloin in cold water and dry with paper towels. Place the meat in a resealable plastic bag or a covered glass dish, and add the marinade, turning the food to coat. Transfer to the refrigerator and allow the meat to marinate for 8 hours or overnight, occasionally turning the tenderloin or massaging the plastic bag to ensure absorption of the marinade into the meat.

3. Remove the tenderloin from the marinade, reserving the marinade. If the tenderloin is in 2 pieces, tie them together using kitchen twine. Start the pellet grill and set the temperature control to 225°F.

4. Transfer the marinade to a saucepan and bring to a rolling boil over high heat. Allow it to remain at a boil for at least 3 minutes before continuing with your recipe.

5. When the grill reaches the desired temperature, transfer the meat to the grill grate, close the door, and smoke for 30 minutes. Increase the temperature to 325°F and continue to grill, basting the meat every 20 to 30 minutes with the boiled marinade until it reaches the desired level of doneness, about 1$\frac{1}{2}$ hours. An instant-read thermometer will read 120°F to 130°F for rare, 135°F to 145°F for medium, or 155°F or greater for well done.

6. When the roast is almost done, warm the barbeque sauce in a small saucepan.

7. Transfer the tenderloin to a cutting board, cover with aluminum foil, and allow to rest for 10 minutes before slicing thinly into serving portions. Serve with the warmed sauce on the side.

The Best Wines for Beef Dishes

In the past, wine and food experts believed that the big, bold taste of beef called for the fuller taste of red wines. Now, most experts agree that that the best wine for any meal is the one that pleases your palate. That being said, it is true that some wines tend to better complement the flavor of beef, and that the way in which you prepare the dish should be considered when you select a beverage. The following list includes some great wines to serve with your next wood pellet-grilled beef.

Cabernet Sauvignon. A dry red wine with medium to heavy tannins, cabernet has aromas of blackberry, black currant, cassis, mint, and plum. This wine is wonderful with grilled, roasted, and braised beef, but is not the best choice for very spicy beef dishes.

Merlot. This dry, fruity red wine is similar to Cabernet Sauvignon, but softer in texture and with a rounder mouth feel. Enjoy it with lightly spiced beef and especially with any dishes that include mushrooms.

Red Zinfandel. A medium- to full-bodied dry red wine, Red Zinfandel has blackberry, boysenberry, and plumy fruit notes. Enjoy it with spiced, smoky dishes like barbequed beef brisket.

Sangiovese. Light- to medium-bodied, this dry red Italian wine can be thin and watery or rich and complex. When young, the wine has some fruit sweetness. As it ages, it can take on earthy flavors like tea and orange peel. Sangiovese is magical with spicy beef dishes, especially those with garlic.

Syrah. This full-bodied dry red wine, which is a little bolder than Cabernet and Merlot, exhibits aromas of blackberry, pepper, and spice, and sometimes offers a little "fruit sweetness." It is excellent with robust fare such as prime rib and highly seasoned beef.

Chardonnay. A dry white wine with a crisp, clean taste, Chardonnay is usually produced in stainless steel barrels, but may be fermented or aged in oak barrels. When fermented in stainless steel, it tends to be medium-bodied. When fermented in oak, it takes on oak and vanilla flavors and develops more body. For your beef dishes, choose oak-fermented Chardonnays, which match well with roast beef, steak, and smoked beef.

Home-Style Beef Brisket

Low cooking temperatures and aromatic smoke turn brisket—a tough, fatty cut of beef—into one of the best barbeque dishes you're ever likely to taste. In my neighborhood, when the sweet smell of the smoke begins wafting through the air, the doorbell rings and neighbors appear with side dishes and enough beverages to keep the fleet afloat. The spices and low and slow cooking contribute significantly to enhancing the flavor and tenderizing this delectable cut of beef. I highly recommended hickory or mesquite pellets for this recipe.

YIELD: 8–10 SERVINGS
RECOMMENDED PELLETS: HICKORY OR MESQUITE
MARINATION/SEASONING TIME: 8 HOURS TO OVERNIGHT
COOKING TIME: 12 HOURS TO OVERNIGHT

10- to 12-pound beef brisket, fat trimmed to ¼ inch

1 cup Home-Style Seasoning Mix (page 26) or commercial hickory smoke-and-spice blend

2 cups Basic Kansas City-Style Barbeque Sauce (page 43) or commercial sweet tomato-based barbeque sauce, warmed (optional)

---

1. Rinse the brisket in cold water and dry with paper towels.

2. Rub the seasoning mix seasoning liberally over all sides of the brisket. Wrap the brisket securely in plastic wrap and refrigerate for 8 hours or overnight. If time does not permit, don't worry. The brisket will absorb the spices during the cooking process.

3. Start the pellet grill and set the temperature control to 180°F or "Smoke."

4. When the grill reaches the desired temperature, remove the brisket from the refrigerator and discard the plastic wrap. Place the brisket in an appropriate size aluminum pan, fat side up, and place the pan on the grill grate. Close the grill door and allow the brisket to smoke uncovered for 8 hours.

5. Cover the pan with heavy-duty aluminum foil and continue to slow-cook the meat for a total of 12 to 14 hours or overnight. The meat will be done when it is tender enough to shred with your fingers and has an internal temperature of 180°F to 190°F. Several factors can affect the cooking time, including the size of the brisket, the heat of the grill, and even the outside temperature.

6. Remove the pan from the grill, and allow the meat to rest for 15 minutes. Transfer the brisket to a cutting board and thinly slice across the grain. Serve with warmed barbeque sauce, if desired.

Good Thyme Beef Tenderloin

Beef tenderloin has a naturally delicious flavor, and this recipe lets it shine through by enhancing it with thyme, parsley, and tarragon. For a truly sublime taste, use maple pellets to fuel your grill.

YIELD: 4–6 SERVINGS
RECOMMENDED PELLETS: MAPLE
MARINATION/SEASONING TIME: NONE
COOKING TIME: 50 MINUTES

4-pound beef tenderloin, trimmed of excess fat	**1 tablespoon finely chopped fresh tarragon**
1 tablespoon dried thyme	**1 tablespoon coarse sea salt**
1/4 cup roughly chopped fresh flat leaf parsley	**1 teaspoon coarsely ground black pepper**

1. Start the pellet grill and set the temperature control to 350°F.

2. Rinse the tenderloin in cold water and dry with paper towels. If the tenderloin is in 2 pieces, tie them together using kitchen twine.

3. Lay out a sheet of waxed paper large enough to hold the meat. Rub the thyme to release the oils, and bruise the parsley and tarragon leaves. Evenly spread the herbs and sea salt on the paper.

4. Rub the black pepper evenly over the beef so that the pepper remains in place. Roll the roast in the salt and herb mixture to coat evenly. Then press the herb mixture into the meat by hand.

5. When the grill reaches the desired temperature, transfer the meat to the grate, close the grill door, and cook until it reaches the desired level of doneness, about 50 minutes. An instant-read thermometer will read 120°F to 130°F for rare, 135°F to 145°F for medium, or 155°F or greater for well done.

6. Transfer the meat to a cutting board, cover with aluminum foil, and allow to rest for 10 minutes before slicing thinly into serving portions. Serve immediately.

QUICK GRILLING FOR BEEF TENDERLOIN

For those occasions when you want to cook Good Thyme Beef Tenderloin more quickly, increase the grill temperature to 400°F and decrease the cooking time to about 35 minutes. Just remember that whenever you turn up the temperature of the grill, you reduce the food's smoky flavor and aroma. (For more information on Quick Grilling, see page 12.)

Texas-Style Beef Brisket

Texans don't care for sweet sauces and seasonings on their barbequed fare. Instead, they flavor their brisket with ground chili peppers and an array of Southwestern-style spices, and allow the meat to absorb the seasonings overnight. The meat is then exposed to smoke and low heat until it virtually falls apart. A spicy sauce served on the side adds a final fiery touch to the meal.

YIELD: 6–8 SERVINGS
RECOMMENDED PELLETS: HICKORY OR MESQUITE
MARINATION/SEASONING TIME: 8 HOURS TO OVERNIGHT
COOKING TIME: 6 TO 8 HOURS

5- to 6-pound beef brisket, fat trimmed to ¼ inch

¼ cup plus 1 tablespoon Texas-Style Rub (page 22) or commercial chili-based rub

½ cup apple juice

½ cup water

1½ cups Spicy Texas-Style Barbeque Sauce (page 46) or commercial Texas-style barbeque sauce, warmed

---

1. Rinse the brisket in cold water and dry with paper towels.

2. Rub the seasoning mix liberally over both sides of the brisket. Wrap the brisket securely in plastic wrap and refrigerate for 8 hours or overnight. If time does not permit, don't worry. The brisket will absorb the spices during the cooking process.

3. Start the pellet grill and set the temperature control to 180°F or "Smoke." Mix the apple juice and water in a spray bottle, and set aside.

4. When the grill reaches the desired temperature, remove the brisket from the refrigerator and discard the plastic wrap. Place the brisket in an appropriate size aluminum pan, fat side up, and transfer the pan to the grill. Close the grill door and allow the meat to smoke uncovered for 6 to 8 hours, basting at least once per hour with the fat and juices from the pan and a light spray of the apple juice-water mixture. The meat will be done when it is tender enough to shred with your fingers and has an internal temperature of 180°F to 190°F. Several factors can affect the cooking time, including the brisket size and even the weather.

5. If desired, prior to removing the brisket from the grill, liberally baste the meat with the barbeque sauce. Turn the meat over, and sauce the other side as well. Close the grill and allow the sauce to bake onto the meat for approximately 20 minutes.

6. Remove the pan from the grill and cover with aluminum foil. Allow the meat to rest for about 15 minutes. Transfer the brisket to a cutting board and thinly slice across the grain. Transfer the meat to a serving platter and, if desired, pour the pan juices directly into a gravy boat and serve with the meat. Serve immediately with warmed barbeque sauce on the side.

Unbelievable Pepper Roast Beef

This recipe, although easy to prepare, results in a roast that's full of flavor and has an indescribably luxurious texture. The longer the herbs and spices remain on the meat, the deeper the flavors penetrate. The recommended pellets for this recipe are maple or cherry.

YIELD: 5–6 SERVINGS
RECOMMENDED PELLETS: MAPLE OR CHERRY
MARINATION/SEASONING TIME: 4 HOURS TO OVERNIGHT
COOKING TIME: ABOUT $2^1/_2$ HOURS

3 tablespoons extra virgin olive oil

3 garlic cloves, finely minced

2 tablespoons coarsely ground black pepper

2 tablespoons fennel seed, crushed or powdered in a spice mill

1 tablespoon dried thyme

1 teaspoon sea salt

1 cup chopped fresh parsley

$2^1/_2$- to 3-pound boneless beef round tip roast

1. Combine the olive oil, garlic, pepper, fennel seed, thyme, and salt in a small bowl. Spread the parsley over a sheet of waxed paper.

2. Rinse the meat in cold water and dry with paper towels. Brush or rub the olive oil mixture over the meat on all sides. Then roll the meat in the chopped parsley to coat evenly.

3. Place the coated meat in a large bowl and cover with plastic wrap to tightly seal. Place in the refrigerator for 4 to 6 hours or overnight.

4. Start the pellet grill and set the temperature control to 225°F.

5. Remove the meat from the refrigerator and discard the plastic wrap. When the grill reaches the desired temperature, place the roast on a roasting pan and transfer the pan to the grill. Close the grill door and allow to smoke uncovered for approximately 45 minutes.

6. Increase the grill temperature to 325°F. Cover the meat with heavy-duty aluminum foil and roast for $1^1/_2$ to 2 hours, or until the meat reaches the desired degree of doneness. An instant-read thermometer will read 120°F to 130°F for rare, 135°F to 145°F for medium, or 155°F or greater for well done.

7. Remove the roasting pan from the grill and allow the meat to rest for 10 minutes. Transfer the meat to a cutting board and carve into $1/_4$-inch slices. Collect the juice from the roasting pan and pour into a gravy boat to serve with the roast beef.

Rock Salt Prime Rib Roast

This roast is generously seasoned before being encased in a "batter" of rock salt. During cooking, the salt hardens into a crust that prevents moisture loss so that the finished dish is juicy and roasted to perfection. Before serving this roast au jus, test the pan juices to make sure that they're not too salty for you. If they are, accompany the roast with just the horseradish.

YIELD: 10–12 SERVINGS
RECOMMENDED PELLETS: MAPLE
MARINATION/SEASONING TIME: 30 MINUTES
COOKING TIME: 3$^1/_2$ HOURS

15-pound prime rib roast (7–9 bones)

1 cup Prime Rib Rub (page 24) or commercial spice blend for beef

1$^1/_2$ tablespoons coarsely ground black pepper

6 cups food-grade rock salt

6 cups all-purpose flour

1 tablespoon crushed dried thyme

1$^1/_2$ cups water

Prepared horseradish

1. Rinse the rib roast in cold water and dry with paper towels.

2. In a small bowl, combine the Prime Rib Rub and pepper. Rub the spice mix liberally over all sides of the roast. Then transfer the roast to an aluminum baking sheet, cover with aluminum foil, and refrigerate for 30 minutes.

3. Start the pellet grill and set the temperature control to 325°F.

4. Mix the rock salt, flour, and thyme in a bowl. Gradually pour the water into the mixture and stir by hand. Continue to mix, adding more water as necessary, until you have a sticky batter or paste.

5. Place a $^1/_2$-inch layer of batter over the bottom of a shallow roasting pan. Remove the roast from the baking sheet and place it, bones side down, in the roaster. Pull the batter up and around the roast, adding extra batter as necessary to ensure that the roast is fully encased in the salt batter. Set a small amount of paste aside for repairs to the shell later in the cooking process.

6. Insert a metal meat thermometer in the roast with the gauge positioned so that it's visible when you open the grill. Ensure that the thermometer probe is not touching any bones.

7. When the grill reaches the desired temperature, place the roasting pan on the grate, close the grill door, and roast for 20 to 25 minutes. Remove the pan from the grill and use the reserved batter to patch any holes or breaks in the coating.

8. Return the pan to the grill and roast for 3 additional hours, or until the roast reaches the desired degree of doneness. The thermometer in the roast should read 120°F to 130°F for rare, 135°F to 145°F for medium, or 155°F or greater for well done.

9. Remove the pan from the grill and cover with aluminum foil. Allow the meat to rest for 20 to 30 minutes.

10. Remove and discard the crust. Transfer the meat to a cutting board, and cut the bones away from the meat. Carve the meat into 1/2-inch slices and serve with the horseradish and, if desired, the roast's natural juices.

Cooking with Rock Salt

Want to try an unusual culinary technique for sealing in both the flavor and moistness of roasts, whole fish, poultry, and even potatoes? Completely encase the food in rock salt during cooking. It is a simple approach that involves just one very important rule—*you must use food-grade rock salt*. Many commercial rock salts contain chemicals and impurities, and unless they are labeled "edible," you cannot use them with food.

When employing this cooking method, there are basically two ways to cover the food. The first is with a thick "batter"—a mixture of water and equal parts of rock salt and flour. After adding a 1/2-inch layer of this batter to the bottom of a roasting pan, place the food on top. Using your hands, completely cover the food with more batter; then cook according to the recipe instructions. (This is the same approach I use in this recipe for Rock Salt Prime Rib Roast.)

The second food-covering method is a little simpler—but you'll need a spray bottle. After lining the bottom of the roasting pan with a generous layer of rock salt, spray it with just enough water to moisten. Place the food on top, then cover the sides and top with more moistened salt until the food is completely coated.

Once the cooking is done, crack the hardened shell with a hammer (a gentle tapping is all you'll need) and remove it from the food. Not only does this technique produce meat and fish that are juicy and delicious, it also offers a fun tableside "presentation" that is sure to impress your guests.

Sirloin Roast with Bacon

Just about everyone loves bacon and roast beef, and when you put them together, the result is outstanding. This recipe further enhances the beef with thyme and the sweet addition of a Spicy Rum Barbeque Sauce, creating a sublime experience.

YIELD: 6–8 SERVINGS
RECOMMENDED PELLETS: HICKORY AND MAPLE
MARINATION/SEASONING TIME: NONE
COOKING TIME: 1$^1/_2$ HOURS

2$^1/_2$-pound boneless sirloin roast (may be tied together), trimmed of excess fat

1 cup Spicy Rum Barbeque Sauce (page 48) or commercial rum-based or honey-bourbon barbeque sauce

$^1/_2$ teaspoon dried thyme

7 or 8 bacon slices

4 sweet white onions, peeled and halved crosswise

2 tablespoons extra virgin olive oil

2 tablespoons Home-Style Seasoning Mix (page 26) or commercial hickory smoke-and-spice blend

8 ounces cherry tomatoes, or 3 regular tomatoes cut into wedges

1. Start the pellet grill and set the temperature control to 350°F.

2. Rinse the roast in cold water and dry with paper towels. Using a sharp knife, cut slits in the roast to allow the bacon drippings to penetrate the meat as it cooks.

3. Brush the barbeque sauce over the meat and sprinkle on the dried thyme. Wrap the bacon around the roast (or across the top, from one side to the other, if not long enough to encircle the roast) and hold in place with toothpicks. You will need about 20 wooden picks.

4. When the grill reaches the desired temperature, place the roast directly on the grill grate (bacon side up if not completely wrapped). Close the grill door and cook uncovered for 1 hour.

5. While the roast is cooking, place the onions on a plate, cut side up. Brush with the olive oil and sprinkle the seasoning mix over the top.

6. After the roast has been on the grill for an hour, arrange the onions on the grill surrounding the roast. Continue to cook for another 30 minutes, or until the meat reaches the desired degree of doneness. An instant-read thermometer will read 120°F to 130°F for rare, 135°F to 145°F for medium, or 155°F or greater for well done. Remove the onions when they are browned and tender when pierced with a sharp knife.

7. Transfer the roast to a cutting board, cover with aluminum foil, and allow to rest for 10 minutes. Leaving the toothpicks in place, cut the roast into $1/2$-inch slices. At this point, remove the toothpicks if desired or necessary for appearance. Arrange the meat on a serving platter with the onions, bacon, and tomatoes, and serve immediately.

Garlic and Pepper Beef Roast

Garlic and pepper were intended to be "married" to beef. In this recipe, the union is sublime and, along with the other herbs and spices, brings out the very best in the roast. I recommend mesquite, hickory, or cherry pellets, but you can change the aromatics and flavor of the meat by blending mesquite and cherry.

YIELD: 4–5 SERVINGS
RECOMMENDED PELLETS: MESQUITE, HICKORY, OR CHERRY
MARINATION/SEASONING TIME: 3 HOURS TO OVERNIGHT
COOKING TIME: ABOUT 2$1/2$ HOURS

$3^1/_2$-pound boneless rump, sirloin, top round, or eye of round beef roast

1 tablespoon coarsely ground black pepper

$1/4$ cup Herb and Garlic Seasoning Blend (page 32) or commercial herb-and-garlic seasoning

1. Rinse the meat in cold water and dry with paper towels.

2. In a small bowl, mix the pepper with the herb seasoning. Sprinkle the mixture over the roast and transfer it to a plastic bag. Refrigerate for at least 3 hours or as long as overnight.

3. Start the pellet grill and set the temperature control to 225°F.

4. Remove the roast from the refrigerator and discard the plastic bag. When the grill reaches the desired temperature, place the roast on the grate, close the grill door, and smoke for 1$1/2$ hours.

5. Increase the grill temperature to 325°F and continue to cook for 30 minutes. Use an instant-read thermometer to check the internal temperature. When it reaches 140°F, wrap the roast in heavy-duty aluminum foil and return it to the grill. Roast for another 20 minutes; then turn off the grill. Allow the roast to rest on the grill for 10 minutes.

6. Transfer the roast to a cutting boat and carve into thin slices. Collect the juices from the foil and place in a gravy boat. Serve the juices with the meat.

Short Ribs Mediterranean

In the Greek Ionian Islands, a dish called Pastitsatha begins with spicy braised beef. In the Greek spirit, Short Ribs Mediterranean unites short ribs with savory Greek additions like cinnamon and cloves, creating a dish that is tender and delectable. Because the meat is braised in a pot, it does not matter which pellets you use. If you like, grill some vegetables while you make the meat, adding them at the end of the cooking period so that the ribs and accompaniments are ready at the same time.

YIELD: 4–6 SERVINGS.
RECOMMENDED PELLETS: YOUR CHOICE
MARINATION/SEASONING TIME: 1 HOUR
COOKING TIME: ABOUT 3$^1/_2$ HOURS

4 pounds lean beef short ribs, or 4 pounds chuck steak cut into strips	1 tablespoon hot pepper sauce
$^1/_4$ cup Mediterranean Spice Seasoning (page 30) or commercial spice blend containing basil, fennel, garlic, lemon, thyme, and cayenne	$^1/_2$ teaspoon celery seeds
	$^1/_2$ teaspoon ground cinnamon
	$^1/_4$ teaspoon ground cloves
1$^1/_2$ cups V8 vegetable juice	2 tablespoons olive oil
1 cup red wine	2 tablespoons butter
$^1/_2$ cup beef stock	1 large onion, sliced into rings
1$^1/_2$ tablespoons Worcestershire sauce	4 garlic cloves, minced
1 tablespoon prepared horseradish	4 carrots, peeled and quartered
	20 medium-size button mushrooms, stems removed

1. Rinse the ribs in cold water and dry with paper towels. Pierce the meat with a fork and liberally season with the Mediterranean Spice blend. Wrap the meat securely in plastic wrap and refrigerate for at least 1 hour.

2. Start the pellet grill and set the temperature control to 180°F or "Smoke." Remove the meat from the refrigerator, remove and discard the plastic wrap, and allow the ribs to warm to room temperature as the grill heats.

3. When the grill reaches the desired temperature, place the ribs directly on the grate, close the grill door, and smoke for 1 hour.

4. In a glass or ceramic mixing bowl, combine the V8 juice, wine, stock, Worcestershire sauce, horseradish, pepper sauce, celery seed, cinnamon, and cloves. Stir well and set aside.

5. Heat an ovenproof Dutch oven or wide shallow pot with lid over medium-high heat on the kitchen stove. Stir in the olive oil and butter until melted; then add the onion and garlic. Cook until the onion softens and begins to brown. Remove the onion mixture from the pan and set aside.

6. Transfer the ribs from the grill to the Dutch oven. Over medium-high heat, lightly brown the meat on all sides in the olive oil and butter.

7. Top the ribs with the reserved onions and the carrots. Pour the vegetable juice mixture over all, and cover.

8. Reset the wood pellet grill temperature control to 275°F. Alternatively, preheat your kitchen oven to 275°F.

9. Remove the Dutch oven from the stovetop and place on the grill grate or in your oven. Braise the ribs for 2 hours.

10. Add the mushroom to the Dutch oven, recover the pot, and continue to braise the ribs for another hour.

11. Serve the ribs with the sauce and vegetables. This dish is especially good when accompanied with white or brown rice or pasta.

A Word About Short Ribs

Short ribs are an affordable luxury. Although the meat starts off fatty and tough, through the magic of the wood pellet grill, it is transformed into a moist, tender, richly flavored beef dish. Unlike spare ribs, which have the majority of meat between the bones, short ribs have a thick layer of meat that sits on top of the bones. They can be cut from three different sections of the cow, with the best cuts coming from the back ribs and the short plate, located on the underbelly.

Whenever you purchase short ribs, be aware that they are sometimes sold as *braising ribs, crosscut ribs,* or *English short ribs.* The meat should be firm and bright red in color with fat thinly marbled throughout. Keep in mind that higher grades of beef will contain thin layers of fat, which result in meat that is more tender and juicy than cuts which contain chunks or thick layers of fat. When determining the amount of ribs to buy, consider the weight of the bones and the fact that the meat is sure to shrink during the cooking process. As a general rule, one pound of short ribs for each adult is recommended.

Roasted Dinosaur Bones

At the supermarket one day, I heard a friend's grandson ask him about the "big dinosaur bones" he had placed in the shopping cart. Displayed next to the pork baby backs, the beef ribs did look ominous. Grandpa laughed and told a tall tale of the battle between the butcher and the beast. Oddly enough, the butcher had suffered a broken arm from a fall at home a couple of days earlier. When the battle-scarred butcher came out from behind the meat counter to visit, the lad's eyes bugged out. Whether called dinosaur bones or ribs, this dish is delicious. I recommend a 60/40 blend of mesquite and maple pellets, or 100 percent of either one, as they both complement the ribs.

YIELD: 4–5 SERVINGS
RECOMMENDED PELLETS: MESQUITE AND MAPLE
MARINATION/SEASONING TIME: NONE
COOKING TIME: ABOUT $3^1/_2$ HOURS

8–10 pounds beef ribs, trimmed of excess fat

$^3/_4$ **cup Prime Rib Rub (page 24) or commercial spice blend for beef**

1 recipe Uncle Bob's Basic Barbeque Sauce (page 47) or commercial spicy barbeque sauce

Sea salt and ground black pepper to taste

---

1. Rinse the ribs in cold water and dry with paper towels. Start the pellet grill and set the temperature control to 180°F.

2. Select a roasting pan that is large enough to hold the ribs and sauce. Spray the inside of the pan with nonstick cooking spray.

3. Season the ribs with the spice blend and arrange them in the prepared pan. When the grill reaches the desired temperature, place the pan in the grill, close the door, and smoke uncovered for 1 to $1^1/_2$ hours.

4. Increase the grill temperature to 350°F and roast the ribs for 45 to 50 minutes. Using a turkey baster or large spoon, remove any accumulated fat from the pan.

5. Pour the barbeque sauce over the ribs and brush to entirely coat the meat. Bake uncovered for 1 to $1^1/_2$ hours additional hours, or until the meat is tender. Baste occasionally with the pan juices, and season with salt and pepper if desired. The ribs are done when the meat pulls away from the ends of the bones and can be easily removed from the bones with a fork.

6. Remove the pan from the grill, cover with foil, and allow to rest for 10 to 15 minutes.

7. Transfer the ribs to a cutting board and carve into serving portions. Serve immediately with additional warmed barbeque sauce.

4.

Between the Buns

Burgers, Hot Dogs, and Sausages

They may not be the most glamorous foods to emerge from the barbeque, but burgers, hot dogs, and sausages are certainly popular—not only at backyard cookouts, but at just about every holiday from Memorial Day to Labor Day. Besides being undeniably delicious and easy to make, burgers and dogs are easy to eat, too, which is why they also make an appearance at year-round sporting events across the country. Who could imagine a ball game without a hot dog and a bottle of something cold?

There's just one problem: These all-American foods can be a little boring, especially by the end of the summer when you've gobbled up burger after burger, sausage after sausage. Sure, you add mustard, ketchup, and other condiments, and maybe even cheese or chopped onion, but beneath it all, burgers and sausages are pretty much always the same. Moreover, not every backyard chef manages to produce a juicy, flavorful burger or a truly delicious dog.

The wood pellet grill offers just the versatility you need to turn same old, same old into something special. This chapter features a variety of hot dogs and sausages, which are often smoked for additional flavor and then cooked in a range of creative ways, involving everything from a simmer in beer to a partnership with onions and peppers. It also provides a bevy of burgers, and whether you opt for an All-American Beef Burger or a meaty Portobello mushroom burger, you can't go wrong. If you're expected a crowd, there's even a special recipe for Party Time Burgers and Hot Dogs. (See the inset on page 74.)

When using a wood pellet grill to prepare foods served "between the buns," it's important to recognize that while these grills excel at many types of cooking, they are not the best at toasting bread. Since the grills use indirect heat, they tend to dry out baked items unless you slather the surface with butter or another moist spread. That's why in each of the following recipes, I direct you to use the broiler in your conventional oven if you want toasted buns. These recipes are all spectacular and worthy of your time and effort whether you choose to toast the bread or use it as is.

Whether summer grilling is just starting up in your neck of the woods or you recently served up your umpteenth burger or dog, this chapter will show you how to transform these simple grilled treats into something that's simply delicious. It's as easy as can be with a wood pellet grill.

Beer-Simmered Sausages

These sausages are lightly smoked, then simmered in beer with onions and garlic to deepen the taste of the meat. The sausages are then returned to the grill for finishing. This is one of our favorite weekend choices and is especially popular when we gather to watch sporting events.

YIELD: 12 SERVINGS
RECOMMENDED PELLETS: YOUR CHOICE
MARINATION/SEASONING TIME: NONE
COOKING TIME: ABOUT 4 HOURS

12 sausage links of your choice (Italian hot or sweet, bratwurst, hot links, chorizo, or others)

1 tablespoon olive or vegetable oil

1 white onion, thinly sliced

1 tablespoon finely minced garlic

1 teaspoon fennel seed

2 bottles (16 ounces each) beer of your choice

12 sourdough or French rolls, sliced in half

Yellow and deli mustards, ketchup, barbeque sauce, or the condiments of your choice (optional)

1. Start the pellet grill and set the temperature control to 180°F or "Smoke." Pierce the sausage casings all over with a fork. This will keep the casings from bursting as the sausages cook.

2. When the grill reaches the desired temperature, arrange the sausages on the grill grate, leaving space between them so that smoke can circulate. Close the lid of the grill and smoke for 20 to 30 minutes.

3. While the sausages are smoking, place a very deep skillet or Dutch oven on your kitchen stove and heat the oil over medium heat. Add the onion, garlic, and fennel seed to the skillet and stir to mix. Continue cooking, stirring occasionally, for about 5 minutes, or until the onions and garlic are translucent.

4. Turn the pellet grill off. Remove the sausages from the grill and arrange them over the onions. Add the beer and bring to a boil. Cover the skillet or pot, reduce the heat, and simmer for 3 to 4 hours. Occasionally check the level of the liquid, adding more beer as necessary.

5. Start the pellet grill and turn the temperature control to 375°F. When the grill reaches the desired temperature, remove the sausages from the skillet and arrange them on the grill. Close the lid and cook for about 15 minutes, turning every 3 or 4 minutes to create grill marks.

6. If you want toasted rolls, preheat your kitchen broiler about 10 minutes before the sausages are done. During the last 5 minutes of grilling, spread the rolls open on a cookie sheet and toast lightly under the broiler.

7. Remove the sausages from the grill, place each in a roll, and spread with the condiments of your choice. Using a slotted spoon, lift the onion mixture out of the skillet, allowing the liquid to drain off, and top each sausage with some of the mixture. Serve immediately.

Cooking with Beer

Along with its classic role as a refreshing beverage, did you know that beer is also a valuable cooking ingredient? Beer offers exceptional flavor and texture to a wide variety of foods, from meat, chicken, and seafood to breads and other baked goods.

First, beer makes a wonderful seasoning agent. Including it in a basting sauce adds richness to roasted, broiled, or grilled meats, poultry, and fish. When used in a marinade, beer not only offers flavor, but also serves as a tenderizer, making it the perfect choice for tougher cuts of meat. Adding some to a pot of simmering stew or chili gives the dish added zing. As a simmering liquid, beer brings out meat's natural richness, as seen in the above recipe for Beer-Simmered Sausages. Although the alcohol content will evaporate during cooking, the wonderful flavor of the beer will remain. Dark ales offer stronger flavor, while lighter lagers lend a more delicate, subtle taste.

Beer can also add a light, airy texture and moistness to baked goods like breads and biscuits, while increasing their shelf life. And when beer is used in batter coatings for fried foods, the yeast it contains causes the batter to puff up into a light, crisp crust.

So don't be afraid to experiment with this tasty age-old brew. Add a splash to your favorite sauce, use it in bastes and marinades, and try some in homemade bread. Check out different types of beers with different recipes. And don't forget to pour yourself a frosty mug while you're cooking!

Party Time Burgers & Hot Dogs

If you want your party to be just a little bit special, try serving up toppings other than the usual ketchup, mustard, and relish. When it's party time at my house, I make one or all of three favorites—a Spicy Guacamole, a tangy Cherry Tomato Relish, and, for the truly adventurous, a Gongonzola and Onion Spread. Because I prepare the spreads and toppings before my guests arrive, I'm able to enjoy the party along with friends and family.

YIELD: 16 SERVINGS
RECOMMENDED PELLETS: YOUR CHOICE
MARINATION/SEASONING TIME: NONE
COOKING TIME: 30 TO 35 MINUTES

2 pounds ground chuck

8 beef hot dogs

8 hamburger buns

8 hot dog buns

Sea salt and ground
black pepper to taste

SPICY GUACAMOLE

4 ripe avocados

1 medium tomato, diced

1/2 medium white onion, chopped

1/2 cup jarred medium-hot salsa

3 tablespoons chopped fresh cilantro

Juice of 1 lemon

Sea salt to taste

CHERRY TOMATO RELISH

1 pint cherry tomatoes, quartered

4 scallions, sliced

1/2 yellow bell pepper, finely chopped

3 tablespoons chopped fresh cilantro

3 tablespoons honey

Juice of 1 lime

Sea salt and ground black pepper
to taste

GORGONZOLA AND ONION SPREAD

12 ounces Gorgonzola cheese

1/2 cup diced white onion

OPTIONAL TOPPINGS

Sliced tomatoes

Sliced red and white onions

Sliced dill and sweet pickles

Ketchup and mustard

1. To make the guacamole, cut each avocado in half, remove the pit, and scrape the flesh out into a large glass, stainless steel, or ceramic bowl. Mash the avocado with a fork until you reach the desired consistency. Add the tomato, onion, salsa, cilantro, and lemon juice, and stir to mix well. Add salt to taste, and adjust the flavor by adding additional salsa, cilantro, or onion as necessary. Transfer the guacamole to a serving bowl, cover *tightly* with plastic wrap (to prevent browning), and refrigerate until ready to serve.

2. To make the cherry tomato relish, place all of the ingredients except for the salt and pepper in a large glass, stainless steel, or ceramic bowl. Stir to mix well and add salt and pepper to taste. Transfer the relish to a serving bowl, cover with plastic wrap, and refrigerate until ready to serve.

3. To make the cheese spread, cut the Gorgonzola into chunks and place in a food processor equipped with a metal mixing blade. Add the onion, and pulse until the mixture has the consistency of a paste. Transfer the cheese spread to a serving bowl, cover with plastic wrap, and refrigerate until ready to serve.

4. Start the pellet grill and set the temperature control to 325°F.

5. While the grill is heating up, divide the ground chuck into 8 equal pieces, each weighing about 4 ounces. Form each piece into a meatball, and turn the balls into patties by tossing them from hand to hand. Each patty should be a little larger than the diameter of the buns and about 3/4 inch thick. Press your thumb into the middle of the meat to leave a depression on one side. This will prevent the burger from puffing up in the center as it cooks. Season both sides with salt and pepper to taste.

6. Arrange the burgers on the grill grate. Close the grill door and cook for 12 to 15 minutes on the first side. Turn the patties and continue to cook for about 18 minutes, or until an instant-read thermometer shows an internal temperature of 160°F.

7. A few minutes after the burgers are turned, arrange the hot dogs on the grill grate. Close the grill door and cook the dogs for a total of 15 to 20 minutes, rotating them occasionally to put grill marks all around.

8. If you want toasted buns, preheat your kitchen broiler about 10 minutes before the burgers and hot dogs are done. During the last 5 minutes of grilling, spread the buns open on a cookie sheet and toast lightly under the broiler.

9. Remove the burgers and hot dogs from the grill and place each in a toasted bun. Serve them with the toppings and condiments of your choice.

The Great All-American Beef Burger

One of my fondest childhood memories is that of burgers grilling on my Dad's barbeque. The smell called me to wherever I was, summoning me to the dinner table. Mom used ground chuck because it was inexpensive, and as it turned out, this cut—which is about 15 percent fat—makes the best burgers because the fat keeps the meat moist and flavorful. I have suggested some toppings below, but you're sure to have your own favorites. Any pellets you have in the hopper will work for this classic American food.

YIELD: 8 SERVINGS
RECOMMENDED PELLETS: YOUR CHOICE
MARINATION/SEASONING TIME: NONE
COOKING TIME: 30 TO 35 MINUTES

---

2 pounds ground chuck

8 hamburger buns

Sea salt and ground black pepper to taste

Ketchup, mustard, pickle relish, onion, tomato, cheese, bacon, or the condiments and toppings of your choice

---

1. Start the pellet grill and set the temperature control to 325°F.

2. Divide the ground beef into 8 equal pieces, each weighing about 4 ounces. Form each piece into a meatball, and turn the balls into patties by tossing them from hand to hand. Each patty should be a little larger than the diameter of the buns and about 3/4 inch thick. Press your thumb into the middle of the meat to leave a depression on one side. This will prevent the burger from puffing up in the center as it cooks. Season both sides with salt and pepper to taste.

3. When the grill reaches the desired temperature, arrange the burgers on the grate. Close the grill and cook for 12 to 15 minutes on the first side. Turn the patties and continue to cook for an additional 18 minutes, or until an instant-read thermometer shows an internal temperature of 160°F.

4. If you want toasted buns, preheat your kitchen broiler about 10 minutes before the burgers are done. During the last 5 minutes of grilling, spread the buns open on a cookie sheet and toast lightly under the broiler.

5. Remove the burgers from the grill and place each in a bun. Serve them with the toppings of your choice.

QUICK GRILLING FOR THE ALL-AMERICAN BURGER

For those occasions when you want to cook The Great All-American Beef Burger more quickly, increase the grill temperature to 400°F and decrease the cooking time to about 10 minutes per side. Just remember that whenever you turn up the temperature of the grill, you reduce the food's smoky flavor and aroma. (For more information on Quick Grilling, see page 12.)

How to Make a Better Burger

Your wood pellet grill, along with the recipes presented in this chapter, will help you prepare burgers that are juicy and bursting with flavor. To enjoy the very best results, you'll want to keep the following guidelines in mind whenever you make burgers:

☐ Select ground meat that has a fat content of 15 to 20 percent. Leaner meat will make a burger that is drier and harder, which is not what you want. For truly great results, select a piece of chuck and ask your butcher to grind it to order, or take it home and coarsely chop it in your food processor. Also consider mixing different meats, such as beef and pork. (See Juicy Burgers and Cheese on page 78.)

☐ Be adventurous and season the ground meat with your favorite spices and flavorings. Salt and pepper are classics, but if you love garlic powder, onion powder, chili powder, or Worcestershire sauce, you may want to add some to your burger mixture. Or consider slathering on your favorite barbeque sauce when the burgers are done. The sky's the limit!

☐ When forming your patties, handle the meat as little as possible so that you don't make the burgers too dense. Once you turn each portion of ground meat into a ball, flatten it by tossing it from hand to hand—not by pressing it between your hands. For my recipes, you'll want the patties to have a $3/4$-inch thickness.

☐ Once each patty is the right thickness, use your thumb to create a $1/4$-inch depression in the middle of one side. This will keep your burger from puffing up in the middle as it cooks.

☐ Cook your burgers until an instant-read thermometer shows an internal temperature of 160°F. This will help ensure that your grilled patties are as safe as they are moist and flavorful.

Juicy Burgers and Cheese

While an all-beef burger is a satisfying classic, sometimes you want something a little different—a burger that's bursting with juice and a wonderful combination of flavors. This burger fits the bill. I combine ground chuck and pork, and to elevate the patty to gourmet status, I add shredded cheese to the mixture so that it melts and blends within the meat rather than ending up on the bun. Choose any cheese you like. I've used Cheddar, Monterey Jack, pepper cheese, Edam, feta, bleu, and Swiss, and they've all melted easily and been delicious. Since this recipe is not about smoke, you can use any pellets that are in the hopper.

YIELD: 8 SERVINGS
RECOMMENDED PELLETS: YOUR CHOICE
MARINATION/SEASONING TIME: NONE
COOKING TIME: 30 TO 35 MINUTES

---

1 pound ground chuck

1 pound ground pork

8 slices (about 8 ounces) Cheddar, Monterey Jack, or other cheese of your choice, chopped or shredded

Sea salt and ground black pepper to taste

8 hamburger buns

Ketchup, mustard, pickle relish, onion, tomato, pickle, or the condiments and toppings of your choice

---

1. Start the pellet grill and set the temperature control to 325°F.

2. In a large mixing bowl, mix the chuck, pork, and cheese until well blended.

3. Divide the meat mixture into 8 equal pieces, each weighing about 5 ounces. Form each piece into a meatball, and turn the balls into patties by tossing them from hand to hand. Each patty should be a little larger than the diameter of the buns and about ³/₄ inch thick. Press your thumb into the middle of the meat to leave a depression on one side. This will prevent the burger from puffing up in the center as it cooks. Season both sides with salt and pepper to taste.

4. When the grill reaches the desired temperature, arrange the burgers on the grate. Close the grill and cook for 12 to 15 minutes on the first side. Turn the patties and continue to cook for an additional 18 minutes, or until an instant-read thermometer shows an internal temperature of 160°F.

5. If you want toasted buns, preheat your kitchen broiler about 10 minutes before the burgers are done. During the last 5 minutes of grilling, spread the buns open on a cookie sheet and toast lightly under the broiler.

6. Remove the burgers from the grill and place each in a toasted bun. Serve them with the toppings of your choice.

QUICK GRILLING FOR BURGERS AND CHEESE

For those occasions when you want to cook Juicy Burgers and Cheese more quickly, increase the grill temperature to 400°F and decrease the cooking time to about 10 minutes per side. Just remember that whenever you turn up the temperature of the grill, you reduce the food's smoky flavor and aroma. (For more information on Quick Grilling, see page 12.)

The Best Wines for Burgers, Hot Dogs, and Sausages

Although soda and beer are popular beverages whenever people gather to grill burgers, hot dogs, and sausages, several wines make wonderful complements to these foods. For me, chilled white wines are perfect during the warmer months, and red wines come into play when the weather gets brisk. The next time you want to raise your burgers or dogs to a whole new level, try one of the following selections.

Pinot Grigio. An easy-drinking crisp white wine that tastes of pear and spice, Pinot Grigio is a good match with mushrooms and cheeseburgers, as well as with vegetables, fruit, and cheese.

Viognier. This well-rounded, medium- to full-bodied dry white wine is very often described as having exotic honeysuckle- and citrus-like characteristics. It pairs well with many foods, including burgers, mushrooms, hot dogs, cheese, and fruit.

Red Zinfandel. A medium- to full-bodied dry red wine, Red Zinfandel has blackberry, boysenberry, and plumy fruit notes. It is great with spicy, smoky dishes, including beef burgers and sausages that have been cooked with onions and peppers.

Rosé. This light red wine is made from red grapes, but exposed to the grape skins for only a short time during fermentation so that only a little of the red pigment is extracted. The fermentation is stopped before all the sugar is converted to alcohol, making the wine slightly sweet. Enjoy this beverage chilled with burgers and hot dogs.

Syrah. This full-bodied dry red wine, a little bolder than a Cabernet or Merlot, exhibits aromas of blackberry, pepper, and spice, and sometimes has a "fruit sweetness." It is excellent with full-flavored cheeseburgers and spicy sausages.

Sausages with Peppers and Onions

Of all the sausages available for grilling, I find bratwurst and hot link sausages particularly satisfying. When exposed to low heat for smoking, the fat melts away while the meat picks up tantalizing flavors and aromas from the wood. This recipe deliciously pairs the two succulent meats with peppers and onions. If you prefer Italian sausages, use them instead for a classic combination. (See "For a Change" at the end of the recipe.) Base your choice of wood pellets on your side dishes. Are baked beans in the offing? Try the maple or oak pellets. How about some potato or macaroni salad? You might use apple or alder pellets.

YIELD: 12 SERVINGS
RECOMMENDED PELLETS: YOUR CHOICE
MARINATION/SEASONING TIME: NONE
COOKING TIME: ABOUT 1 HOUR

6 bratwurst sausage links	1 medium white onion, sliced
6 hot link sausages	Sea salt and coarsely ground pepper to taste
1 tablespoon extra virgin olive oil	
1 teaspoon fennel seed	12 hot dog buns or raised rolls, sliced in half
1 green bell pepper, sliced into rings or strips	Ketchup, mustard, pickle relish, or the condiments of your choice (optional)
1 red bell pepper, sliced into rings or strips	

1. Start the pellet grill and set the temperature control to "Smoke" or 180°F. Pierce the sausage casings all over with a fork. This will keep the casings from bursting as the sausages cook.

2. When the grill reaches the desired temperature, arrange the sausages on the grill grate, leaving space between them so that the smoke can circulate. Close the lid of the grill and smoke for 25 to 35 minutes.

3. Increase the grill temperature to 325°F. Continue cooking the sausages with the lid closed, turning occasionally, for 20 to 25 minutes, or until they are fully cooked. An instant-read thermometer should show an internal temperature of 160°F, and when cut with a knife, the center of the sausage should no longer be pink.

4. While the sausages are cooking at the higher temperature, place the olive oil and fennel seed in a large skillet over medium heat. Add the peppers and onions and cook, stirring occasion-

ally, for about 10 minutes, or until the vegetables are soft. Add salt and pepper to taste, and cover to keep warm.

5. If you want toasted rolls, preheat your kitchen broiler about 10 minutes before the sausages are done. During the last 5 minutes of grilling, spread the rolls open on a cookie sheet and toast lightly under the broiler.

6. Remove the sausages from the grill and place each in a toasted roll. Top with peppers and onions, and serve with the condiments of your choice.

For a Change

■ If you love Italian sausages and peppers, simply replace the bratwurst and hot links with sweet or hot Italian links, and cook as directed above. Be sure to use crusty rolls—not hot dog buns—for a true Italian-American experience.

QUICK GRILLING FOR SAUSAGES WITH PEPPERS

For those occasions when you want to cook Sausages with Peppers and Onions more quickly, increase the grill temperature to 400°F (skip the smoking) and decrease the cooking time to about 15 minutes. Just remember that whenever you turn up the temperature of the grill, you reduce the food's smoky flavor and aroma. (For more information on Quick Grilling, see page 12.)

A Worldwide Staple

Virtually every country in the world enjoys sausage, which comes in hundreds of different varieties that are great for grilling. The following choices are among my favorites:

Bratwurst. Hailing from Germany, bratwurst is traditionally prepared with pork, although some varieties contain beef or veal. Available precooked or raw, this sausage is sometimes simmered in dark beer before grilling.

Chorizo. This staple Mexican-style sausage is made with fresh ground pork and lots of spices—primarily chile peppers and garlic. It is very different from Spanish chorizo, which is a dried sausage, similar to pepperoni.

Hot links. These highly spiced sausages are generally made from a combination of beef, pork, and sometimes chicken. Cayenne pepper, hot paprika, coriander, and garlic are among the many spices they contain.

Italian sausages. These fresh pork sausages come in two main varieties—sweet and hot. Mild-tasting sweet sausage is often flavored with garlic and fennel or cheese and parsley, while the hot, spicy links get their fiery taste from crushed red chile peppers.

Grilled Portobello Mushroom Burgers

The Portobello mushroom is a remarkable vegetable. As large as a beef burger, it is also deliciously meaty in taste and texture when grilled. Add the right condiments—in this case, a sophisticated aioli (garlic mayonnaise), lettuce, onion, tomato, and perhaps some cheese— and you're sure to satisfy both vegetarians and meat-eaters. This recipe doesn't include smoking, but if you'd like to enhance the mushrooms with a smoky taste, start the grill at a lower temperature (180°F) and smoke for about 30 minutes before finishing the caps over higher heat. Any of the wood pellets will work for this recipe, but I think that apple and alder best complement the Portobello.

YIELD: 4 SERVINGS
RECOMMENDED PELLETS: APPLE OR ALDER
MARINATION/SEASONING TIME: 1 HOUR
COOKING TIME: 10 TO 12 MINUTES

4 Portobello mushroom caps (about 5 inches across), cleaned and trimmed

4 hamburger buns

4 slices (1 ounce each) Cheddar or provolone cheese (optional)

4 slices onion

1 large tomato, thinly sliced

4 large lettuce leaves

MARINADE

$^1/_2$ cup balsamic vinegar

3 tablespoons extra virgin olive oil

$1^1/_2$ tablespoons minced garlic

1 teaspoon chopped fresh basil

1 teaspoon chopped fresh oregano

Sea salt and ground black pepper to taste

AIOLI SAUCE

$^1/_4$ cup plus 2 tablespoons mayonnaise

1 tablespoon fresh lemon juice

$^3/_4$ teaspoon dry mustard

$^1/_2$ teaspoon minced garlic

Sea salt and ground black pepper to taste

1. To prepare the marinade, place all the marinade ingredients in a small bowl and whisk until the salt is dissolved.

2. Brush the marinade over the gills (underside) of the mushrooms. Then spoon some marinade into a baking dish and arrange the mushrooms in the dish, cap side up. Brush the marinade over the tops, reserving the leftover marinade. Cover the mushrooms with plastic wrap and allow to marinate at room temperature for about 1 hour.

THE COMPLETE WOOD PELLET BARBEQUE COOKBOOK

3. Start the pellet grill and set the temperature control to 350°F. While the grill is heating up, make the aioli by stirring all the ingredients together in a small bowl. Cover and refrigerate until needed.

4. When the grill reaches the desired temperature, remove the mushrooms from the marinade and arrange them on the grill grate, cap side up. Brush the tops of the mushrooms with additional marinade. Close the lid and cook for 5 to 6 minutes.

5. If you want toasted buns, preheat your kitchen broiler when you put the mushrooms on the grill. During the last 5 minutes of grilling, spread the buns open on a cookie sheet and toast lightly under the broiler.

6. Turn the mushrooms over, brush some marinade onto the gill side, and continue to cook for 5 to 6 minutes, or until the mushrooms can be easily pierced with a fork. If desired, about 2 minutes before the mushrooms are done, turn them over so the cap is up and top with a slice of cheese.

7. Transfer the toasted buns to a serving platter, and spread both sides with the prepared aioli. Place a grilled mushroom on each bottom half, and top with the onion, tomato, and lettuce. Serve immediately.

The Portobello

Flavorful and succulent, the meaty Portobello mushroom is an excellent choice for the grill. In Northern Italy, Portobellos are called *cappellone*, which translates as "big cap"—an appropriate name considering their firm round caps can grow to be as large as six inches in diameter. Due to their satisfying taste and texture, Portobellos are favorites among vegetarians and meat-eaters alike. These Grilled Portobello Mushroom Burgers, for instance, are always a hit no matter who is coming to dinner.

Portobellos are typically sold fresh and are available year-round. Select those that are firm and plump with a clean earthy smell. If the caps are limp, appear shriveled and dried, or have a slightly moist, slippery feel, they are past their prime and should be avoided. It is also best to use Portobellos shortly after buying them. If, however, you have to store them, place the mushrooms in a brown paper bag or wrap them in dry paper towels. Then store them in the refrigerator, where they should keep for up to a week.

Before using the caps, gently wipe them clean with a slightly damp kitchen towel. If they need to be rinsed, do so directly before using. Use cold water and then pat the caps dry. Like all mushrooms, once Portobellos are cooked, they can be frozen for several months.

The Plain Ol' Hot Dog

The hot dog has a long, proud history. It began as a sausage in Frankfurt, Germany over five hundred years ago. In the 1800s, American street vendors began placing the sausage, or frankfurter, in a roll, and in 1893, the new treat was popularized at the Chicago World's Fair. Soon, college students were buying sausages in buns from "dog carts," and it didn't take long for Americans everywhere to embrace a food that was inexpensive, a snap to make, and fun to eat. Now an American icon, it makes an appearance at ball games, picnics, county fairs, and backyard barbeques. Here's a way to prepare the "dog" with all of the respect due.

YIELD: 8 SERVINGS
RECOMMENDED PELLETS: YOUR CHOICE
MARINATION/SEASONING TIME: NONE
COOKING TIME: 15 TO 20 MINUTES

8 hot dogs	**Ketchup, mustard, pickle relish,**
8 hot dog buns	**pickles, onion, cheese, or the condiments and toppings of your choice**

1. Start the pellet grill and set the temperature control to 375°F.

2. When the grill reaches the desired temperature, arrange the hot dogs on the grate. Close the grill door and cook for 15 to 20 minutes, rotating the franks every 3 minutes or so to create grill marks.

3. If you want toasted buns, preheat your kitchen broiler when you put the dogs on the grill. During the last 5 minutes of grilling, spread the hot dog buns open on a cookie sheet, and toast lightly under the broiler.

4. Remove the hot dogs from the grill and place each in a bun. Serve them with the toppings of your choice.

THE COMPLETE WOOD PELLET BARBEQUE COOKBOOK

5.

Plentiful Pork

When true master grillers get together, the meat they most love to cook and share is pork. Pork is generally lean, lends itself to an amazing variety of seasonings and sauces, and always satisfies. Even if you aren't a master at the grill, chances are that you can't resist perfectly seasoned baby back pork ribs or a mound of smoky pulled pork.

This chapter shows you how to create a range of pork dishes using different cuts of meat, different rubs and sauces, and, most important, the incredibly versatile wood pellet grill. The recipes begin with a meltingly tender pork tenderloin seasoned with both dried spices and Kansas City-style sauce. I then present a selection of roasts, and from an elegant stuffed loin to a satisfying apple wood-smoked butt, every dish is sure to please.

If you love pork chops, you'll be delighted to find several ways of preparing them. Choose among chops that are deliciously paired with pineapple, spiced apples, or cranberries, or create a batch of hearty stuffed pork chops.

For many people, the word "barbeque" brings to mind a plate of savory ribs. For them, this chapter offers ribs inspired by three barbeque regions: Kansas City, Memphis, and Texas. Each style has its unique flavors and aromas, and each is delicious.

If you have a little more time and a big appetite, you'll want to prepare my Pulled Pork. Making the most of an inexpensive cut of meat, this spicy, slightly sweet dish is slow-cooked with smoke until it can be shredded with two forks and piled on a bun. The aroma will drive you crazy during the long hours of cooking, but the marvelous results will be well worth the wait.

Although grill masters love the creative opportunities that pork offers, anyone armed with a wood pellet grill and a few ingredients can enjoy mouth-watering results when using this versatile meat. This chapter will start you on your own rewarding culinary adventures with pork.

Barbequed Pork Tenderloin

Pork tenderloin is a luxurious cut of meat that's always a pleasure to present at the dinner table. When seasoned properly—in this recipe, with gentle spices, sesame oil, and garlic—it turns any meal into a special occasion. Enhance the smokiness of the seasoning blend with maple pellets, and you'll have a little slice of heaven on your plate.

YIELD: 7–8 SERVINGS
RECOMMENDED PELLETS: MAPLE
MARINATION/SEASONING TIME: 8 HOURS TO OVERNIGHT
COOKING TIME: 1 1/2 TO 2 HOURS

2 pork tenderloins (about 1 pound each), trimmed of excess fat

MARINADE

1/4 cup Barbeque Seasoning Blend (page 28) or your favorite commercial barbeque seasoning

1/4 cup sesame oil

3 garlic cloves, minced

SAUCE

1 cup Basic Kansas City-Style Barbeque Sauce (page 43) or commercial sweet tomato-based barbeque sauce

1/4 cup sesame oil

1/4 cup red wine vinegar

1 garlic clove, finely minced

1. Blend the marinade ingredients in a small bowl.

2. Rinse the tenderloins in cold water and dry with paper towels. Place the meat in a resealable plastic bag or covered glass dish, and add the marinade, turning the food to cover. Place in the refrigerator for at least 8 hours or as long as overnight, occasionally turning the tenderloins or massaging the plastic bag to ensure absorption of the marinade into the meat.

3. Remove the tenderloins from the marinade, reserving the marinade. Start the pellet grill and set the temperature control to 225°F.

4. Transfer the marinade to a saucepan and bring to a rolling boil over high heat. Allow it to remain at a boil for at least 3 minutes before continuing with your recipe.

5. When the grill reaches the desired temperature, transfer the meat to the grill, close the lid, and cook for 1½ to 2 hours, basting every 20 to 30 minutes with the boiled marinade. Cook the meat until it reaches the desired state of doneness or until an instant-read thermometer shows an internal temperature of 120°F to 130°F for rare, 135°F to 145°F for medium, or 155°F or greater for well done.

6. During the last hour of cooking, place the sauce ingredients in a medium-size saucepan and stir to mix. Simmer gently for about 30 minutes to allow the flavors to blend. Cover to keep warm, and remove from the heat.

7. Transfer the tenderloins to a cutting board, cover with aluminum foil, and allow to rest for 10 minutes before carving into ½-inch slices. Serve with the warmed sauce on the side.

QUICK GRILLING FOR PORK TENDERLOIN

For those occasions when you want to cook Barbequed Pork Tenderloin more quickly, increase the grill temperature to 350°F and decrease the cooking time to 50 to 60 minutes. Just remember that whenever you turn up the temperature of the grill, you reduce the food's smoky flavor and aroma. (For more information on Quick Grilling, see page 12.)

Is It a Loin or a Tenderloin?

This chapter includes recipes for both pork loins (see page 88) and pork tenderloins (see recipe above). Is there a difference between the two cuts? Absolutely, and you'll want to understand the distinction before you shop for ingredients.

The *pork loin* is the large, thick cut of meat that runs along the pig's back. Usually, the loin is sold in sections called *loin roasts,* each of which is several pounds in weight.

The *pork tenderloin* is actually part of the loin. (Sometimes a loin sold in a store contains the tenderloin, which appears darker than the rest of the roast.) A long, narrow strip of meat, the tenderloin is very lean and very tender. In addition to being sold as part of the larger loin, tenderloins are sold separately and are often vacuum-packed in pairs, with each piece of meat weighing in at about a pound. The prepackaged pork tenderloins are offered plain or are infused with marinade. When using the recipes in this book, you'll want meat that has not been marinated as this will allow you to season it to taste. Be assured that whether you choose a loin or a tenderloin, it will cook up juicy, flavorful, and simply sensational on your wood pellet grill.

Pork Loin with Apple Stuffing

This roast is well-seasoned and then stuffed with a sweet-and-spicy mixture of apples, walnuts, sugar, and spice. Although easy to prepare, it is perfect for a special occasion—impressive in appearance with a unique blend of flavors and aromas. The finishing touch is provided by a fifty-fifty blend of apple and maple smoke.

YIELD: 5–6 SERVINGS
RECOMMENDED PELLETS: APPLE AND MAPLE
MARINATION/SEASONING TIME: NONE
COOKING TIME: ABOUT 1 1/2 HOURS

5-pound pork loin, trimmed of excess fat	**APPLE STUFFING**
1 1/2 teaspoons sea salt	**3 Granny Smith apples (unpeeled), chopped into 1/4-inch dice**
1/4 teaspoon ground cloves	**3 scallions, chopped**
1/4 teaspoon ground allspice	**2 tablespoons grated fresh ginger root, or 1 tablespoon ground ginger**
1/2 cup apple juice	**2 1/2 tablespoons butter, softened**
1/2 cup water	**2 1/2 tablespoons brown sugar**
	2 tablespoons Dijon-style mustard
	1/4 cup chopped walnuts

1. Start the pellet grill and set the temperature control to 300°F.

2. Rinse the pork loin in cold water and dry with paper towels. Place the roast on a cutting board and use a sharp knit to cut the pork loin into approximately 3/4-inch-thick *partial* slices. Do *not* cut all the way through.

3. In a small bowl, mix the sea salt, cloves, and allspice. Sprinkle the mixture over the outer surfaces of the pork. (This works best if you put the spices in a small shaker.) Be cautious about increasing the spice amounts, as ground clove and allspice can be very powerful.

4. Transfer the loin to a shallow aluminum roasting pan.

5. To make the stuffing, place all of the stuffing ingredients in a medium-size bowl, and toss to mix well. Spoon equal amounts of stuffing between the slices of the loin. If any of the mixture remains, spoon it around the roast.

6. Mix the apple juice and water in a spray bottle, and set aside.

7. When the grill reaches the desired temperature, transfer the aluminum pan to the grill, close the lid, and cook for 30 minutes. To help keep the roast moist, spray the loin with the apple juice mixture. Spraying the roast every 15 minutes or so, continue to cook for another 30 minutes or until an instant-read thermometer shows an internal temperature of at least 155°F.

8. Open the grill door to release some of the heat and reset the temperature control to 180°F or "Smoke." Close the door and continue to cook the roast for an additional 30 minutes.

9. Transfer the roast to a cutting board, cover with aluminum foil, and allow it to rest for 10 minutes. Then use a knife to separate each slice from the roast. Serve the pork with the apple dressing on top.

Why Use an Apple Juice Spray During Cooking?

You'll find that many of the recipes in this chapter direct you to periodically spray the cooking meat with apple juice that has been diluted with water. Most lean pork has a tendency to dry out as it's cooked, and pork chops—because they are generally lean and relatively thin—are especially prone to dryness. I've found that one of the best ways to prevent this is to fill a clean spray bottle with a fifty-fifty solution of apple juice and water, and spray the meat with the solution every fifteen to thirty minutes during cooking. This simple strategy helps to keep the meat moist, adds wonderful flavor, and may even help tenderize tougher cuts. It should be noted that the longer and hotter the meat is cooked, the more moisture it will tend to lose.

Should you always use an apple juice-and-water solution when making pork on your wood pellet grill? Not always. If you're slow-cooking a fatty cut of meat such as a pork butt, the combination of the fat and low temperatures will prevent the meat from drying out. If you are basting the meat during cooking with a tasty mop sauce or another liquid, a spray of apple juice will, again, not be necessary. Lastly, if you have decided to brine the meat before cooking (see the inset on page 38 of Chapter 2), the meat will remain moist without any additional help. But when you are preparing very lean cuts of pork without brining or basting sauces, the apple juice spray will provide you with an easy way to ensure moist, flavorful results.

Hawaiian Pineapple Loin Chops

When I returned from my first trip to Hawaii, I sought to recreate the wonderful flavors and aromas I had experienced there. This dish—which uses a marinade of teriyaki sauce, soy sauce, scallions, and a citrusy spice mix—is as close as you can get to Island cuisine without boarding a plane. Don't skip the pineapple slice, which adds flavor, color, and a distinctive Hawaiian touch.

YIELD: 4 SERVINGS
RECOMMENDED PELLETS: MAPLE
MARINATION/SEASONING TIME: I HOUR TO OVERNIGHT
COOKING TIME: ABOUT 45 MINUTES

2$\frac{1}{2}$–3 pound pork loin roast, or 4 boneless pork chops, each 1$\frac{1}{2}$ inches thick (do not trim off fat)

4 fresh pineapple rings (about $\frac{1}{2}$ inch thick), or 4 canned

(unsweetened) pineapple rings, well drained

1 cup Hawaiian Marinade (page 37) or commercial teriyaki and soy sauce marinade

1. Rinse the meat in cold water and dry with paper towels. If you purchased a roast, slice it into 4 chops, each about 1$\frac{1}{2}$ inches thick.

2. Place the chops in a resealable plastic bag or covered glass dish, and add the marinade, turning the food to cover. Place in the refrigerator for at least 1 hour or as long as overnight, occasionally turning the chops or massaging the bag to ensure absorption of the marinade.

3. Start the pellet grill and set the temperature control to 300°F.

4. Remove the meat from the marinade, discarding the marinade. When the grill reaches the desired temperature, arrange the chops directly on the grill and cook, without turning, for 15 minutes. Arrange the pineapple rings on the grill, and continue to cook the chops and the pineapple for another 30 minutes, until the meat reaches the desired state of doneness, or until an instant-read thermometer shows an internal temperature of 120°F to 130°F for rare, 135°F to 145°F for medium, or 155°F or greater for well done.

5. Transfer the chops to a serving platter with the grill marks facing up. Top with the pineapple rings, grill marks up, and serve immediately.

QUICK GRILLING FOR LOIN CHOPS

For those occasions when you want to cook Hawaiian Loin Chops more quickly, increase the grill temperature to 400°F and decrease the cooking time to about 30 minutes. Remember that whenever you turn up the temperature of the grill, you reduce the food's smoky flavor and aroma. (For more information on Quick Grilling, see page 12.)

Savory Roast Pork

This pork roast is one of life's simple pleasures. Seasoned with a unique blend of Mediterranean and Southwestern herbs and spices, its flavors and aromas are further enhanced with gentle apple smoke. Although a commercial Mediterranean seasoning blend will give you delicious results, for this recipe, I recommend that you put together my easy-to-make but distinctive spice mix for an out-of-this-world treat.

YIELD: 6–8 SERVINGS
RECOMMENDED PELLETS: APPLE
MARINATION/SEASONING TIME: 3 HOURS TO OVERNIGHT
COOKING TIME: ABOUT 3 HOURS

5–6 pound rolled (boneless) Boston-style pork butt	**¹/₄ cup plus 1 tablespoon Savory Spice Rub and Seasoning Blend (page 24)**
¹/₂ cup apple juice	**¹/₂ cup water**

1. Rinse the roast in cold water and dry with paper towels. Trim the heavy fat from the roast, leaving no more than ¹/₄ inch of fat. Leave any lacing in place.

2. Sprinkle the spice blend over the roast, and massage it into all surfaces of the meat. Wrap the roast securely in plastic wrap and refrigerate for at least 3 to 4 hours, or as long as overnight.

3. Start the pellet grill and set the temperature control to 225°F. Mix the apple juice and water in a spray bottle, and set it aside.

4. When the grill reaches the desired temperature, remove the roast from the refrigerator and discard the plastic wrap. Place the meat in a shallow aluminum roasting pan, fat side up, and transfer the pan to the grill grate. Close the lid of the grill and cook for 1 hour.

5. Increase the temperature control to 300°F. To help keep the roast moist, lightly spray it with the apple juice mixture every 30 minutes or so for about 2 hours, until the meat reaches the desired degree of doneness, or until an instant-read thermometer shows an internal temperature of 120°F to 130°F for rare, 135°F to 145°F for medium, or 155°F or greater for well done. Turn off the grill, cover the roast with aluminum foil, and allow it to rest in the closed grill for 15 minutes.

6. Transfer the roast to a cutting board, carve into ¹/₂-inch slices, and serve immediately.

Apple-Stuffed Pork Chops

Some form of apples has accompanied our pork dishes for as long as I can remember because this fruit so beautifully complements the flavor of pork. This particular pairing works very well, especially when you use apple pellets as the heat and smoke source. Johnny Appleseed would be envious.

YIELD: 4 SERVINGS
RECOMMENDED PELLETS: APPLE
MARINATION/SEASONING TIME: NONE
COOKING TIME: ABOUT 1 HOUR

$^{1}/_{2}$ **cup apple juice**

$^{1}/_{2}$ **cup water**

2$^{1}/_{2}$–3 pound pork loin roast, or 4 boneless pork chops, each 1$^{1}/_{2}$ inches thick, trimmed of excess fat

2–3 tablespoons Herb and Garlic Seasoning Blend (page 32) or commercial herb and garlic seasoning

APPLE STUFFING

3 Granny Smith apples, peeled and chopped into $^{1}/_{4}$-inch dice

1 tablespoon fresh lemon juice

$^{3}/_{4}$ **teaspoon ground cinnamon**

$^{1}/_{4}$ **teaspoon ground cloves**

1 tablespoon sugar

1. Start the pellet grill and set the temperature control to 300°F. Mix the apple juice and water in a spray bottle, and set aside.

2. Rinse the meat in cold water and dry with paper towels. If you purchased a roast, slice it into 4 chops, each about 1$^{1}/_{2}$ inches thick. Cut a pocket into one side of each pork chop, leaving the other three sides intact to hold the stuffing.

3. Sprinkle the seasoning blend into the pocket and over the exterior of each chop. Set the chops aside.

4. To make the stuffing, place the diced apples in a medium-sized bowl. In a small bowl, combine the lemon juice, cinnamon, cloves, and sugar. Stir the mixture into the apples.

5. Using a spoon, place an equal portion of the apple mixture in the pocket of each pork chop. To secure the apples in the meat, insert a toothpick on the diagonal through the open edges of the chop. If necessary, add a second toothpick, slanted in the opposite direction, to keep the stuffing from falling out during cooking.

6. When the grill reaches the desired temperature, arrange the pork chops directly on the grate, close the grill door, and cook, without turning, for about 1 hour. Keep the meat moist by spraying the chops with the apple juice mixture every 15 minutes. Grill until the chops reach the desired state of doneness or until an instant-read thermometer shows an internal temperature of at least 155°F.

7. Transfer the chops to a serving platter, cover with aluminum foil, and allow to rest for 10 minutes before serving.

Southwestern-Style Roast Pork

In this simple but delicious dish, Southwestern spices like cumin, chili, and cayenne combine with mesquite smoke to enhance a hearty pork roast. To complete your menu, accompany the succulent meat with Spanish rice, refried beans, and corn tortillas.

YIELD: 6–8 SERVINGS
RECOMMENDED PELLETS: MESQUITE
MARINATION/SEASONING TIME: 3 HOURS TO OVERNIGHT
COOKING TIME: ABOUT 3 HOURS

5–6 pound rolled (boneless) Boston-style pork butt	**$1/4$ cup plus 1 tablespoon Southwestern Seasoning Blend and Rub (page 27) or commercial Southwestern seasoning blend**
$1/2$ cup apple juice	
$1/2$ cup water	

1. Rinse the roast in cold water and dry with paper towels. Trim the heavy fat from the roast, leaving no more than $1/4$ inch of fat. Leave any lacing in place.

2. Sprinkle the seasoning over the roast, and massage it into all surfaces of the meat. Wrap the roast securely in plastic wrap and refrigerate for at least 3 to 4 hours, or as long as overnight.

3. Start the pellet grill and set the temperature control to 225°F. Mix the apple juice and water in a spray bottle, and set it aside.

4. When the grill reaches the desired temperature, remove the roast from the refrigerator and discard the plastic wrap. Place the meat in a shallow aluminum roasting pan, fat side up, and transfer the pan to the grill grate. Close the lid of the grill and cook for 1 hour.

5. Increase the temperature control to 300°F. To help keep the roast moist, lightly spray it with the apple juice every 20 minutes for about 2 hours, until the meat reaches the desired state of done-ness, or until an instant-read thermometer shows an internal temperature of 120°F to 130°F for rare, 135°F to 145°F for medium, or 155°F or greater for well done. Turn the pellet grill off, cover the roast with aluminum foil, and allow it to rest in the closed grill for 15 minutes.

6. Transfer the roast to a cutting board, carve into $1/2$-inch slices, and serve immediately.

Cranberry Glazed Pork Chops

Simple and extremely satisfying, these chops are guaranteed to please your entire family. The glaze is not only beautiful but also adds the tantalizing aromas of fruit, cinnamon, and clove. If a juicier chop is desired, before cooking, brine the meat overnight by following the directions on page 38. For this recipe, cherry or maple pellets are highly recommended.

YIELD: 4 SERVINGS
RECOMMENDED PELLETS: CHERRY OR MAPLE
MARINATION/SEASONING TIME: NONE
COOKING TIME: ABOUT 45 MINUTES

2$^1/_2$–3 pound pork loin roast, or 4 boneless pork chops, each 1$^1/_2$ inches thick (do not trim off fat)

1 tablespoon garlic salt

1 tablespoon ground black pepper

CRANBERRY GLAZE

1 cup cranberry juice cocktail

$^1/_2$ cup dried cranberries

$^1/_2$ teaspoon ground cinnamon

$^1/_4$ teaspoon ground cloves

1 teaspoon cornstarch

1 tablespoon cold water

1. Start the grill and set the temperature control to 300°F.

2. Rinse the meat in cold water and dry with paper towels. If you purchased a roast, slice it into 4 chops, each about 1$^1/_2$ inches thick. Sprinkle the garlic salt and pepper on both sides of the chops.

3. When the grill reaches the desired temperature, arrange the chops directly on the grate and close the grill door. Cook, without turning, for 45 to 50 minutes, until the meat has reached the desired degree of doneness, or until an instant-read thermometer shows an internal temperature of 120°F to 130°F for rare, 135°F to 145°F for medium, or 155°F or greater for well done. Turn off the grill and allow the chops to rest on the closed grill for 10 minutes.

4. While the chops are cooking, prepare the cranberry glaze by placing the cranberry juice, dried cranberries, cinnamon, and cloves in a small saucepan. Place over low heat and cook, stirring occasionally, for about 20 minutes, or until the liquid has reduced by half.

5. Place the cornstarch and water in a small dish, and stir until smooth. Add the mixture to the glaze and stir until thickened. Remove the glaze from the heat and cover to keep warm. (This glaze can be prepared a day in advance and stored in the refrigerator until needed. Warm the glaze over low heat before serving.)

6. Arrange the chops on individual plates, spoon the glaze over the top, and serve.

QUICK GRILLING FOR GLAZED PORK CHOPS

For those occasions when you want to cook Cranberry Glazed Pork Chops more quickly, increase the grill temperature to 400°F and decrease the cooking time to about 30 minutes. Just remember that whenever you turn up the temperature of the grill, you reduce the food's smoky flavor and aroma. (For more information on Quick Grilling, see page 12.)

The Best Wines for Pork Dishes

Because pork can be prepared on the pellet grill in so many ways, with such a huge range of spices and sauces, there is an equally large assortment of wines—both white and red—that can harmonize with your pork dishes. The following recommendations are based on my personal experience.

Champagne. A sparkling white wine, Champagne begins as a blending of "still" (non-sparkling) wines—usually Chardonnay and Pinot Noir. Once a balance of body and flavors has been achieved, the wine goes through a second fermentation to produce the characteristic bubbles. The resulting libation is marvelous with a wide range of foods, including pork roasts and many other pork dishes, but is not the best choice for spicy foods.

Chardonnay. A dry white wine with a crisp, clean taste, Chardonnay is usually produced in stainless steel barrels, but may be fermented or aged in oak barrels. When fermented in stainless steel, it tends to be medium-bodied. When fermented in oak, it takes on oak and vanilla flavors and develops more body. Offer a "big" Chardonnay—one fermented in oak—with highly smoked or seasoned pork dishes. Stainless steel-fermented versions are lighter and best suited for mildly seasoned, lightly smoked dishes.

Sauvignon Blanc. A light- to medium-bodied dry white wine, Sauvignon Blanc is taut and herbal with sharp acidity. Served chilled, this wine is amazingly adaptable and will complement a large assortment of lightly seasoned pork dishes, including roasts, chops, and tenderloin.

Viognier. This medium- to full-bodied white wine has been described as having exotic honeysuckle- and citrus-like characteristics. It beautifully complements both pork loins and chops.

Merlot. This dry red wine is similar to Cabernet Sauvignon, but softer in texture with a rounder mouth feel. It is best with lightly spiced pork dishes like pork loin, tenderloin, roasts, and chops.

Syrah. This full-bodied dry red wine, which is a little bolder than a Cabernet and Merlot, exhibits aromas of blackberry, pepper and spice, and sometimes has a little "fruit sweetness." It is a wonderful choice when serving roast pork, pork tenderloin, and spicy barbequed dishes such as ribs and pulled pork.

Red Zinfandel. A medium- to full-bodied red wine, Red Zinfandel has blackberry, boysenberry, and plumy notes. Enjoy it with highly spiced, smoky dishes such as pulled pork.

Kansas-Style Baby Back Pork Ribs

These ribs are marvelous. Perfectly seasoned with mustard, herbs and spices, and a sweet Kansas City-style sauce—and slowly infused with hickory or mesquite smoke—they have an appealing crust and meat so moist and tender that it virtually falls off the bone.

YIELD: 4 SERVINGS ($^1/_2$ RACK PER SERVING)
RECOMMENDED PELLETS: HICKORY OR MESQUITE
MARINATION/SEASONING TIME: 4 HOURS TO OVERNIGHT
COOKING TIME: 4 TO 5 HOURS

2 racks baby back pork ribs (about 4 pounds)

$^1/_4$ cup Home-Style Seasoning Mix (page 26) or commercial hickory smoke-and-spice blend

1 cup prepared yellow mustard

2 cups Basic Kansas City-Style Barbeque Sauce (page 43) or commercial sweet tomato-based barbeque sauce

1. Remove the thin membrane from the back of each rack of ribs by pulling it off in a sheet using a sharp knife and paper towels. Rinse the ribs in cold water and dry with paper towels.

2. Using a pastry or silicone brush, coat both sides of the ribs with the mustard. Sprinkle on the seasoning mix and massage the mustard and spices into the meat. Wrap the ribs in plastic wrap and refrigerate for 4 hours to as long as overnight.

3. Start the pellet grill and set the temperature control to 180°F or "Smoke." When the grill reaches the desired temperature, remove the ribs from the refrigerator and discard the plastic wrap. Arrange the ribs directly on the grill grate, or place the ribs on a rib rack, and set the rack on the grill. Leave sufficient room between the ribs to allow the smoke to flow freely. Close the lid of the grill and smoke uncovered for 1 hour.

4. Increase the grill temperature to 225°F and continue to cook for 2½ to 3 hours, or until the meat has pulled back from the bones. Check the meat by lifting one end of the rib rack with tongs. When done, the rib meat will start to crack on the surface, and the rack will be pliable and close to breaking between the bones.

5. Liberally brush the barbeque sauce over the ribs. Close the lid of the grill and allow the sauce to caramelize for about 10 minutes. Turn the ribs over and apply the sauce to the second side. Turn the grill off and allow the ribs to rest in the closed grill for 10 to 15.

6. Transfer the ribs to a carving board and cut into serving pieces, each containing 2 to 3 bones, or cut each rack in half to create a dramatic appearance on the serving plate. Serve immediately.

Memphis-Style Pork Ribs

In Memphis, the grill masters are not big fans of sugary sauces. Instead, they apply savory dry rubs before cooking and, to balance the flavors, they brush on a vinegar-based mop sauce a short time before the meat is done. The result is tender, flavorful meat that can be served as is or accompanied by the barbeque sauce of your choice.

YIELD: 4 SERVINGS ($^1/_2$ RACK PER PERSON)
RECOMMENDED PELLETS: APPLE, HICKORY, OR MESQUITE
MARINATION/SEASONING TIME: 6 HOURS TO OVERNIGHT
COOKING TIME: 3 TO 4 HOURS

---

2 racks baby back pork ribs (about 4 pounds)

1 cup Memphis-Style Rub (page 20) or commercial Memphis-style rub, divided

1 recipe Basic Memphis-Style Mop Sauce (page 42)

Barbeque sauce of your choice (optional)

1. Remove the thin membrane from the back of each rack of ribs by pulling it off in a sheet using a sharp knife and paper towels. Rinse the ribs in cold water and dry with paper towels.

2. Sprinkle two-thirds of the rub over both sides of the ribs, and rub into the meat. Wrap the ribs securely in plastic wrap and refrigerate for at least 6 to 8 hours, or as long as overnight.

3. Start the pellet grill and set the temperature control to 225°F.

4. When the grill reaches the desired temperature, remove the ribs from the refrigerator and discard the plastic wrap. Arrange the ribs directly on the grill grate, or place the ribs on a rib rack, and set the rack on the grill. Leave sufficient room between the ribs to allow the smoke to flow freely. Close the lid of the grill and cook for 1 hour.

5. Brush the mop sauce over the surface of the ribs, and continue to cook for 30 minutes. Brush the sauce over the ribs again, and, brushing the sauce on every 30 minutes, continue to cook for 2 more hours, or until the meat has pulled back from the ends of the bones. Check the meat by lifting one end of the rib rack with tongs. When done, the rib meat will start to crack on the surface, and the rack will be pliable and close to breaking between the bones. Before removing the ribs from the grill, mop the ribs gently one more time and sprinkle the remaining rub mixture over the meat.

6. Transfer the ribs to a carving board, cover with aluminum foil, and allow to rest for 10 to 15 minutes. Cut into serving pieces, each containing 2 to 3 bones, or cut each rack in half to create a dramatic appearance on the serving plate. Serve immediately with barbeque sauce on the side, if desired.

Stuffed Pork Chops

For most of us, the smell of stuffing brings back happy childhood memories. In this recipe, for ease and simplicity, I stuff pork loin chops with prepared stuffing mix and then roast the chops on the pellet grill. The result—moist, flavorful chops filled with savory bread stuffing—is sure to be the start of some new and wonderful memories in your family.

YIELD: 4 SERVINGS
RECOMMENDED PELLETS: APPLE OR CHERRY
MARINATION/SEASONING TIME: NONE
COOKING TIME: ABOUT 1 HOUR

$^1/_2$ cup apple juice

$^1/_2$ cup water

$2^1/_2$–3 pound pork loin roast, or 4 pork chops, each $1^1/_2$ inches thick (do not trim off fat)

2–3 tablespoons Herb and Garlic Seasoning Blend (page 32) or commercial herb and garlic seasoning

2 cups prepared seasoned bread stuffing mix or homemade stuffing

---

1. Start the pellet grill and set the temperature control to 300°F degrees. Mix the apple juice and water in a spray bottle, and set aside.

2. Rinse the meat in cold water and dry with paper towels. If you purchased a roast, slice it into 4 chops, each about $1^1/_2$ inches thick. Cut a pocket into one side of each pork chop, leaving the other three sides intact to hold the stuffing.

3. Sprinkle the seasoning blend into the pocket and over the exterior of each chop.

4. Using a spoon, place an equal portion of the stuffing in each pork chop. To secure the stuffing in the meat, insert a toothpick on the diagonal through the open edges of the chop. If necessary, add a second toothpick, slanted in the opposite direction, to keep the stuffing from falling out during cooking.

5. When the grill reaches the desired temperature, arrange the stuffed chops on the grill, close the door, and cook, without turning, for about an hour. Keep the meat moist by spraying the chops with the apple juice mixture every 15 minutes. Grill until the chops reach the desired state of doneness or until an instant-read thermometer shows an internal temperature of 120°F to 130°F for rare, 135°F to 145°F for medium, or 155°F or greater for well done.

6. Transfer the chops to a serving platter, cover with aluminum foil, and allow to rest for 10 minutes before serving.

Texas-Style Pork Ribs

In Texas, this delicious dish is spiced with seasonings and sauces that include hot peppers, which bring both a unique flavor and quite a bit of heat to the party. Although this recipe—which is a good representative of Southwestern cuisine—does have a little kick, it will not send you running for a glass of water. I recommended mesquite pellets to round out the flavors.

YIELD: 4 SERVINGS ($^1/_2$ RACK PER PERSON)
RECOMMENDED PELLETS: MESQUITE
MARINATION/SEASONING TIME: 4 HOURS TO OVERNIGHT
COOKING TIME: 3 TO 4 HOURS

2 racks baby back pork ribs (about 4 pounds)

$^1/_4$ cup Southwestern Seasoning Blend and Rub (page 27) or commercial Southwestern seasoning blend

$1^3/_4$ cups Spicy Texas-Style Barbeque Sauce (page 46) or commercial Texas-style barbeque sauce

1. Remove the thin membrane from the back of each rack of ribs using a sharp knife and paper towels. Rinse the ribs in cold water and dry with paper towels.

2. Sprinkle the seasoning blend over both sides of the ribs, and rub into the meat. Wrap the ribs securely in plastic wrap and refrigerate for at least 4 to 6 hours, or as long as overnight.

3. Start the pellet grill and set the temperature control to 225°F.

4. When the grill reaches the desired temperature, remove the ribs from the refrigerator and discard the plastic wrap. Arrange the ribs directly on the grill grate, or place them on a rib rack, and set the rack on the grill. Leave sufficient room between the ribs to allow the smoke to flow freely.

5. Close the lid of the grill and cook for $2^1/_2$ to 3 hours, or until the meat has pulled back from the ends of the bones. Check the meat by lifting one end of the rib rack with tongs. When done, the rib meat will start to crack on the surface, and the rack will be pliable and close to breaking between the bones.

6. Liberally brush the barbeque sauce over the ribs. Close the lid of the grill and allow the sauce to caramelize for about 10 minutes. Turn the ribs over and apply the sauce to the second side. Turn the grill off and allow the ribs to rest in the closed grill for 10 to 15 minutes so that the sauce has a chance to set.

7. Transfer the ribs to a carving board and cut into serving pieces, each containing 2 to 3 bones, or cut each rack in half to create a dramatic appearance on the serving plate. Serve immediately, accompanying the ribs with more sauce if desired.

Pulled Pork

Fork-tender and delicious, this spicy, slightly sweet version of pulled pork is delightful by itself or on a potato roll, with or without barbeque sauce. Although it takes a long time to cook—up to 15 hours of low heat and slow smoking—the results are well worth the wait. I prefer getting the grill ready in the evening and putting the meat on the grate just before bedtime. Use apple pellets if you want to add a light smoke flavor, or, for a more distinct taste and aroma, use mesquite or hickory. Have fun with this one.

YIELD: ABOUT 5 POUNDS SHREDDED PORK (8 SERVINGS)
RECOMMENDED PELLETS: APPLE, MESQUITE, OR HICKORY
MARINATION/SEASONING TIME: 8 HOURS TO OVERNIGHT
COOKING TIME: 12 TO 15 HOURS

7–8 pound pork butt (shoulder), bone in with skin and fat

1 cup Pulled Pork Rub (page 23) or commercial pulled pork spice blend

Barbeque sauce of your choice (optional)

---

1. Rinse the meat in cold water and dry with paper towels. Sprinkle the rub over the entire butt, and rub into the meat. Wrap the meat securely in plastic wrap and refrigerate for at least 8 hours, or as long as overnight.

2. Start the pellet grill and set the temperature control to 180°F or "Smoke." While it's heating up, remove the meat from the refrigerator and discard the plastic wrap. Place the roast in an appropriately sized disposable aluminum pan. Allow the meat to warm to room temperature, about 30 minutes.

3. When the grill reaches the desired temperature, transfer the pan to the grill, close the lid, and smoke for 10 to 12 hours. Use an instant-read thermometer to check the internal temperature of the meat, which should be near 180°F. If not, increase the grill temperature to 225°F and continue roasting for another 1 1/2 to 2 hours. Then measure the temperature again. Note that the internal temperature may plateau but will eventually increase. Continue cooking until the meat can be easily shredded with 2 forks. This can take up to 15 hours total cooking time, depending on the weight of the meat.

4. Using 2 forks, remove the meat from the bone and place it in a serving dish or a glass baking dish. Serve immediately or cover the meat with foil and place in a low-temperature oven until you're ready to serve. If desired, accompany the pork with some of Uncle Bob's Basic Barbeque Sauce (page 47), Spicy Texas-Style Barbeque Sauce (page 46), or the sauce of your choice. Because the meat is flavorful and moist, you may not need to add sauce.

6.
Championship Chicken

The pellet grill is absolutely magical when it comes to preparing chicken. Because both the grill and chicken itself are so versatile, endless combinations of marinades, seasonings, sauces, wood pellets, and cooking techniques are possible. Season your chicken with just a little salt and pepper, and the results are superb. Place some fresh rosemary or thyme under the skin and cook with smoke, and the chicken reinvents itself as a gourmet delight. Add a few spices and change the wood pellets, and the chicken is different again. Infuse the meat with citrus and choose a complementary wood source, and chicken is transformed into something truly sublime.

This chapter shows you just how to prepare chicken in a variety of ways, both simple and sophisticated. You'll start by learning how to roast a whole chicken, and as you'll see, the pellet grill makes it easy to produce a bird that's moist, flavorful, and delicious, inside and out. Following this, you'll learn how to prepare a range of different chicken pieces, and whether you opt for basic Barbequed Grilled Chicken, spicy Buffalo Wings, or savory Chicken Legs 'n Bacon, you'll be delighted by the results.

If you want a dish that's a bit more elegant, try Cornish Game Hens with Rice Stuffing. Stylish yet satisfying, this entrée is as much a treat for the eyes as it is for the taste buds.

Chicken is such a universal favorite that most of us prepare it often. Unfortunately, it's easy to get into a rut and serve the same old poultry dishes over and over again. But it doesn't have to be that way. Armed with a pellet grill and the recipes that follow, you can serve a different chicken dish—each fit for a champion—every single night of the week.

Herbed Chicken with Lemon

This chicken is infused with aromatic thyme and the tang of lemon juice, lemon rind, and a sweet lemony spice mixture. The dish is incredible when it comes off the grill, and is even better the next day—if you're lucky enough to have leftovers! Apple pellets pair perfectly with this out-of-the-world treat. This is a classic way to prepare a whole chicken in your pellet grill, and can easily be modified so that you'll never get bored. Below the recipe, you'll find that with a few changes, Herbed Chicken with Lemon can be transformed into Rosemary Chicken or smoky Southwest Spiced Chicken.

YIELD: 6 SERVINGS
RECOMMENDED PELLETS: APPLE
MARINATION/SEASONING TIME: NONE
COOKING TIME: ABOUT 1 1/2 HOURS

4–5 pound roasting chicken

$2^1/_4$ tablespoons Sweet Lemon Spice (page 32), commercial lemon-based spice blend, or your favorite spice blend, divided

2 pats butter, about 1 teaspoon each

4 sprigs fresh thyme

2 lemons

16-ounce can beer (optional)

$^1/_4$ cup melted butter

---

1. Start the pellet grill and set the temperature control to 325°F.

2. Remove and discard the giblet packet from inside the chicken. Rinse the chicken, inside and out, in cold water and pat dry with paper towels.

3. Liberally sprinkle about 1 tablespoon of the Sweet Lemon Spice inside the chicken. Using your fingers, carefully separate the skin from the chicken breast, and place 1 pat of butter and 2 sprigs of thyme under each side of the breast. Ensure that the thyme sprigs are distributed evenly so that the oils will permeate the entire breast area.

4. Cut the lemons in half and squeeze the juice into the body cavity of the chicken. Then drop the lemon rinds into the cavity.

5. Place the chicken breast-side-up on a work surface. To truss the bird, tuck the wings under the body and use kitchen twine to tie the legs together. This should help the chicken maintain an appealing shape as it cooks.

6. Set the chicken on a vertical roasting rack or a half-empty 16-ounce can of beer. Brush the chicken liberally with the melted butter and sprinkle the skin with the remaining Sweet Lemon Spice.

7. When the grill reaches the desired temperature, position the chicken vertically on the middle of the grate. Close the grill door, making sure that it does not make contact with the chicken.

8. Roast the chicken for at least 1½ hours, until the juices run clear when the meat is pierced with a sharp knife, or until an instant-read thermometer inserted in the breast reads 165°F. Make sure that the thermometer is not touching bone. The cooking time should be about 20 minutes per pound, but if you are using a beer can, allow an extra 20 to 30 minutes of cooking time, as the can prevents the heat from flowing through the chicken.

9. Transfer the chicken from the grill to a cutting board. Cover with aluminum foil, and allow to rest for 10 minutes. Remove and discard the twine, and discard the lemon rinds. Carve the chicken into pieces and serve.

For a Change

■ To make Rosemary Chicken, follow the directions for Herbed Chicken with Lemon, but omit the lemon; replace the thyme sprigs with sprigs of rosemary; and replace the Sweet Lemon Spice with an equal amount of Herb and Garlic Seasoning Blend (see page 32).

■ To prepare Southwest Spiced Chicken, follow the directions for Herbed Chicken with Lemon, but omit the lemon, butter, and fresh herbs. Instead, season the bird with Southwestern Seasoning Blend and Rub (see page 27). Also replace the apple pellets with mesquite.

The Safe Handling of Chicken

Like all raw food, chicken and other types of poultry can carry bacteria like *salmonella, listeria,* and *E. coli*—major causes of food-borne illness. Following a few commonsense handling and cooking guidelines can destroy and prevent the spread of these microorganisms.

☐ After buying chicken, refrigerate it promptly and keep it refrigerated until preparation time. Make sure the raw juice does not touch or drip onto other foods. If you are not using the chicken within two days, freeze it.

☐ To avoid cross contamination, wash your hands in hot soapy water after handling raw chicken. Also wash any utensils, equipment, bowls, platters, and countertops that have come in contact with it. If you rinse the chicken before cooking, be sure to scrub the sink with hot soapy water afterwards. If possible, use a separate cutting board for raw chicken.

☐ Defrost frozen chicken in the refrigerator, not on the kitchen countertop at room temperature.

☐ After marinating chicken, either discard the marinade or boil it for at least three minutes before using it with cooked food.

☐ Cook chicken to an internal temperature of at least 165°F. The meat should have no sign of pinkness.

☐ Never leave cooked chicken at room temperature longer than two hours. Refrigerate leftovers as soon as possible.

Apple Glazed Smoked Chicken

This chicken is first salted on the inside, then basted with an apple-and-cinnamon glaze. The result is sweet, spicy, and pretty darn good! Make this chicken for your next backyard barbeque or picnic. Apple pellets are recommended for the smoke in this recipe.

YIELD: 6 SERVINGS
RECOMMENDED PELLETS: APPLE
MARINATION/SEASONING TIME: NONE
COOKING TIME: ABOUT 1 1/2 HOURS

4–5 pound roasting chicken

2 cups apple juice, divided

1/4 cup plus 2 tablespoons apple jelly

1/4 teaspoon ground cinnamon

1 tablespoon sea salt

1. Remove and discard the giblet packet from inside the chicken. Rinse the chicken, inside and out, in cold water and pat dry with paper towels. Set aside.

2. Combine 1 1/4 cups of the apple juice and all of the apple jelly and cinnamon in a small saucepan. Place the pan over medium heat and cook, stirring often, for about 20 minutes, or until the mixture is reduced by half. Remove the saucepan from the heat.

3. While the glaze is cooking, start the pellet grill and set the temperature control to 225°F.

4. Liberally sprinkle the inside of the chicken with the sea salt. Place the chicken breast-side-up on a work surface. To truss the bird, tuck the wings under the body and use kitchen twine to tie the legs together. This should help the chicken maintain an appealing shape as it cooks.

5. Set the chicken on a vertical roasting rack or an empty 16-ounce beer can that has been partially filled with the remaining 3/4 cup of apple juice. If using a vertical roasting rack that has a reservoir, fill the reservoir with the apple juice.

6. When the grill reaches the desired temperature, position the chicken vertically on the middle of the grill grate. Close the grill door, making sure that the door does not make contact with the chicken.

7. Roast the chicken for 30 minutes. Increase the grill temperature to 325°F, and roast for another 30 minutes.

8. Baste the chicken liberally with the apple glaze. Close the grill door and cook for another 20 minutes; then baste again. If you are using a roasting rack, the total cooking time will be about 20 minutes per pound. If you are using a beer can, allow an extra 20 to 30 minutes of cooking time, as the can prevents the heat from flowing through the chicken. About 15

THE COMPLETE WOOD PELLET BARBEQUE COOKBOOK

minutes before the chicken is done, baste it for the last time. Cook until the juices run clear when the meat is pierced with a knife, or until an instant-read thermometer inserted in the breast reads 165°F. Make sure that the thermometer is not touching bone.

9. When the chicken is done, turn off the grill and allow the chicken to rest in the closed grill for 10 minutes. Discard any remaining apple glaze.

10. Transfer the chicken from the grill to a cutting board, and remove and discard the twine. Carve the chicken into pieces and serve.

Buffalo Wings

These wings make a memorable addition to any celebration, but if you want a little more heat, sprinkle on my Cajun Spice blend and you'll have Hot Wings in an instant. If you really want to wow your friends, serve the wings along with the Chicken Legs 'n Bacon (page 109). You'll hit a grand slam!

YIELD: About 12 servings
RECOMMENDED PELLETS: Cherry or hickory
MARINATION/SEASONING TIME: None
COOKING TIME: About 45 minutes

12 chicken wings (about 1 pound), tips removed

1 cup Basic Buffalo Wing Sauce (page 42) or commercial chicken wing sauce

2 tablespoons Cajun Spice (page 29) or commercial Cajun spice mix (optional)

1 cup ranch-style dressing (optional)

1. Start the pellet grill and set the temperature control to 325°F.

2. Rinse the chicken wings in cold water and pat dry with paper towels.

3. When the grill reaches the desired temperature, arrange the wings on the grill grate, leaving space between the pieces. Close the grill door and cook for 15 minutes.

4. Baste the wings with the Buffalo Wing Sauce, and, if desired, sprinkle with the spice blend. Turn the wings over and baste again with the sauce and seasoning. Continue to turn and baste every few minutes for about 30 additional minutes, until the juice runs clear when the meat is pierced with a sharp knife, or until an instant-read thermometer shows an internal temperature of 165°F. (Avoid coming in contact with a bone while checking the temperature.)

5. Transfer the chicken to a serving platter and serve with additional sauce and ranch dressing, if desired.

Barbeque Grilled Chicken

This dish pairs chicken with both a spicy seasoning blend and a sweet and tangy sauce. Add potato salad and some Texas-style baked beans, and you'll have a meal to remember. I recommend mesquite pellets for this dish.

YIELD: 6 SERVINGS
RECOMMENDED PELLETS: MESQUITE
MARINATION/SEASONING TIME: 30 MINUTES
COOKING TIME: ABOUT 1 HOUR AND 20 MINUTES

4–5 pound roasting chicken, cut into 10 pieces

3 tablespoons Barbeque Seasoning Blend (page 28) or your favorite commercial barbeque seasoning

1 cup Spicy Texas-Style Barbeque Sauce (page 46) or commercial Texas-style barbeque sauce

1. Rinse the chicken in cold water and dry with paper towels. Sprinkle the seasoning blend over the chicken, cover, and refrigerate for 30 minutes.

2. Spray the grill grate with nonstick cooking spray. Start the pellet grill and set the temperature control to 325°F.

3. When the grill reaches the desired temperature, arrange the chicken pieces on the grill, allowing space between the pieces so that smoke and heat can circulate. Close the grill door and cook for 30 minutes; then turn. Grill for 30 additional minutes, until the juices run clear when the meat is pierced with a knife, or until an instant-read thermometer inserted in the thickest part of the chicken reads 165°F.

4. Brush the barbeque sauce over the chicken and allow the chicken to sit on the grill for 10 minutes. Turn the chicken, apply sauce to the other side, and cook for 10 additional minutes.

5. Turn the pellet grill off and allow the chicken to rest on the grate for 15 more minutes before removing it from the grill. Serve immediately or at room temperature.

THE COMPLETE WOOD PELLET BARBEQUE COOKBOOK

Greek Lemon Chicken Breasts

If you like your chicken flavored with lemon, oregano, and garlic, you will adore these moist, tender chicken breasts, which are based on a great recipe found on the Kalyn's Kitchen website. (Visit www.kalynskitchen.com.) I once prepared this dish for a large social event, and it was the highlight of the luncheon. No commercial products can replace the piquant homemade marinade, but you'll find that it comes together quickly.

YIELD: 6 SERVINGS
RECOMMENDED PELLETS: APPLE OR ALDER
MARINATION/SEASONING TIME: 8 HOURS TO OVERNIGHT
COOKING TIME: ABOUT 1 1/2 HOURS

---

6 large boneless, skinless chicken breast halves (about 3 pounds total), trimmed of excess fat

3/4 cup Greek-Style Lemon Marinade (page 36)

---

1. Rinse the chicken in cold water and dry with paper towels. Use a fork to puncture the chicken breasts liberally over both sides to allow the marinade to penetrate the meat.

2. Place the chicken in a resealable plastic bag or a shallow covered glass dish. Add the marinade, turning the chicken to coat. Transfer to the refrigerator and allow the breasts to marinate for at least 8 hours or as long as overnight, occasionally turning the chicken pieces or massaging the plastic bag to ensure absorption of the marinade.

3. Start the pellet grill and set the temperature control to 250°F.

4. When the grill reaches the desired temperature, remove the chicken from the marinade, discarding the marinade. Arrange the chicken breasts directly on the grill grate, leaving space between the pieces, and cook for 35 to 40 minutes. Turn the chicken over and cook for another 35 minutes, until the juices run clear when the meat is pierced with a sharp knife, or until an instant-read thermometer inserted in the chicken reads 165°F.

5. Transfer the chicken to a glass baking dish or bowl and cover with aluminum foil. Allow the breasts to rest for 15 minutes before serving.

For a Change

■ To make Greek Lemon Chicken Sandwiches, split 6 ciabatta rolls and spread each side with a mixture of 1/2 cup mayonnaise, 1/2 cup sour cream, 1/4 cup fresh lemon juice, and 3 tablespoons chopped chives. Thinly slice the cooked chicken, and arrange a portion over the bottom of each roll. Top with lettuce, tomato, and the second half of the roll. Pair the sandwiches with a Greek salad and a chilled glass of Sauvignon Blanc for a tantalizing summer meal.

Cornish Game Hens with Rice Stuffing

Cornish game hens are one of life's simple pleasures. Once enjoyed only by the wealthy, this culinary offering is now available to everyone and can be purchased at any grocery store. The seasonings and sauces used in this recipe complement one another beautifully, and also harmonize with the rice. This combination is one of our favorites, and I hope that it becomes one of yours as well. I recommend a fifty-fifty blend of hickory and cherry pellets.

YIELD: 4 SERVINGS
RECOMMENDED PELLETS: HICKORY AND CHERRY
MARINATION/SEASONING TIME: NONE
COOKING TIME: ABOUT 1$^1/_4$ HOURS

4 Cornish game hens (about 1 pound each), thawed

2 tablespoons Home-Style Seasoning Mix (page 26) or commercial hickory smoke-and-spice blend, divided

3 tablespoons melted butter

1 cup Spicy Rum Barbeque Sauce (page 48) or commercial rum-based or honey-bourbon barbeque sauce

RICE STUFFING

2 tablespoons extra virgin olive oil

2 tablespoons butter

$^1/_2$ cup chopped onion

$^1/_2$ cup chopped celery

3 cups cooked long grain and wild rice

1 cup chopped mushrooms

$^1/_2$ cup sliced scallions

3 tablespoons soy sauce

1 teaspoon ground black pepper

1. To make the stuffing, place the olive oil and butter in a large skillet over medium heat. Add the onion and celery, and cook, stirring occasionally, until softened, about 3 minutes.

2. Add the rice, mushrooms, scallions, soy sauce, and pepper to the vegetable mixture, and stir to combine. Remove the skillet from the heat and set aside.

3. Start the pellet grill and set the temperature control to 325°F.

4. Remove and discard the packet of giblets from inside each game hen. Rinse the hens, inside and out, with cold water and dry them thoroughly with paper towels. Sprinkle approximately $^1/_2$ teaspoon seasoning mix inside each hen and rub inside to distribute evenly.

5. Place an equal amount of the rice stuffing (approximately $^3/_4$ to 1 cup) in each hen. Do not pack tightly. Arrange the stuffed hens on a roasting rack inside a disposable roasting pan.

THE COMPLETE WOOD PELLET BARBEQUE COOKBOOK

6. Brush the hens with the melted butter and sprinkle each with approximately 1 teaspoon of the remaining seasoning mix.

7. Place the roasting pan on the grill grate, close the lid, and allow to roast for 1 hour.

8. Using an instant-read thermometer, check the internal temperature of the meat. When the thermometer shows a temperature of 165°F or the juices run clear when the meat is pierced with a sharp knife, liberally brush the hens with the barbeque sauce.

9. Allow the hens to roast for 15 additional minutes. Remove the roasting pan from the grill, cover with aluminum foil, and let rest for 10 minutes.

10. Arrange the hens on a serving platter or individual plates and serve immediately with additional barbeque sauce on the side.

Chicken Legs 'n Bacon

Bacon makes nearly anything taste better, and when you wrap seasoned chicken legs with this tasty meat, you have a winning combination that you'll want to make time and time again.

YIELD: About 10 servings
RECOMMENDED PELLETS: Cherry or hickory
MARINATION/SEASONING TIME: None
COOKING TIME: About 25 minutes

10 chicken legs, thighs removed	3 tablespoons chopped fresh parsley
Olive oil	2 tablespoons chopped fresh thyme
$1\frac{1}{2}$ teaspoons sea salt	2 garlic cloves, minced
$1\frac{1}{2}$ teaspoons ground black pepper	10 bacon slices

1. Start the pellet grill and set the temperature control to 400°F.

2. Rinse the chicken legs in cold water and dry with paper towels. Brush the legs with the olive oil, and sprinkle with salt and paper.

3. Mix the herbs and garlic together in a small bowl, and press the mixture onto the skin of the legs. Then wrap each leg with a strip of bacon, starting at the top and winding the bacon around in a spiral. Secure each end with a toothpick.

4. Arrange the legs on the grill grate, leaving space between the pieces. Close the grill door and cook, turning occasionally, for 25 minutes, until the juice runs clear when the meat is pierced, or until an instant read thermometer shows an internal temperature of 165°F. Remove the chicken from the grill and serve.

Jamaican Jerk Chicken

This chicken is hot and spicy, flavored with regional seasonings like allspice, ginger, cinnamon, nutmeg, and a bit of rum. Mix yourself a piña colada, put on some Bob Marley reggae music, and take a backyard trip to the island of Jamaica.

YIELD: 4 SERVINGS
RECOMMENDED PELLETS: MESQUITE AND MAPLE
MARINATION/SEASONING TIME: 1 HOUR TO OVERNIGHT
COOKING TIME: ABOUT 1 HOUR

4 large boneless, skinless chicken breast halves (about 2 pounds total), trimmed of excess fat

¼ cup prepared mustard

3 tablespoons dark rum

½ cup Jamaican Jerk Rub (page 25) or commercial Jamaican Jerk blend

1. Rinse the chicken in cold water and dry with paper towels.

2. Combine the mustard and rum in a small bowl, and brush the mixture over the chicken breasts. Sprinkle the rub over the mustard, pressing to make it adhere. Arrange the chicken in a glass or ceramic bowl or dish, cover with plastic wrap, and place in the refrigerator for at least 1 hour or as long as overnight.

3. Spray the grill with nonstick cooking spray to prevent sticking. Start the pellet grill and set the temperature control to 325°F.

4. When the grill reaches the desired temperature, remove the chicken from the refrigerator and discard the plastic wrap. Arrange the chicken on the grill grate, leaving space between the pieces. Close the grill lid and cook for 40 minutes. Turn the chicken and cook for another 20 minutes, or until the juices run clear when the meat is pierced or an instant-read thermometer shows an internal temperature of 165°F.

5. Transfer the chicken to a serving platter and cover with aluminum foil. Allow the chicken to rest for 10 minutes before serving.

THE COMPLETE WOOD PELLET BARBEQUE COOKBOOK

The Best Wines for Chicken Dishes

Perhaps the most versatile food of all, chicken can be prepared in many different ways. Because the dishes can range from mild to bold, from sweet to spicy, the list of wine pairings is virtually endless. The following recommendations should get you started.

Champagne. A sparkling white wine, Champagne begins as a blending of "still" (non-sparkling) wines—usually Chardonnay and Pinot Noir. Once a balance of body and flavors has been achieved, the wine goes through a second fermentation to produce the characteristic bubbles. The resulting libation is marvelous with a wide variety of lightly spiced or roasted chicken dishes, but is not recommended when serving highly spiced dishes such as chicken wings.

Chardonnay. A dry white wine with a crisp, clean taste, Chardonnay is usually produced in stainless steel barrels, but may be fermented or aged in oak barrels. When fermented in stainless steel, it tends to be medium-bodied. When fermented in oak, it takes on oak and vanilla flavors and develops more body. Reserve Chardonnay for mildly flavored chicken dishes, which match up well with medium-bodied (stainless steel-fermented) versions of the wine.

Chenin Blanc. A light- to medium-bodied white wine that can be dry or lightly sweet, Chenin Blanc has flavors of apricots, pears, melons, and peaches. This wine pairs well with just about any chicken dish.

Pinot Grigio. An easy-drinking light- to medium-bodied white wine, Pinot Grigio is crisp and tastes of pear and spice. It goes well with light to moderately seasoned smoked, roasted, or barbequed chicken dishes.

Sauvignon Blanc. A light- to medium-bodied dry white wine, Sauvignon Blanc is taut and herbal with sharp acidity. Served chilled, this wine is amazingly adaptable and complements a wide variety of lightly seasoned smoked or roasted chicken dishes.

Viognier. This well-rounded, medium- to full-bodied dry white wine has been described as having exotic honeysuckle- and citrus-like flavors. It pairs well with many foods, including virtually any chicken dish.

Pinot Noir. A light- to medium-bodied dry red wine, the earthy yet elegant Pinot Noir exhibits flavors that have been compared to warm baked cherries, plums, mushrooms, and chocolate. Highly versatile, it mates well with all chicken dishes.

Red Zinfandel. A medium- to full-bodied dry red wine, Red Zinfandel has blackberry, boysenberry, and plumy fruit notes. It is great with spicy, smoky chicken dishes.

Sangiovese. Light- to medium-bodied, this dry red Italian wine can be thin and watery or rich and complex. When young, the wine has some fruit sweetness. As it ages, it can take on earthy flavors like those of tea and orange peel. Sangiovese is magical with spicy chicken dishes.

Syrah. This full-bodied dry red wine, which is a little bolder than Cabernet and Merlot, exhibits aromas of blackberry, pepper, and spice, and sometimes has a little "fruit sweetness." It is excellent with any barbequed chicken dish.

"Slow Mo" BBQ Chicken

Cooked low and slow, this chicken is permeated with mesquite smoke as well as a spicy barbeque seasoning blend and a rich sauce prepared Kansas City-style. The result is a mouth-watering down-home delight.

YIELD: 6 SERVINGS
RECOMMENDED PELLETS: MESQUITE
MARINATION/SEASONING TIME: 3 HOURS
COOKING TIME: 1 1/2 HOURS

6 large boneless, skinless chicken breast halves (about 3 pounds total), trimmed of excess fat

1/4 cup plus 2 tablespoons extra virgin olive oil

1/4 cup Barbeque Seasoning Blend (page 28) or your favorite commercial barbeque seasoning

1 cup Basic Kansas City-Style Barbeque Sauce (page 43) or commercial sweet tomato-based barbeque sauce

1. Rinse the chicken in cold water and dry with paper towels. Use a fork to puncture the chicken breasts liberally over both sides to allow the olive oil and seasonings to penetrate the meat.

2. Brush both sides of each chicken breast with olive oil. Then sprinkle the barbeque blend over all. Arrange the chicken in a glass or ceramic bowl or dish, cover with plastic wrap, and place in the refrigerator for up to 3 hours.

3. Start the pellet grill and set the temperature control to "Smoke" or 180°F.

4. When the grill reaches the desired temperature, arrange the chicken directly on the grate, leaving space between the pieces. Close the cover of the grill and smoke for 35 to 40 minutes.

5. Increase the grill temperature to 300°F, and allow the chicken to roast for 40 minutes.

6. When the juices run clear when the meat is pierced with a fork or an instant-read thermometer shows an internal temperature of 165°F, brush the barbeque sauce over the top. Roast for another 10 to 12 minutes, turn the chicken, and brush the second side with the sauce. Turn off the pellet grill and allow the chicken to remain on the grill for 15 minutes before serving.

7.
Terrific Turkey

Turkey isn't just for Thanksgiving anymore. It is available year-round, and your local supermarket or butcher can supply not only whole birds, but also boneless and bone-in turkey breasts, as well as wings, drumsticks, and cutlets. So if you love turkey, there's no reason why you can't enjoy it at any special occasion or even when there's no holiday in sight! The wood pellet grill makes it easy and gives you so many ways to enjoy this culinary treat.

The chapter begins with a tried-and-true recipe for roasted stuffed turkey. By using a boxed stuffing mix, I've taken the fuss out of preparation, and by adding a blend of apple and cheery pellets, I've infused the meat with sensational flavor. Now a roast turkey is not just easy to make; it's out of this world!

Turkey breasts make it practical to enjoy this versatile all-American bird even during the week. This chapter includes a wide range of turkey breast recipes, each with its own unique seasonings and wood pellet choices. If you're looking for a traditional (but sensational) flavor, try Thyme and Garlic Turkey Breast. Feeling a little more adventurous? Consider Honey Lime Breast of Turkey. If you love spicier fare, by all means prepare your turkey Cajun-style. Creative recipes for turkey cutlets, legs, and wings round out this chapter's offerings, providing new ways for you to enliven your cookouts and family dinners.

So if you think that turkey can be enjoyed only during a winter chill, think again. With a wood pellet grill, a variety of wood pellets, and the seasonings of your choice, this succulent meat can be enjoyed at any time of the year and can please even the most demanding of barbeque aficionados.

Roasted Stuffed Turkey

As a child, the aroma of a stuffed turkey roasting in the oven filled our home with anticipation of the meal to come. But this holiday meal came at a price: lengthy preparations followed by an even longer cleanup. Now, the pellet grill has made it easy to enjoy a roasted turkey at any time—without a lot of work or a lot of mess. If you want to enjoy Thanksgiving in July, or if you want your holiday bird to be a little out of the ordinary this year, load the apple and cherry wood pellets into your grill, gather the family, and get ready to build some new and wonderful memories.

YIELD: 10–12 SERVINGS
RECOMMENDED PELLETS: APPLE AND CHERRY
MARINATION/SEASONING TIME: 24 HOURS FOR BRINING, IF DESIRED
COOKING TIME: 5 TO 6 HOURS

12–15 pound whole turkey, brined if desired (see the inset on page 38)

1 tablespoon sea salt

1 tablespoon ground black pepper

8–10 cups prepared seasoned bread stuffing mix * or homemade stuffing, at room temperature

1/2 cup melted butter

2 tablespoons Herb and Garlic Seasoning Blend (page 32) or commercial herb and garlic seasoning

*You will probably have to use more than one package of stuffing mix to make the necessary amount of prepared stuffing. Follow the servings guide and manufacturer's instructions on the stuffing mix of your choice.

1. If the turkey was *not* brined, remove the giblet packet from inside the turkey, and discard the giblets or keep them for future use. Rinse the turkey, inside and out, in cold water and pat dry with paper towels. If the turkey *was* brined, rinse the brine off with cold water, drain the turkey, and dry it thoroughly. Place the dried turkey on a work surface and set aside.

2. Start the pellet grill and set the temperature control to 225°F.

3. Liberally sprinkle the inside of the bird with salt and pepper, massaging the seasonings thoroughly into the flesh.

4. Loosely spoon the prepared stuffing into the turkey. (Stuffing expands as it cooks.) If the wings are "flying away" from the turkey, truss the bird. (See the inset on page 115 for directions.)

5. Place the stuffed turkey, breast side up, on a roasting rack set in a roasting pan. Brush the melted butter over the turkey breast, wings, thighs, and legs. Liberally sprinkle the seasoning mixture over the entire bird.

6. When the grill reaches the desired temperature, transfer the roasting pan to the grate and close the grill cover. Allow the turkey to smoke for approximately 1 hour.

7. Increase the pellet grill temperature to 325° F and roast the turkey for an additional 4 to 5 hours, or about 20 minutes per pound, basting every 40 to 45 minutes with the pan juices or with melted butter. When done, an instant-read thermometer will indicate an internal temperature of 165°F at the leg joint (avoid the bone), and the juices will run clear when the meat is pierced with a sharp knife or fork.

8. Remove the roasting pan from the grill, cover with aluminum foil, and allow the turkey to rest for 25 minutes. Scoop out the stuffing, transferring it to a serving bowl. Carve the turkey into serving pieces and enjoy.

For a Change

- To make sausage stuffing, sauté a pound of loose hot or sweet Italian sausage until thoroughly cooked. Drain off the fat, stir the meat into the prepared stuffing, and stuff and cook the turkey as directed in the recipe.

- To make fruit stuffing, peel and dice 2 to 3 Granny Smith apples. Stir the apples into the prepared stuffing, and stuff and cook the turkey as directed in the recipe.

Trussing a Turkey

While trussing a turkey isn't necessary for cooking, it does create a compact shape and a more attractive presentation. Here's how it's done.

1. Once the bird has been stuffed, place it on a cookie sheet or roasting rack so that the neck is away from you and the breast is facing up. Cut a 5-foot piece of kitchen twine.

2. Center the twine under the turkey, across the back. Pull the twine around the wings and over the turkey breast to bring the wings close to the body. Cross the ends of the twine over the breast and tie a knot to hold the wings in place.

3. Pull the ends of the string downward towards the legs, and pass under and around the ends of the drumsticks. Pull the legs together so that the ends touch, and tie another knot.

4. Trim off and discard any excess twine.

Thyme and Garlic Turkey Breast

Aromatic thyme and pungent garlic create a magic that "ignites" the mild flavor of turkey. Add cherry pellets to the mix, and you have a truly special dish that's sure to please.

YIELD: 8–10 SERVINGS
RECOMMENDED PELLETS: CHERRY
MARINATION/SEASONING TIME: NONE
COOKING TIME: ABOUT 2 HOURS

5–6 pound boneless turkey breast	1½ tablespoons finely minced garlic
¼ cup melted butter	½ teaspoon sea salt
1½ tablespoons dried thyme	½ teaspoon ground black pepper

1. Start the pellet grill and set the temperature control to 300°F.

2. Rinse the turkey breast in cold water and pat it dry with paper towels. Place it on a work surface.

3. Combine the butter, thyme, and garlic in a small bowl. Carefully run your fingers between the skin and the flesh of the turkey breast, and brush the butter mixture under the skin. Brush more of the mixture over the outside of the breast, and season with salt and pepper.

4. When the grill reaches the desired temperature, place the turkey breast directly on the grill grate, skin side up, or place in a shallow roasting pan and set the pan on the grate. Close the grill cover and roast the turkey for 2 hours, or about 20 minutes per pound, brushing on additional butter mixture every 20 to 30 minutes.

5. Use an instant-read thermometer to check the internal temperature of the meat. When the temperature reaches 165°F and the juices run clear when the meat is pierced, transfer the turkey to a cutting board and cover with aluminum foil. Allow the turkey to rest for 10 minutes before slicing thinly and serving.

Honey Lime Breast of Turkey

This recipe balances honey with fresh lime and thyme to create a full-flavored dish that's sweet and tangy, with an herbal finish. Your family and friends will enjoy this unique pleasure while you appreciate the no-fuss recipe. I recommend using cherry or maple pellets. If you can't decide between them, use a fifty-fifty blend.

YIELD: 8–10 SERVINGS
RECOMMENDED PELLETS: CHERRY OR MAPLE
MARINATION/SEASONING TIME: NONE
COOKING TIME: ABOUT 2$^1/_2$ HOURS

5–6 pound boneless turkey breast

$^1/_2$ teaspoon sea salt

$^1/_2$ teaspoon ground black pepper

HONEY-LIME BASTING SAUCE

$^1/_2$ cup honey

Juice of 2 limes

3 tablespoons extra virgin olive oil

1 tablespoon brown sugar

1 teaspoon sea salt

$^3/_4$ teaspoon dried thyme

$^1/_2$ teaspoon coarsely black pepper

---

1. To make the basting sauce, place all of the sauce ingredients in a small bowl and whisk thoroughly to blend. Set aside.

2. Start the pellet grill and set the temperature control to 225°F.

3. Rinse the turkey breast in cold water and pat it dry with paper towels. Place it on a work surface, and sprinkle the breast with salt and pepper.

4. When the grill reaches the desired temperature, place the turkey breast directly on the grill grate, skin side up, and close the grill cover. Smoke the meat for 30 minutes.

5. Brush the turkey with the basting sauce and increase the grill temperature to 300°F. Roast the breast for about 2 more hours, or 20 minutes per pound, brushing on the sauce every 30 minutes.

6. Use an instant-read thermometer to check the internal temperature of the meat. When the temperature reaches 165°F and the juices run clear when the meat is pierced, transfer the turkey to a cutting board and cover with aluminum foil. (Discard any remaining basting sauce.) Allow the turkey to rest for 10 minutes before slicing thinly and serving.

Cajun-Style Turkey Breast

Cajun cooking has had an enormous influence on mainstream American cuisine in recent years. In the Gulf Coast area, it rivals Tex-Mex for spiciness and "heat"—as well as popularity. This recipe pairs the vibrant flavors of Cajun food with cherry wood smoke to create a turkey breast that is tantalizing in both flavor and aroma.

YIELD: 8–10 SERVINGS
RECOMMENDED PELLETS: CHERRY
MARINATION/SEASONING TIME: NONE
COOKING TIME: ABOUT 2 HOURS

5–6 pound boneless turkey breast
¹/₄ cup melted butter or olive oil

¹/₄ cup Cajun Spice (page 29) or commercial Cajun seasoning

1. Start the pellet grill and set the temperature control to 325° F.

2. Rinse the turkey breast in cold water and pat it dry with paper towels. Place it on a work surface.

3. Carefully run your fingers between the skin and the flesh, and brush the butter or olive oil under the skin. Sprinkle with the Cajun spice mix, and rub it into the meat. Then brush more of the butter or oil over the outside of the breast and sprinkle with the spice mix. Massage the seasoning into the skin and exterior flesh.

4. When the grill reaches the desired temperature, place the turkey breast directly on the grill grate, skin side up, or place in a shallow roasting pan and set the pan on the grate. Close the grill cover and roast the turkey for about 2 hours, or about 20 minutes per pound. Brush additional butter or oil over the turkey every 30 minutes.

5. Use an instant-read thermometer to check the internal temperature of the meat. When the temperature reaches 165°F and the juices run clear when the meat is pierced, transfer the turkey to a cutting board and cover with aluminum foil. Allow the turkey to rest for 10 minutes before slicing thinly and serving.

For a Change

■ If Cajun seasoning is not to your taste or if you simply want a change of pace, follow the recipe instructions for Cajun-Style Turkey Breast, but replace the spice mix with an equal amount of the Dijon Spice Blend (see page 33) or the Home-Style Seasoning Mix (see page 26).

Hickory Smoked Turkey Breast

Smoked meat has been a staple for hundreds of years and is a favorite in the barbeque world. In this recipe, hickory smoke is used to accentuate a home-style spice blend, and the result is a culinary work of art. This turkey makes a wonderful entrée accompanied by mashed potatoes and grilled vegetables, or you can use it in an open-faced sandwich, swabbed with barbeque sauce and served with potato salad and baked beans. The choices are virtually endless and limited only by your imagination.

YIELD: 8–10 SERVINGS
RECOMMENDED PELLETS: HICKORY
MARINATION/SEASONING TIME: NONE
COOKING TIME: ABOUT 3 HOURS

5–6 pound boneless turkey breast

¹/₄ cup extra virgin olive oil

¹/₄ cup Home-Style Seasoning Mix (page 26) or commercial hickory smoke-and-spice blend

1. Start the pellet grill and set the temperature control to "Smoke" or 180°F.

2. Rinse the turkey breast in cold water and pat it dry with paper towels. Place it on a work surface. Brush the breast with olive oil, and season it liberally with the seasoning mix.

3. When the grill reaches the desired temperature, place the turkey breast directly on the grill grate, skin side up, and close the grill cover. Smoke the meat for 1 hour.

4. Brush the turkey with additional olive oil, and increase the grill temperature to 225°F. Roast the breast for about 2 more hours, or about 20 minutes per pound, brushing on olive oil every 30 to 45 minutes. Add additional seasoning if desired.

5. Use an instant-read thermometer to check the internal temperature of the meat. When the temperature reaches 165° F and the juices run clear when the meat is pierced, transfer the turkey to a cutting board and cover with aluminum foil. Allow the turkey to rest for 10 minutes before slicing thinly and serving.

Grilled Turkey Cutlets with Mango Pepper Salsa

Enlivened with a citrus marinade and topped with a sweet and spicy salsa, this dish is not only full of flavor but also a treat for the eye with its medley of bright colors. Add a simple side dish of brown rice, and your meal will be complete.

YIELD: 4 SERVINGS
RECOMMENDED PELLETS: YOUR CHOICE
MARINATION/SEASONING TIME: 2 HOURS
COOKING TIME: ABOUT 1 HOUR

---

8 turkey cutlets (about 4 ounces each)

$^1/_4$ cup Greek-Style Lemon Marinade (page 36) or commercial lemon-pepper marinade

MANGO PEPPER SALSA

1 tablespoon extra virgin olive oil

$^1/_2$ cup chopped onion

1 small red bell pepper, seeded and chopped fine

1 small yellow bell pepper, seeded and chopped fine

1 small green bell pepper, seeded and chopped fine

1 cup mango, peeled and chopped

1 tablespoon chopped cilantro

1 jalapeño pepper, seeded and chopped fine

1 tablespoon cider or wine vinegar

1. Rinse the turkey cutlets in cold water and pat them dry with paper towels.

2. Place the turkey cutlets in a resealable plastic bag or a shallow covered glass dish. Add the marinade, turning the turkey to coat. Transfer to the refrigerator and allow the cutlets to marinate for at least 2 hours, occasionally turning the turkey pieces or massaging the plastic bag to ensure absorption of the marinade.

3. While the cutlets are marinating, make the salsa by placing the olive oil in a medium-size skillet over medium heat. Add the onions to the pan and sauté until translucent, about 5 minutes. Add the bell peppers and cook just until tender-crisp, about 1 minute. Transfer the vegetable mixture to a medium-size bowl, and allow to cool. Stir in the remaining ingredients, cover with plastic wrap, and refrigerate for at least 1 hour before serving.

4. Start the pellet grill and set the temperature control to 250°F.

5. Remove the turkey from the refrigerator and allow it to warm for 30 minutes. When the grill reaches the desired temperature, remove the cutlets from the marinade, discarding the remaining marinade.

6. Arrange the cutlets directly on the grill grate, allowing space between the pieces so that smoke and heat can circulate. Close the grill door and cook for 1 hour, or until an instant-read thermometer shows an internal temperature of 165°F and the juices run clear when the meat is pierced.

7. Turn the grill off and allow the cutlets to rest for 10 minutes in the closed grill before serving with the Mango Pepper Salsa.

QUICK GRILLING FOR GRILLED TURKEY CUTLETS

For those occasions when you want to cook Grilled Turkey Cutlets with Mango Pepper Salsa more quickly, increase the grill temperature to 325°F and decrease the cooking time to about 30 minutes. Just remember that whenever you turn up the temperature of the grill, you reduce the food's smoky flavor and aroma. (For more information on Quick Grilling, see page 12.)

The Best Wines for Turkey Dishes

Like chicken and pork, turkey is a versatile food that can be highly or mildly seasoned and then cooked in a number of ways, including smoking, roasting, and grilling. The following list suggests both white and red wines that can be deliciously paired with a variety of wood pellet grill-prepared turkey dishes.

Champagne. A sparkling white wine, Champagne begins as a blending of "still" (non-sparkling) wines—usually Chardonnay and Pinot Noir. Once a balance of body and flavors has been achieved, the wine goes through a second fermentation to produce the characteristic bubbles. The resulting libation is absolutely marvelous with roasted turkey.

Chardonnay. A dry white wine with a crisp, clean taste, Chardonnay is usually produced in stainless steel barrels, but may be fermented or aged in oak barrels. When fermented in stainless steel, it tends to be medium-bodied. When fermented in oak, it takes on oak and vanilla flavors and develops more body. It is great with all types of turkey dishes.

Sauvignon Blanc. A light- to medium-bodied dry white wine, Sauvignon Blanc is taut and herbal with sharp acidity. Amazingly adaptable, it pairs well with a variety of foods, including whole roasted or smoked turkey, lightly smoked or spiced turkey breast, and turkey cutlets.

Viognier. This well-rounded, medium- to full-bodied dry white wine has been described as having exotic honeysuckle- and citrus-like flavors. It complements many turkey dishes and is especially good with those that include a fruit stuffing, sauce, or salsa.

Red Zinfandel. A medium- to full-bodied dry red wine, Red Zinfandel has blackberry, boysenberry, and plumy fruit notes. It is great with spiced, smoky dishes like turkey legs and wings.

Citrus Turkey Cutlets

Citrus juice add zing to this dish, and the combination of cilantro, chili powder, cumin, and mild apple smoke rounds out the flavors, making these cutlets anything but dull.

YIELD: 4 SERVINGS
RECOMMENDED PELLETS: APPLE
MARINATION/SEASONING TIME: 2 HOURS
COOKING TIME: ABOUT 1 HOUR

8 turkey cutlets (about 4 ounces each)

$^1/_4$ cup Citrus Marinade (page 36) or commercial lemon-pepper or chili-lime marinade

1. Rinse the turkey cutlets in cold water and pat them dry with paper towels.

2. Place the turkey cutlets in a resealable plastic bag or a shallow covered glass dish. Add the marinade, turning the turkey to coat. Transfer to the refrigerator and allow the cutlets to marinate for at least 2 hours, occasionally turning the turkey pieces or massaging the plastic bag to ensure absorption of the marinade.

3. Start the pellet grill and set the temperature control to 250°F.

4. Remove the turkey from the refrigerator and allow it to warm for 30 minutes. When the grill reaches the desired temperature, remove the cutlets from the marinade, discarding the remaining marinade.

5. Arrange the cutlets directly on the grill grate, allowing space between the pieces so that smoke and heat can circulate. Close the grill door and cook for 1 hour, or until an instant-read thermometer shows an internal temperature of 165°F and the juices run clear when the meat is pierced.

6. Turn the grill off and allow the cutlets to rest for 10 minutes in the closed grill before serving.

QUICK GRILLING FOR CITRUS TURKEY CUTLETS

For those occasions when you want to cook Citrus Turkey Cutlets more quickly, increase the grill temperature to 325°F and decrease the cooking time to about 30 minutes. Just remember that whenever you turn up the temperature of the grill, you reduce the food's smoky flavor and aroma. (For more information on Quick Grilling, see page 12.)

THE COMPLETE WOOD PELLET BARBEQUE COOKBOOK

Smoked Turkey Legs

Because the special brine infuses turkey with wonderful flavor, and hickory smoke works its own magic, you won't have to rub any seasonings on these drumsticks to enjoy great flavor. Serve as a special treat at backyard barbeques and picnics.

YIELD: 4 SERVINGS
RECOMMENDED PELLETS: HICKORY
MARINATION/SEASONING TIME: 24 HOURS FOR BRINING
COOKING TIME: 4–5 HOURS

---

4 turkey legs (about 3 pounds), brined overnight (see page 39)

1. Rinse the brine off the turkey legs with cold water, and dry the legs with paper towels. Start the pellet grill and set the temperature to 225°F.

2. When the grill reaches the desired temperature, arrange the legs on the grill grate, allowing space between the pieces so that smoke and heat can circulate. Close the grill door and smoke for 4 to 5 hours, or until an instant-read thermometer shows an internal temperature of 165°F and the juices run clear when the meat is pierced. The legs should be deeply browned on the outside and may have a pinkish hue under the skin. (This color results from a chemical reaction between the brine and the smoke.)

3. Remove the legs from the grill and serve immediately.

For a Change

■ To vary the flavor of your Smoked Turkey Legs, use the brine variations described under "For a Change" on page 39.

Saucy Smoked Turkey Wings

Smoked turkey wings are a great alternative to chicken wings. Not only are they bigger and more substantial, but when brined, seasoned with Cajun Spice, and basted with a hot sauce, they become bold, flavorful, and downright irresistible.

YIELD: 8 SERVINGS
RECOMMENDED PELLETS: HICKORY
MARINATION/SEASONING TIME: 24 HOURS FOR BRINING
COOKING TIME: ABOUT 1 1/2 HOURS

8 whole turkey wings (about 4 pounds), cut apart at the joints and wing tips removed, brined overnight (see page 39) **1/4 cup extra virgin olive oil**	**3 tablespoons Cajun Spice (page 29) or commercial Cajun seasoning** **1 1/2 cups Uncle Bob's Basic Barbeque Sauce, prepared according to the "For a Change" variation (page 47), or commercial spicy barbeque sauce**

1. Start the pellet grill and set the temperature control to 225°F.

2. Rinse the brine off the wings with cold water, and dry with paper towels. Arrange them in a single layer on a baking sheet. Brush with olive oil and sprinkle with half of the Cajun Spice. Turn the wings over, brush the second side with oil, and season with the remaining spice blend.

3. When the grill has reached the desired temperature, arrange the wings on the grate, allowing space between the pieces so that smoke and heat can circulate. Close the grill door and smoke for 1 hour, or until an instant-read thermometer shows an internal temperature of 165°F and the juices run clear when the meat is pierced.

4. Brush the barbeque sauce on the wings, close the door, and allow the sauce to caramelize for 15 minutes. Turn the wings over, baste again, and allow to caramelize for 10 minutes. Turn the grill off and allow the wings to rest in the closed grill for 10 minutes before serving. Serve with additional barbeque sauce on the side.

For a Change

■ For a different combination of flavors, replace the Cajun Spice with Southwestern Seasoning Blend and Rub (see page 27) or Home-Style Seasoning Mix (page 26), and use Spicy Rum Barbeque Sauce (page 48) instead of the basic barbeque sauce.

8.

Scrumptious Seafood

Whether you live near the ocean or miles away, chances are that your local markets offer a variety of seafood, providing you with a wealth of culinary possibilities. And because the wood pellet grill makes available so many cooking methods and smoke sources, those possibilities are multiplied, making them virtually endless and always delicious.

The recipes in this chapter show you how to prepare nearly any culinary gift from the sea on your wood pellet grill. The chapter begins with shellfish, including classic baked lobster tails, shrimp and scallop dishes, and even savory crab cakes prepared East Coast-style. Some of these recipes make use of vibrant spices to excite your palate, while others prepare the seafood as simply as possible

to let the natural flavors shine through. Because you're cooking on a pellet grill, even the plainest of foods will taste fabulous.

The remainder of the chapter guides you through the preparation of many different types of fish, including catfish, cod, tuna, halibut, orange roughy, salmon, tilapia, and swordfish. Whether you choose Crispy Catfish, Northwest Grilled Salmon, or Grilled Orange Roughy with Spicy Mango Relish, the final dish will be outstanding.

In paging through this chapter, you may notice that the wood pellets have been chosen very carefully so that they enhance each food without overwhelming it. That's why mild-tasting fish such as cod are usually cooked with the gentle smoke of alder or apple wood, while stronger woods like cherry and maple are reserved for more assertively flavored selections such as swordfish, or for highly seasoned dishes like Cajun Spiced Shrimp. Once you understand this basic principle, you'll be able to take your own favorite seafood dishes and prepare them on your grill with great results.

Seafood is always a wonderful choice, especially if you're looking for healthful but satisfying fare, and the gifts of the sea are beautifully suited for cooking over a wood fire. So relax and enjoy the simple pleasures of wood pellet grilling.

Plain Ol' Scallops

This recipe grills scallops simply and beautifully, allowing the natural flavor of the seafood to shine through. The heat caramelizes the surface of the scallops, adding to their sweetness, but enough moisture remains to capture the salt that's sprinkled on at the end of cooking. For this recipe, I recommend alder wood pellets.

YIELD: 4 SERVINGS
RECOMMENDED PELLETS: ALDER
MARINATION/SEASONING TIME: NONE
COOKING TIME: 15 TO 20 MINUTES

1 pound medium-size sea scallops (about 25 per pound)   Sea salt to taste

1. Rinse the scallops in cold water and pat dry with paper towels. Set aside.

2. If you don't have a perforated grilling pan, place aluminum foil on the grill so that the scallops won't fall through the grating. Start the pellet grill and set the temperature control to 325°F.

3. When the grill reaches the desired temperature, arrange the scallops on the foil-covered grill or in a perforated grilling pan, close the grill door, and cook for 15 to 20 minutes, or until the scallops begin to brown. To check for doneness, remove one scallop from the grill and slice it in half. The center of the scallop should be barely translucent.

4. Transfer the scallops to a serving platter, sprinkle lightly with the salt, and serve.

Baked Lobster Tails

How do you make an evening at home as special as a night out on the town? The answer is simple: Serve baked lobster tails and a bottle of champagne. To round out the meal, prepare a green salad with Riesling vinaigrette dressing. What a life! I highly recommend maple pellets for this recipe.

YIELD: 4 SERVINGS
RECOMMENDED PELLETS: MAPLE
MARINATION/SEASONING TIME: NONE
COOKING TIME: 15 TO 18 MINUTES

4 whole lobster tails

1 recipe French Lobster Sauce, warmed (page 44)

BASTING BUTTER

$^1/_4$ cup melted butter

$^1/_2$ teaspoon dried tarragon or rosemary

1 teaspoon dry mustard

1 teaspoon sea salt

$^1/_4$ teaspoon ground black pepper

1. Start the pellet grill and set the temperature control to 375°F.

2. To prepare the basting butter, place the melted butter in a bowl and stir in the remaining ingredients. Place the bowl in a small saucepan partially filled with warm water to keep the butter melted.

3. Rinse the lobster tails in cold water and pat dry with paper towels. Place the tails with the back (shell) side down on a cutting board, and use a chef's knife to split each one in half from below the fan end through the other end of the tail. (You want to keep the fan end intact.) Once you cut through the flesh, you may have to rock the knife back and forth to cut through the shell on the back. Using your fingers, gently separate the meat from the shell, pulling it away from the shell so that it can be basted. Arrange the lobster tails in a shallow roasting pan or cookie sheet, shell side down, and baste the top with the flavored butter.

4. When the grill reaches the desired temperature, set the roasting pan on the grate, close the cover, and bake for 15 to 18 minutes or until the meat is opaque and white. Baste the tails once more.

5. Transfer the cooked lobster to a warm platter, pour any remaining butter over the top, and serve immediately with the warmed lobster sauce on the side.

Fiesta Lime Shrimp

If you're planning a Mexican-theme party or if you simply love Mexican fare, you'll want to grill up a batch of these easy-to-make shrimp. Infused with lime and South-of-the-Border spices, this dish is perfect served with yellow rice and refried beans. Use cherry pellets to add another layer of flavor and aroma.

YIELD: 3–4 SERVINGS
RECOMMENDED PELLETS: CHERRY
MARINATION/SEASONING TIME: NONE
COOKING TIME: 20 TO 25 MINUTES

1½ pounds large shrimp, peeled and deveined

½ cup Fiesta Lime Spice Butter (page 45)

1. Spray the grill with nonstick cooking spray. Start the pellet grill and set the temperature control to 325°F.

2. Rinse the shrimp in cold water and pat dry with paper towels. Determine the number of shrimp you'll use for each serving, and divide the shrimp among metal or bamboo skewers. (If you choose bamboo, soak the skewers in water before use.) Skewer the shrimp by forcing the skewers through the underside of the shrimp. Use 2 skewers per serving so that the shrimp will be easier to turn.

3. When the grill reaches the desired temperature, arrange the skewers on the grate and baste with the butter mixture. Turn the shrimp and baste the other side.

4. Close the door of the grill and allow the shrimp to cook for 10 to 15 minutes. Turn the skewers over, repeat the basting, and continue to cook until the shrimp turn opaque and are pink in color, another 10 to 12 minutes. Do not overcook.

5. Transfer the skewers to individual plates and serve.

THE COMPLETE WOOD PELLET BARBEQUE COOKBOOK

Cajun Spiced Shrimp

The Cajun Spice mix used to flavor these shrimp includes chili powder, lemon peel, cayenne pepper, and other vibrant ingredients. Should your family like a little more spice, pass a shaker of the Cajun blend around the table. I recommend maple or cherry wood pellets for this recipe.

YIELD: 3–4 SERVINGS
RECOMMENDED PELLETS: MAPLE OR CHERRY
MARINATION/SEASONING TIME: NONE
COOKING TIME: 20 TO 25 MINUTES

1½ pounds large shrimp, peeled and deveined

2 tablespoons chopped flat leaf parsley for garnish

BASTING BUTTER

½ cup melted butter

1 tablespoon Cajun Spice (page 29) or commercial Cajun seasoning

½ teaspoon celery seed

2 garlic cloves, finely minced

1. Spray the grill grate with nonstick cooking spray. Start the pellet grill and set the temperature control to 325°F.

2. Rinse the shrimp in cold water and pat dry with paper towels. Determine the number of shrimp you'll use for each serving, and divide the shrimp among metal or bamboo skewers. (If you choose bamboo, soak the skewers in water before use.) Skewer the shrimp by forcing the skewers through the underside of the shrimp. Use 2 skewers per serving so that the shrimp will be easier to turn.

3. To prepare the basting butter, place the melted butter in a bowl and stir in the remaining ingredients. Place the bowl in a small saucepan partially filled with warm water to keep the butter melted.

4. When the grill reaches the desired temperature, arrange the skewers on the grate and baste with the butter mixture. Turn the shrimp and baste the other side.

5. Close the door of the grill and allow the shrimp to cook for 10 to 15 minutes. Turn the skewers over, repeat the basting, and continue to cook until the shrimp turn opaque and are pink in color, another 10 to 12 minutes. Do not overcook.

6. Transfer the shrimp to a serving dish, sprinkle with the parsley, and serve, passing extra Cajun spice mix or cayenne pepper. Accompany with dirty rice and seasoned mixed vegetables, like celery, carrots, and onion.

Eastern Grilled Crab Cakes

On the East Coast, crabmeat is a popular seafood that's served in a variety of ways. These crab cakes are out of this world and so easy to put together. Flavored with a popular seafood seasoning and highlighted with mustard, the dish works well as an appetizer or an entrée.

YIELD: 4 SERVINGS
RECOMMENDED PELLETS: YOUR CHOICE
MARINATION/SEASONING TIME: NONE
COOKING TIME: ABOUT 20 MINUTES

½ cup plain bread crumbs	1 teaspoon fresh lemon juice
1 egg	1 teaspoon Old Bay Seasoning
2 tablespoons prepared yellow mustard	½ teaspoon dry mustard
1 tablespoon mayonnaise	8–10 ounces crabmeat, fresh or canned
1 tablespoon chopped fresh parsley	1 tablespoon butter
1½ teaspoons melted butter	Lemon wedges for garnish
1 teaspoon Worcestershire sauce	

1. Start the pellet grill and set the temperature control to 350°F.

2. Place all of the ingredients except the crabmeat, tablespoon of butter, and lemon wedges in a large bowl, and stir to combine well. Carefully fold in the crabmeat. Shape the mixture into four cakes, each about 3 inches in diameter.

3. Place a 10- or 12-inch skillet (regular or nonstick) on the grill grate, close the door, and allow the skillet to heat for about 10 minutes. Place the butter in the skillet and allow it to melt. Brush the butter over the bottom of the skillet.

4. Arrange the cakes in the skillet, close the grill door, and allow to bake for 10 minutes, or until the bottom is browned. Turn the cakes over and cook for another 10 minutes, or until the second side is browned.

5. Transfer the cakes to individual serving plates and garnish each plate with a lemon wedge. Serve with tartar sauce, if desired. (See the inset on page 131.)

Tartar Sauce

With its creamy mayonnaise base and its piquant flavor, tartar sauce is a favorite accompaniment to all kinds of seafood, including several dishes that are presented in this chapter. If you have time, whip this sauce up a few hours before dinner so that the flavors can blend and develop.

YIELD: ABOUT 3/4 CUP

$1/2$ cup plus 2 tablespoons mayonnaise

2 tablespoons ketchup

2 tablespoons prepared mustard of your choice

2 tablespoons sweet pickle relish

Pinch garlic salt

Pinch celery salt

Sweet pickle juice (optional)

---

1. Place the mayonnaise in a small bowl, and whisk until smooth and creamy. Add all of the remaining ingredients except the pickle juice, and whisk to blend. If the sauce seems too thick, whisk in a little pickle juice until you have the desired consistency.

2. Use the tartar sauce immediately, or cover and refrigerate until ready to serve.

Tips for Buying the Freshest Fish

Shopping for seafood should not be taken lightly. Fish is highly perishable, so it's important to make sure that you purchase it at its freshest. The following guidelines will help you make the best selection.

☐ Make sure that the fish is displayed on ice. This helps to keep it fresh.

☐ Ask to smell the fish. Aroma is the primary indication of fish quality, so make sure it has a clean briny aroma—a sign of freshness. Strong odors indicate that the fish may have been stored or handled improperly or is no longer at its peak.

☐ When buying a whole fish, make sure that the eyes are bright, clear, and full. As the fish ages and loses moisture, the eyes will sink back into the head and begin to cloud to some degree. Also make sure that the gills have a red or maroon color and are fresh and moist in appearance. Gray or brown gills indicate that oxidation (aging) has taken place.

☐ When buying fish fillets, look for firm fillets that are dense and moist. The flesh should be translucent rather than opaque.

☐ When buying shrimp, do not use color as an indication of freshness, as this seafood can be light gray, brownish pink, or red when raw. Instead, choose shrimp that are firm and dry.

☐ Look for scallops that are firm and sweet smelling. An odor of ammonia or sulfur is a sure sign that the scallops are not fresh.

Italian-Style Scallops

Garlic, parsley, oregano, and Parmesan cheese give these scallops Italian flair, and the wood pellet grill makes them utterly delicious. This aromatic dish is a great entrée on its own or can be served over pasta for heartier fare.

YIELD: 4 SERVINGS
RECOMMENDED PELLETS: APPLE OR ALDER
MARINATION/SEASONING TIME: 30 MINUTES TO 1 HOUR
COOKING TIME: 15 TO 20 MINUTES

1 pound medium-size sea scallops (about 25 per pound)

2 tablespoons extra virgin olive oil

2 tablespoons chopped fresh parsley

1 tablespoon Herb and Garlic Seasoning Blend (page 32) or commercial herb and garlic seasoning

1 teaspoon minced garlic

1/2 teaspoon dried oregano

1/4 cup grated Parmesan cheese

1. Rinse the scallops in cold water and pat dry with paper towels. Set aside.

2. In a large bowl, combine the olive oil, parsley, seasoning blend, garlic, and oregano. Add the scallops and stir gently to coat evenly. Cover the bowl with plastic wrap and place in the refrigerator for at least 30 minutes or as long as an hour.

3. If you don't have a perforated grilling pan, place aluminum foil on the grill grate so that the scallops won't fall through the grating. Start the pellet grill and set the temperature control to 325°F.

4. When the grill reaches the desired temperature, remove the scallops from the marinade, discarding the marinade. Arrange the scallops on the foil-covered grill or in a perforated grilling pan, close the grill door, and cook for 15 to 20 minutes, or until the scallops begin to brown. To check for doneness, remove one scallop from the grill and slice it in half. The center of the scallop should be barely translucent.

5. Transfer the scallops to a serving platter, sprinkle with the Parmesan cheese, and serve.

Mediterranean Swordfish

With its firm texture, swordfish stands up well to grilling. And when it's enhanced with lemon juice, dill, and a blend of French-inspired seasonings, the result is a satisfying dish that pairs perfectly with rice, vinaigrette-dressed salads, or fresh vegetables touched with lemon pepper. Use cherry or maple pellets to make this hearty dish.

YIELD: 6 SERVINGS
RECOMMENDED PELLETS: CHERRY OR MAPLE
MARINATION/SEASONING TIME: 30 MINUTES TO 1 HOUR
COOKING TIME: 30 MINUTES

6 swordfish steaks, 1 inch thick (about 2 pounds)

$^1/_4$ cup chopped scallions for garnish (optional)

MARINADE

$^1/_4$ cup fresh lemon juice

2 tablespoons extra virgin olive oil

$1^1/_2$ tablespoons Classic French Spice (page 31), commercial mustard-based spice blend, or favorite seafood seasoning

1 teaspoon minced garlic

$^1/_4$ teaspoon dried dill

1. Rinse the swordfish steaks in cold water and pat dry with paper towels. Place them in a glass or ceramic dish, and set aside.

2. Place all of the marinade ingredients in a small bowl, and whisk to mix. Pour the marinade over the fish and turn to coat. Cover with plastic wrap and place in the refrigerator for at least 30 minutes or up to 1 hour.

3. Spray the grill grate with nonstick cooking spray. Start the pellet grill and set the temperature control to 350°F.

4. Remove the steaks from the marinade and discard the marinade. When the grill reaches the desired temperature, arrange the steaks on the grate, close the grill door, and roast the fish for 15 minutes. Turn the steaks over and cook for another 15 minutes, or until the swordfish can be flaked easily with a fork.

5. Transfer the steaks to a serving platter or individual plates, sprinkle with the scallions, if desired, and serve immediately.

For a Change

■ This dish works equally well with shark or halibut steaks, which are also firm-fleshed and meaty. Simply replace the swordfish with the fish steak of your choice and cook as directed above.

Halibut Suprema

This recipe takes dense, firm halibut steaks, seasons them with a lemony spice mixture, smokes them lightly, and grills them just until flaky. Accompanied by colorful vegetables cooked alongside the fish, the results are superb. All you need is a side of plain rice and your meal is complete.

YIELD: 4 SERVINGS
RECOMMENDED PELLETS: APPLE OR ALDER
MARINATION/SEASONING TIME: 1 HOUR
COOKING TIME: ABOUT 45 MINUTES

4 halibut steaks, 1 inch thick (about 2 pounds)

Extra virgin olive oil

1 tablespoon Lemon and Herb Spice Blend (page 30) or commercial lemon and herb blend

GRILLED VEGETABLES

$^1/_2$ green bell pepper, cut into $^1/_2$-inch strips

$^1/_2$ yellow bell pepper, cut into $^1/_2$-inch strips

$^1/_2$ red bell pepper, cut into $^1/_2$-inch strips

$^1/_2$ zucchini, cut crosswise into $^1/_4$-inch rounds

$^1/_2$ white or yellow onion, cut into $^1/_4$-inch slices

2 tablespoons extra virgin olive oil

$^1/_8$ teaspoon sea salt

$^1/_8$ teaspoon ground black pepper

Chopped fresh parsley for garnish

1. Rinse the halibut steaks in cold water and pat dry with paper towels. Arrange the steaks in a single layer on a large platter, brush the top with olive oil, and sprinkle with the spice blend. Turn the fish over and repeat on the second side. Cover the dish with plastic wrap and place in the refrigerator for 1 hour.

2. Spray the grill grate with nonstick cooking spray. Start the pellet grill and set the temperature control to 225°F.

3. While the grill is heating up, place all of the vegetables in a shallow bowl. Add the olive oil and toss to coat. Season with salt and pepper to taste, and transfer the mixture to a perforated grilling pan.

4. When the grill reaches the desired temperature, arrange the halibut steaks directly on the grate, and place the grilling pan filled with vegetables next to the fish. Close the door of the grill and allow the food to smoke for 30 minutes.

5. Increase the pellet grill temperature to 325°F. Cook the fish and veggies for 10 to 15 additional minutes or until the fish is no longer translucent and can be easily flaked with a fork.

If the vegetables are not yet tender-crisp, remove the fish and keep it warm. Stir the vegetables, close the grill door, and check again in 5 to10 minutes.

6. Transfer the halibut to a serving platter and surround it with the grilled vegetables. Sprinkle parsley over all and serve immediately.

Crispy Catfish

A meaty, solid fish, catfish can be prepared in many ways. On the Gulf Coast, it is battered and deep-fried, but we scrapped the oil for a hot grill and added a flavorful coating of crisp panko bread crumbs and nuts. If you want to taste the nut meats, opt for plain bread crumbs; seasoned panko will make the nut flavor less discernible. I recommend cherry wood pellets for this recipe.

YIELD: 4 SERVINGS
RECOMMENDED PELLETS: CHERRY
MARINATION/SEASONING TIME: NONE
COOKING TIME: 15 TO 20 MINUTES

4 catfish fillets (about 1¹/₂ pounds)	¹/₂ cup panko bread crumbs, plain or seasoned
¹/₄ cup buttermilk	
3 tablespoons Dijon-style mustard	¹/₂ teaspoon sea salt
¹/₄ cup finely minced pecans or walnuts	¹/₂ teaspoon ground black pepper
	Lemon wedges for garnish

1. Rinse the fish fillets in cold water and pat dry with paper towel. Set aside.

2. Spray a shallow aluminum pan with nonstick cooking spray, and set aside. Start the pellet grill and set the temperature control to 375°F.

3. Mix the buttermilk and mustard in a dish large enough to dip the fish fillets. Set aside.

4. In another large dish, mix together the minced nuts, bread crumbs, salt, and pepper.

5. Dip each fillet first in the buttermilk mixture to coat, and then in the bread crumb mixture. Arrange the fillets in the prepared aluminum pan.

6. When the grill reaches the desired temperature, place the aluminum pan on the grill grate, close the grill door, and bake for 15 to 20 minutes, or until the fish can be easily flaked with a fork. Serve with lemon wedges.

Grilled Orange Roughy with Spicy Mango Relish

With its mild nature, orange roughy takes on the flavors of other ingredients. In this recipe, the tartness of the marinade is balanced by the sweet and spicy relish, which also adds a cascade of colors. I recommend apple or alder pellets, or use a fifty-fifty mix of both. You can't lose.

YIELD: 4 SERVINGS
RECOMMENDED PELLETS: APPLE, ALDER, OR BOTH
MARINATION/SEASONING TIME: 1 HOUR
COOKING TIME: 12 TO 15 MINUTES

4 orange roughy fillets (approximately 2 pounds)

MARINADE
$1/4$ cup white wine vinegar
$1/4$ cup sesame oil
2 tablespoons Worcestershire sauce
$1/2$ teaspoon sea salt
$1/4$ teaspoon coarsely ground black pepper

SPICY MANGO RELISH
2 cups diced fresh, jarred, or frozen (thawed) mango (about 2 mangos)

$1/2$ cup quartered cherry tomatoes
$1/2$ cup diced roasted red bell pepper
$1/2$ cup finely chopped sweet white onion
1 jalapeño pepper, seeded and finely minced
2 tablespoons chopped fresh cilantro
$1/2$ teaspoon dried thyme
$1/2$ teaspoon sea salt
$1/4$ teaspoon coarsely ground black pepper
$1/4$ teaspoon ground ginger

1. To make the Spicy Mango Relish, combine all of the relish ingredients in a mixing bowl. Cover with plastic wrap and place in the refrigerator for 2 hours so that the flavors will marry and develop.

2. Rinse the fish fillets in cold water and pat dry with paper towels. Place them in a glass or ceramic dish, and set aside.

3. Place all of the marinade ingredients in a small bowl, and whisk to mix. Pour the marinade over the fillets and turn to coat. Cover with plastic wrap and place in the refrigerator for 1 hour.

4. Spray the grill grate with nonstick cooking spray. Start the pellet grill and set the temperature control to 375°F.

THE COMPLETE WOOD PELLET BARBEQUE COOKBOOK

5. Remove the fish from the marinade and discard the marinade. When the grill reaches the desired temperature, arrange the fillets directly on the grate, close the cover, and cook for 12 to 15 minutes, or until the fish is no longer translucent and is easily flaked with a fork. Do not overcook the fish.

6. Transfer the fillets to a serving platter, top with the relish, and serve immediately.

Northwest Grilled Salmon

Salmon from the Pacific Northwest is nothing short of fantastic. This recipe, which is simplicity itself, seasons the fish with a citrusy spice blend and then cooks it low and slow over alder, allowing the smoke to penetrate the fish and impart a subtle woodsy aroma and flavor. Grilling over a higher temperature finishes the dish. Whether you choose Coho, Chinook (king), or Sockeye salmon, these fillets will be a hit.

YIELD: 6–8 SERVINGS
RECOMMENDED PELLETS: ALDER
MARINATION/SEASONING TIME: NONE
COOKING TIME: ABOUT 1 HOUR

3–4 pound salmon fillet, skin intact, cut into 6 to 8 serving pieces

2 tablespoons Sweet Lemon Spice (page 32) or commercial lemon-based spice blend

1. Spray the grill grate with nonstick cooking spray. Start the pellet grill and set the temperature control to 180°F or "Smoke."

2. Rinse the salmon in cold water and pat dry with paper towels. Lightly sprinkle the spice mixture over the side where the flesh is exposed.

3. When the grill reaches the desired temperature, arrange the salmon fillets on the grate, skin side down. Close the grill door and allow the fish to smoke for about 30 minutes.

4. Increase the grill temperature to 225°F and cook the salmon for an additional 30 to 40 minutes, or until the flesh can be flaked easily with a fork.

5. Transfer the salmon to a serving platter or individual plates and serve immediately.

Grilled Tuna Steaks

In this recipe, tuna comes alive when seasoned with aromatic fresh herbs, olive oil, lemon, and garlic. The alder pellets work their magic without dominating the dish.

YIELD: 4 SERVINGS
RECOMMENDED PELLETS: ALDER
MARINATION/SEASONING TIME: 30 TO 45 MINUTES
COOKING TIME: 15 TO 25 MINUTES

4 tuna steaks, 1 inch thick (about $1^1/_2$ pounds)

3 tablespoons chopped fresh parsley for garnish

Lemon wedges for garnish

HERB MARINADE

$1/_2$ cup extra virgin olive oil

3 tablespoons fresh lemon juice

2 tablespoons chopped fresh oregano, or 1 tablespoon dried

2 tablespoons chopped fresh basil, or 1 tablespoon dried

2 garlic cloves, minced

$1^1/_2$ teaspoons sea salt

1. Rinse the tuna steaks in cold water and pat dry with paper towels. Place them in a glass or ceramic dish, and set aside.

2. Place all of the marinade ingredients in a small bowl and whisk to mix. Pour the marinade over the tuna and turn to coat. Cover with plastic wrap and place in the refrigerator for 30 to 45 minutes.

3. Spray the grill with nonstick cooking spray. Start the pellet grill and set the temperature control to 350°F.

4. Remove the tuna steaks from the marinade, reserving the marinade. Transfer the marinade to a saucepan and bring to a rolling boil over high heat. Allow it to remain at a boil for at least 3 minutes before continuing with the recipe.

5. When the grill reaches the desired temperature, arrange the tuna steaks directly on the grate, close the grill door, and cook for 10 minutes. Turn the fish carefully, baste with the marinade, and close the grill. Cook for an additional 4 to 5 minutes for rare; another 10 minutes for medium (the fish will flake slightly); or another 15 minutes for well done (the fish will flake easily).

6. Transfer the steaks to a serving platter or individual plates, sprinkle with the parsley, and garnish with the lemon wedges. Serve immediately.

Lime-Glazed Tuna Steaks

Meaty in texture, tuna steaks are satisfying fare, and the mild flesh readily soaks up the flavors of other ingredients. This recipe coats the tuna with a delicious glaze that includes lime, garlic, ginger, and sesame oil. The gentle smoke of alder beautifully enhances the flavors without overwhelming them.

YIELD: 4 SERVINGS
RECOMMENDED PELLETS: ALDER
MARINATION/SEASONING TIME: 30 TO 45 MINUTES
COOKING TIME: 15 TO 25 MINUTES

4 tuna steaks, 1 inch thick (about 1½ pounds)	1 tablespoon grated fresh ginger root
	1 tablespoon finely minced garlic
LIME GLAZE	1 teaspoon sea salt
½ cup sesame oil	1 teaspoon sugar
3 tablespoons fresh lime juice	1 jalapeño pepper, seeded and finely minced (optional)

1. Rinse the tuna steaks in cold water and pat dry with paper towels. Place them in a glass or ceramic dish, and set aside.

2. Place all of the glaze ingredients in a small bowl, and whisk together. Pour the mixture over the tuna and turn to coat. Cover with plastic wrap and place in the refrigerator for 30 to 45 minutes.

3. Spray the grill grate with nonstick cooking spray. Start the pellet grill and set the temperature control to 350°F.

4. Remove the tuna steaks from the marinade, reserving the marinade. Transfer the marinade to a saucepan and bring to a rolling boil over high heat. Allow it to remain at a boil for at least 3 minutes before continuing with the recipe.

5. When the grill reaches the desired temperature, arrange the tuna steaks directly on the grate, close the grill door, and cook for 10 minutes. Carefully turn the fish, baste with the boiled marinade, and grill for an additional 4 to 5 minutes for rare; another 10 minutes for medium (the fish will flake slightly); or another 15 minutes for well done (the fish will flake easily). Before removing the fish from the grill, baste it once more.

6. Transfer the steaks to individual plates and serve immediately.

The Best Wines for Seafood Dishes

Seafood and wine make a beautiful couple. The key is pairing white wines with mild-flavored fare like tilapia, cod, and shrimp, and serving full-flavored reds with heartier fare like tuna, swordfish, and any fish that has been highly seasoned. The following list will guide you in selecting wines that will enhance your seafood choices without overwhelming them.

Champagne. A sparkling white wine, Champagne begins as a blending of "still" (non-sparkling) wines—usually Chardonnay and Pinot Noir. Once a balance of body and flavors has been achieved, the wine goes through a second fermentation to produce the characteristic bubbles. The resulting libation is marvelous with most seafood, and especially lobster and crab.

Chardonnay. A dry white wine with a crisp, clean taste, Chardonnay is usually produced in stainless steel barrels, but may be fermented or aged in oak barrels. When fermented in stainless steel, it tends to be medium-bodied. When fermented in oak, it takes on oak and vanilla flavors and develops more body. This wine is great with most seafood choices, especially when butter is involved.

Pinot Grigio. Easy-drinking, dry, and crisp, this light- to medium-bodied white wine tastes of pear and spice. Pinot Grigio goes well with all types of seafood, and is especially delicious with shrimp.

Riesling. A light- to medium-bodied white wine, with intense flavors of ripe peaches, apricots, and melons, a Riesling can be sweet (look for an alcohol level between 10 and 11 percent) or dry (look for a higher alcohol content). Rieslings are very good with shellfish and also complement lighter catches such as cod and tilapia.

Sauvignon Blanc. A light- to medium-bodied dry white wine, Sauvignon Blanc is taut and herbal with sharp acidity. This versatile wine is truly exceptional when served with cod, shrimp, and scallops.

Viognier. This well-rounded, medium- to full-bodied dry white wine has been described as having exotic honeysuckle- and citrus-like flavors. It nicely complements many types of seafood, including salmon, swordfish, tuna, and lobster.

Merlot. This dry red wine is similar to Cabernet Sauvignon, but softer in texture with a rounder mouth feel. It is best when served with full-flavored fare like tuna and well-seasoned halibut.

Pinot Noir. A light- to medium-bodied dry red wine, the earthy yet elegant Pinot Noir exhibits flavors that have been compared to warm baked cherries, plums, mushrooms, and chocolate. The lighter-bodied Pinots complement shrimp and mild-flavored fish like cod and orange roughy. Bolder Pinots pair well with heartier seafood like swordfish, salmon, tuna, and halibut.

Grilled Alder Wood Cod with Lemon and Tartar Sauce

Fresh tasting and mild, cod can be prepared in so many different and exciting ways. This recipe makes excellent use of the character of the fish, which readily accepts alder wood aroma and flavor. Lightly smoked and then grilled over higher heat, the meat is flaky and tender. For a healthy yet tantalizing meal, pair the fish with steamed seasonal vegetables, long grain and wild rice, and a glass of dry sauvignon blanc.

YIELD: 4–5 SERVINGS
RECOMMENDED PELLETS: ALDER
MARINATION/SEASONING TIME: 20 MINUTES
COOKING TIME: 35 MINUTES

4–5 Atlantic cod fillets (about 2 pounds)

Extra virgin olive oil

1 recipe Classic French Spice (page 31), commercial mustard-based spice blend, or favorite seafood seasoning

1 recipe Tartar Sauce (see the inset on page 131)

Lemon wedges for garnish

---

1. Rinse the cod fillets with cold water and pat dry with paper towels. Arrange the fillets on a platter, brush the top with olive oil, and sprinkle with the spice blend. Turn the fish over and repeat on the second side. Cover with plastic wrap and refrigerate for at least 20 minutes to allow the seasoning to penetrate the meat.

2. While the fish is in the fridge, spray the grill grate with nonstick cooking spray. Start the pellet grill and set the temperature control to 180°F or "Smoke."

3. When the grill reaches the desired temperature, arrange the fillets directly on the grate, close the cover, and allow the fish to smoke for 20 minutes.

4. Increase the pellet grill temperature to 375°F and allow the fish to cook for 15 additional minutes, or until it can be easily flaked with a fork.

5. Transfer the fish to a platter or individual serving plates, and serve immediately with tartar sauce and lemon wedges.

Kelly's Salmon Supreme with Lemon Caper Sauce

This is a favorite of my daughter, Kelly. The fish is delicately flavored with herbs, a hint of citrus, and a touch of dill. A blend of alder and apple wood further enhances the salmon, and a creamy lemon caper sauce completes the delicious package.

YIELD: 4 SERVINGS
RECOMMENDED PELLETS: ALDER AND APPLE
MARINATION/SEASONING TIME: NONE
COOKING TIME: ABOUT 1 HOUR

3 tablespoons Lemon and Herb Spice Blend (page 30) or commercial lemon and herb blend

½ teaspoon dried dill

2-pound salmon fillet, skin intact, cut into 4 serving pieces

Chopped parsley for garnish

LEMON CAPER SAUCE

2 tablespoons butter

2 tablespoons all-purpose flour

2 cups milk or half-and-half

1 teaspoon sea salt

1 teaspoon ground black pepper

2 tablespoons capers, drained

1 teaspoon grated lemon zest

1. Mix the spice blend and dill weed in a small dish. Set aside.

2. Spray the grill grate with nonstick cooking spray. Start the pellet grill and set the temperature control to 180°F or "Smoke."

3. Rinse the salmon in cold water and pat dry with paper towels. Lightly sprinkle the seasoning over the side where the flesh is exposed.

4. When the grill reaches the desired temperature, arrange the salmon on the grate, skin side down. Close the grill door and allow the fish to smoke for approximately 30 minutes.

5. Increase the grill temperature to 225°F and cook the fish for an additional 30 to 40 minutes, or until the flesh can be flaked easily with a fork.

6. When the salmon is almost ready to be served, prepare the lemon caper sauce. Melt the butter in a medium-size saucepan over low heat. Stir in the flour, and continue to cook and stir until you have a paste and the flour is lightly browned. Whisking constantly, add the milk or

half-and-half in a steady stream, stirring until the mixture begins to thicken. Add salt and pepper to taste. Then stir in the capers and lemon zest.

7. Transfer the salmon to individual plates, and spoon the sauce over the fish so that it spills onto the plate. Sprinkle with chopped parsley and serve.

Lemon Herbed Tilapia

Mild in taste, tilapia readily absorbs the flavors of other ingredients. In this recipe, it is prepared with butter and spices and then enhanced with gentle apple or alder smoke. Simple, but delicious.

YIELD: 4 SERVINGS
RECOMMENDED PELLETS: APPLE OR ALDER
MARINATION/SEASONING TIME: NONE
COOKING TIME: 15 TO 20 MINUTES

4 tilapia fillets (approximately 1 1/2 pounds)

1/4 cup butter, softened

2 tablespoons Lemon and Herb Spice Blend (page 30) or commercial lemon and herb blend

Lemon wedges for garnish

1. Start the pellet grill and set the temperature control to 350°F. Spray a shallow aluminum pan with nonstick cooking spray.

2. Rinse the fish fillets in cold water and pat dry with paper towels. Arrange the fish in the prepared pan.

3. In a small bowl, combine the butter with the seasoning blend until well mixed. Spread the butter mixture over the top of the fish fillets.

4. When the grill reaches the desired temperature, place the aluminum pan on the grate. Close the door of the grill and bake for 15 to 20 minutes, or until the fish is no longer translucent and can be easily flaked with a fork.

5. Transfer the fish to a serving platter or individual plates, garnish with the lemon wedges, and serve immediately.

Lemon Zest Halibut

This is one of our favorites. A light sprinkling of seasoning is enhanced with lemon zest, which adds a citrus tang to the halibut. Cherry pellets kick the flavor up another notch, making this dish truly spectacular despite ease of preparation. Serve the halibut with a baked potato, a tossed salad, and a glass of sauvignon blanc.

YIELD: 4 SERVINGS
RECOMMENDED PELLETS: CHERRY
MARINATION/SEASONING TIME: 30 MINUTES
COOKING TIME: ABOUT 25 MINUTES

---

4 halibut steaks, 1 inch thick (about 2 pounds)

2 tablespoons Lemon and Herb Spice Blend (page 30) or commercial lemon and herb blend

1 tablespoon grated lemon zest

2 tablespoons finely chopped fresh parsley for garnish

Lemon wedges for garnish

1. Rinse the halibut steaks in cold water and pat dry with paper towels.

2. Arrange the steaks in a glass dish or plate, and sprinkle with the seasoning blend. Turn the steaks over and season the second side. Cover with plastic wrap and place in the refrigerator for 30 minutes.

3. Spray the grill grate with nonstick cooking spray. Start the pellet grill and set the temperature control to 325°F.

4. When the grill reaches the desired temperature, arrange the fish steaks directly on the grill grate. Close the grill door and cook for 10 minutes. Carefully turn the fish over, sprinkle with the lemon zest, and cook for an additional 10 to 15 minutes, or until the fish is no longer translucent and can be easily flaked with a fork.

5. Transfer the fish to a serving platter or individual plates. Sprinkle with parsley, garnish with lemon wedges, and serve.

9.

Venue of Vegetables

Vegetables have a bad reputation, but it's not their fault. Too often, they are cooked in a bland or boring manner that washes away their natural flavors (and their nutrients) in cooking water. Once you start preparing produce on the wood pellet grill, though, your vegetables will never be dull again. Roasting caramelizes the sugars in the veggies, making them sweet and flavorful, while smoke infuses the dish with another layer of taste and aroma. Add a little seasoning and perhaps a touch of olive oil or butter, and you have veggies that can rival any entrée for mouth-watering appeal.

Besides making vegetables delicious, the pellet grill makes it easy to prepare main and side dishes at the same time, without a lot of extra fuss—and without turning on your kitchen oven. Although all of the following recipes specify an ideal cooking temperature, I know that you will often be cooking sides along with a meat entrée. When you're using a pellet grill, coordinating these separate dishes is a snap. Simply set the grill to the temperature required by the meat, and adjust the cooking time of the vegetables as necessary. When your veggies can be easily pierced with a fork, you'll know that they're ready.

The following recipes show you how to prepare a range of vegetables on your pellet grill. The chapter begins with a great barbeque favorite, corn. Whether it's dressed simply with butter and seasoning or wrapped in strips of savory bacon, this popular side is sure to be a hit. Following this, I guide you in grilling and roasting onions and garlic (so good with beef!), Brussels sprouts, eggplant and zucchini, asparagus, and mushrooms. For each dish, the cooking method, herbs, and spices have been carefully chosen to complement the vegetable being prepared so that flavors are enhanced and intensified. Last, but certainly not least, I present five recipes for the much-loved potato. Smoke-Roasted Potatoes, which are so simple to prepare, take the baked potato to new heights with their crunchy skin and fluffy interior. These treats pair well with any entrée, from beef and pork to poultry and fish. Other dishes, like Roasted Potatoes with Rosemary and Garlic, add a little more spice and flair to the menu, and Mexican Stuffed Potatoes are so hearty and satisfying that each is a meal in itself.

Everyone knows that vegetables round out a meal by adding important vitamins, minerals, and fiber, as well as vibrant color. In the pages that follow, you'll find that veggies can also provide a new and delicious reason for your family to gather around the dinner table.

Grill-Roasted Corn

If this is not the best roasted corn on the cob you have ever had, I will eat it all! This is, in fact, the most requested food we make at our backyard parties. Any pellet choice will do, and although I do recommend an ideal cooking temperature, you can successfully grill the corn alongside any entrée, regardless of the temperature being used.

YIELD: 6 SERVINGS
RECOMMENDED PELLETS: YOUR CHOICE
MARINATION/SEASONING TIME: NONE
COOKING TIME: 25 TO 30 MINUTES

6 ears corn
$^1/_4$ cup butter, softened
$^1/_2$ teaspoon sugar

$^1/_4$ teaspoon sea salt
$^1/_4$ teaspoon ground paprika

1. Start the pellet grill and set the temperature control to 300°F.

2. Remove the husks and silk from each ear of corn, rinse the corn in cold water, and dry thoroughly with paper towels.

3. Place the butter, sugar, salt, and paprika in a small bowl, and cream with a fork until smooth. Spread the butter evenly over the corn.

4. Wrap each ear loosely in heavy-duty aluminum foil, and seal carefully. When the grill reaches the desired temperature, arrange the corn on the grill, close the grill door, and cook for 25 to 30 minutes, or until tender, turning occasionally.

5. Serve the corn in the foil to keep hot, and let each diner unwrap when ready to eat.

Bacon-Wrapped Barbequed Corn

Who doesn't love the tantalizing aroma of bacon cooking in the morning alongside eggs? Fortunately, bacon isn't just for breakfast, but can be wrapped around corn for an out-of-this-world side dish. You can throw these enticing treats on the grill at any time while barbequing an entrée such as ribs or chops, but they will be at their best if cooked right before serving.

YIELD: 6 SERVINGS
RECOMMENDED PELLETS: HICKORY OR MESQUITE
MARINATION/SEASONING TIME: NONE
COOKING TIME: 25 TO 30 MINUTES

---

6 large ears of corn	**$1/_2$ teaspoon sea salt**
$1/_4$ cup melted butter or extra virgin olive oil	**$1/_4$ cup chopped chives or scallion tops**
	8–10 slices bacon

1. Start the pellet grill and set the temperature control to 350°F.

2. Pull off and discard the outside husks of the corn. Gently peel back the inner husks to the bottom, and remove and discard all of the silk.

3. Brush the corn with butter or olive oil, and sprinkle with the salt and the chopped chives or scallions. Wrap the bacon completely around the corn in a spiral. You may need more than 1 slice per ear, depending on the size of the corn. Replace the husks and fasten them with toothpicks or kitchen twine.

4. Arrange the corn on the grill, close the door, and roast for 25 to 30 minutes, depending on how well you like your bacon cooked.

5. Transfer the corn to a serving platter and serve inside the husks, allowing each diner to remove them just before eating.

Baked Sweet Onions and Garlic

Grilling transforms onions, making them sweeter and rendering them soft and silky in texture. Garlic, too, undergoes a marvelous change on the grill, becoming mellow and spreadable. This dish is a delicious accompaniment to any barbequed entrée. Choose any wood pellets you have on hand, as in this case, the wood is there to provide heat, not smoke.

YIELD: 8 SERVINGS
RECOMMENDED PELLETS: YOUR CHOICE
MARINATION/SEASONING TIME: NONE
COOKING TIME: 30 TO 35 MINUTES

2 pounds sweet onions (Vidalia, Walla Walla, or Maui), peeled

2 large heads garlic, separated into cloves and peeled

4 ounces pearl onions, peeled

6 large scallions, trimmed

$^1/_4$ cup extra virgin olive oil

$^1/_2$ teaspoon sea salt

$^1/_4$ teaspoon coarsely ground black pepper

2 tablespoons chopped fresh parsley for garnish

1. Start the pellet grill and set the temperature control to 375°F.

2. Quarter some of the onions and slice others to $^3/_4$-inch thickness. (Leave the pearl onions whole.)

3. Thread the onion quarters onto several metal or bamboo skewers. (If you choose bamboo skewers, soak them for several minutes before use.) Also thread the garlic cloves onto skewers.

4. Place the loaded skewers, sliced onions, pearl onions, and scallions on a perforated grilling pan. Brush all the vegetables liberally with olive oil, and sprinkle with salt and pepper.

5. When the grill reaches the desired temperature, set the grilling pan on the grate, close the grill door, and roast for 30 to 35 minutes, or until the garlic is soft and the onions are tender.

6. Transfer the vegetables to a serving platter, sprinkle with the chopped parsley, and serve.

Brussels Sprouts with Citrus Sauce

I love Brussels sprouts and make no bones about it. They do require a bit of parboiling before they hit the grill, but are oh so delicious when served with this easy-to-prepare butter and citrus sauce.

YIELD: 6 SERVINGS
RECOMMENDED PELLETS: YOUR CHOICE
MARINATION/SEASONING TIME: NONE
COOKING TIME: ABOUT 30 MINUTES

1 pound Brussels sprouts, trimmed

1/4 cup butter

2 teaspoons fresh lime or lemon juice

1/2 teaspoon coarse sea salt

1/4 teaspoon ground black pepper

1. Start the pellet grill and set the temperature control to 275°F.

2. Place the sprouts in a large saucepan of boiling salted water, and boil for 5 minutes. Drain well, and transfer the sprouts to an oiled perforated grilling pan or vegetable basket. Close the grill door and cook for 20 to 25 minutes.

3. While the sprouts are grilling, place the butter and lime or lemon juice in a small saucepan and cook over low heat for 3 to 5 minutes, or until the butter has melted and has begun to brown around the edges. Remove the butter from the heat.

4. Brush the Brussels sprouts with the butter sauce, turn the sprouts, and brush the second side. Cook for another 5 minutes, or until the sprouts are tender when pierced with a fork. Baste the sprouts once more, and sprinkle with salt and pepper to taste.

5. Transfer the vegetables to a warmed dish and serve.

For a Change

■ If you like Brussels sprouts as much as I do, you may want to change them up now and then. To make Curried Brussels Sprouts with Brown Butter, follow the recipe above, but omit the citrus juice and add a pinch or two of curry to the butter as it browns. If you like plain butter on your vegetables, leave out both the curry and the citrus juice.

Grilled Eggplant and Zucchini

When eggplant and zucchini are cooked on a wood pellet grill, the heat caramelizes the sugars in the vegetables and the smoke brings out their hidden flavors, resulting in a dish that's anything but boring. These veggies make frequent visits to our dinner table, and I'm sure they'll win your heart, too.

YIELD: 6 SERVINGS
RECOMMENDED PELLETS: YOUR CHOICE
MARINATION/SEASONING TIME: NONE
COOKING TIME: 20 TO 25 MINUTES

---

2 eggplants (about 1 pound each), cut crosswise into $1/2$-inch slices

2 tablespoons coarse kosher salt

2–3 medium zucchini (about 1 pound total), cut crosswise into $1/2$-inch slices

3 tablespoons finely minced garlic

3 tablespoons extra virgin olive oil

$1/2$ teaspoon sea salt

$1/2$ teaspoon ground black pepper

1 tablespoon dried oregano or Italian seasoning

3 tablespoons chopped fresh parsley for garnish

1. Arrange the eggplant slices in a single layer on baking sheets, and sprinkle the kosher salt evenly over both sides. Set the eggplant aside for 30 minutes, allowing the salt to extract any bitter juices.

2. Start the pellet grill and set the temperature control to 325°F.

3. Place the eggplant in a colander and rinse with cold water to remove the salt and juices. Dry thoroughly with paper towels.

4. Place the eggplant, zucchini, and garlic in a large bowl. Drizzle with the olive oil, sea salt, and pepper, and toss gently to coat. Sprinkle the oregano or Italian seasoning over the vegetables, and toss once again to mix.

5. Arrange the vegetables in a single layer on a perforated grilling pan. When the grill reaches the desired temperature, place the pan on the grill grate, close the grill door, and roast for 20 to 25 minutes, or until the vegetables are tender when pierced with a fork.

6. Transfer the vegetables to a serving platter, sprinkle with the parsley, and serve immediately.

Roasted Garlic

If you've ever enjoyed roasted garlic spread on warm bread or stirred it into mashed potatoes, you know how roasting transforms garlic into a magical substance. The pellet grill, with its ability to cook low and slow, is a great way to bring out the best in garlic. Roast the garlic while you're cooking your entrée, and use it any way you choose. Don't worry about the wood pellets; any wood you select will enhance the flavor of the finished purée. This recipe guides you in roasting one head of garlic, but you can easily roast as many heads as you like.

YIELD: About 2 tablespoons of roasted garlic purée
RECOMMENDED PELLETS: Your choice
MARINATION/SEASONING TIME: None
COOKING TIME: 1 ½ hours

---

1 head garlic, cut in half crosswise to expose the middle of the cloves

1 teaspoon extra virgin olive oil

---

1. Start the pellet grill and set the temperature control to 180°F or "Smoke."

2. Using a brush or a small spoon, coat the exposed garlic with olive oil. Then wrap each half head in aluminum foil.

3. When the grill reaches the desired temperature, place the wrapped garlic on the grate and close the lid. Cook for about 1 hour, or until it is easy to penetrate a garlic clove with a toothpick.

4. Open the aluminum foil so that the smoke can penetrate the garlic, and smoke for 30 additional minutes.

5. Use a small knife to scoop out each half-clove and spread on bread, or squeeze the garlic out of the skins and mash to a paste that can be used in mashed potatoes or the dish of your choice.

Dad's Grilled Asparagus

My father was a machine operator for the electric and gas supplier in Colorado, and his assignments would take him all over the Denver area, including farmland. On weekends in the spring, we'd harvest the asparagus that he had seen growing wild during the week. When we got home, Dad would make his special barbequed beef, and he'd grill the tender asparagus, as well. This dish reminds me of my father every time I prepare it.

YIELD: 4 SERVINGS
RECOMMENDED PELLETS: YOUR CHOICE
MARINATION/SEASONING TIME: NONE
COOKING TIME: 25 TO 30 MINUTES

---

1 pound asparagus spears, trimmed

1–2 tablespoons melted butter

1 tablespoon Savory Spice Rub and Seasoning Blend (page 24)

1. Start the pellet grill and set the temperature control to 300°F.

2. Arrange the asparagus in a shallow pan, brush with the melted butter, and sprinkle with the spice blend.

3. When the grill reaches the desired temperature, arrange the asparagus directly on the grate, perpendicular to the bars so that they don't fall through. Close the door of the grill and cook for 25 to 30 minutes, or until the asparagus can be easily pierced with a fork.

4. Transfer the asparagus to a platter or bowl and serve immediately.

Tips for Buying and Storing Asparagus

Every spring, young, tender asparagus appear at garden stands and supermarkets. This is the best time to buy them, prepare them, and perhaps store them for future use. The following tips will help you make the most of fresh asparagus.

☐ When shopping for asparagus, look for bright green vegetables with stalks that are approximately the same thickness so that they cook uniformly, and cut ends that are not dry. The asparagus tip ends should be tightly closed, firm, and compact.

☐ Always store asparagus in the refrigerator. For best results, place the stalks loose inside a re-sealable plastic bag, and place the bag in the vegetable crisper.

Asparagus with Lemon

Asparagus and citrus are a culinary match made in heaven. Pair the resulting dish with beef, pork, or seafood, and you have a winning combination. The type of pellet doesn't matter, so use anything you have in the hopper.

YIELD: 6 SERVINGS
RECOMMENDED PELLETS: YOUR CHOICE
MARINATION/SEASONING TIME: NONE
COOKING TIME: 25 TO 30 MINUTES

1½ pounds asparagus spears, trimmed

2 tablespoons extra virgin olive oil

⅓ cup fresh lemon juice

½ teaspoon sea salt

¼ teaspoon ground black pepper

Lemon wedges or slices for garnish

1. Start the pellet grill and set the temperature control to 275°F.

2. Arrange the asparagus on a shallow pan. Set aside.

3. In a small bowl, mix together the olive oil, lemon juice, salt, and pepper. Brush the mixture over the asparagus or toss them with the mixture until they are coated.

4. When the grill reaches the desired temperature, arrange the asparagus directly on the grate, perpendicular to the bars so that they do not fall through. If desired, brush any remaining oil mixture over the vegetables. Close the door of the grill and cook for 25 to 30 minutes, or until the asparagus can be easily pierced with a fork.

5. Transfer the asparagus to a serving platter or bowl, garnish with lemon wedges or slices, and serve.

☐ To trim fresh asparagus before cooking, snap off the woody ends so that only the tender stalks and heads are used. Simply bend each spear until it snaps at its natural breaking point.

☐ If you cannot use asparagus within a few days of their purchase, store them in the freezer. For best results, first blanch the asparagus by placing them in boiling water for 2 to 5 minutes, just until the stalks turn bright green. Then transfer the asparagus to a bowl of ice water to stop the cooking. Remove them from the water bath and dry to remove most of the surface moisture. Place the spears in date-labeled freezer-safe zip-lock plastic bags, eliminating as much air as possible. Be sure to use the asparagus within eight months of freezing, and do not thaw before cooking.

Smoky Grilled Mushrooms

Mushrooms complement many foods, and are especially delicious with roast beef and steak. When seasoned with a flavored butter, these tasty morsels reach a whole new level. Use any wood pellets you like, and if you're cooking meat on the grill, use the recommended temperature for the meat and adjust the cooking time for the mushrooms as needed.

YIELD: 4 SERVINGS.
RECOMMENDED PELLETS: YOUR CHOICE
MARINATION/SEASONING TIME: NONE
COOKING TIME: 25 MINUTES

1/4 cup melted butter

1/2 teaspoon garlic salt

1/2 teaspoon dried dill

1 pound medium-sized mushrooms, your favorite type, cleaned and trimmed

1. Start the pellet grill and set the temperature control to 275°F.

2. In a small bowl, mix the melted butter with the garlic salt and dill.

3. Slide the mushrooms onto metal or bamboo skewers. (If you choose bamboo, soak them in water for a few minutes before using.) Brush the seasoned butter over all sides of the mushrooms.

4. Arrange the skewers on the grill grate, allowing space between them so that the heat and smoke can circulate around the mushrooms. Close the grill door and cook for about 25 minutes, turning the mushrooms and brushing them with more butter every 10 minutes or so. When done, you will be able to easily pierce the mushrooms with a sharp knife or fork.

5. Transfer the skewers to a large platter and serve.

Grilled Portobello Mushrooms

The Portobello mushroom is a remarkably versatile vegetable. Meaty in taste and texture and utterly delicious, it can be served as a side dish or a light entrée. In this recipe, the mushroom is first smoked and then grilled to create a unique flavor. If you prefer to enjoy your mushrooms without a smoky nuance, start the grill at the higher temperature. Any wood pellets will work for this recipe, but I think that apple and alder best complement the natural characteristics of the Portobello.

YIELD: 4 SERVINGS
RECOMMENDED PELLETS: ALDER OR APPLE
MARINATION/SEASONING TIME: NONE
COOKING TIME: 25 TO 30 MINUTES

3 tablespoons melted butter

$1/2$ teaspoon sea salt

$1/2$ teaspoon ground black pepper

4 Portobello mushroom caps (about 5 inches across), cleaned and trimmed

1. Start the pellet grill and set the temperature control to 180°F or "Smoke."

2. Mix the melted butter, salt, and pepper in a small bowl.

3. Arrange the mushrooms gill side up in a baking dish. Brush the butter mixture over the gills of the mushrooms. Turn the mushrooms over and brush the butter over the caps.

4. When the grill reaches the desired temperature, arrange the mushrooms directly on the grill grate, cap side up. Close the grill door and smoke for 15 minutes.

5. Reset the temperature control to 275°F. Turn the mushrooms over, brush the butter over the gill side, and close the grill door. Cook for 10 to 15 additional minutes, or until the cap is easily pierced with a fork. Serve immediately.

Smoke-Roasted Potatoes

My wife will opt for a baked potato over any meat entrée, and these are her favorites. Smoke-roasted, they have a crisp skin and a fluffy interior that explodes with flavor when you add butter or sour cream and chives. Enjoy these potatoes on their own or with your favorite grilled meat.

YIELD: 4 SERVINGS
RECOMMENDED PELLETS: YOUR CHOICE
MARINATION/SEASONING TIME: NONE
COOKING TIME: ABOUT 1 1/2 HOURS

---

4 large russet potatoes, scrubbed

3 tablespoons melted butter

1/2 teaspoon sea salt

1/2 teaspoon ground black pepper

1. Start the pellet grill and set the temperature control to 225°F.

2. Using a small sharp knife, pierce the potatoes in several places to allow the steam to escape. Brush them with the melted butter and sprinkle with salt and pepper.

3. When the grill reaches the desired temperature, arrange the potatoes on the grate, close the grill door, and smoke for about 30 minutes.

4. Increase the temperature to 375°F and roast for about 1 hour, or until the skins are crisp, the potatoes give slightly when squeezed on the sides, and you can easily pierce the flesh with a skewer.

5. Split the potatoes open and serve with the condiments of your choice, such as sour cream, butter, chopped chives, crumbled cooked bacon, or shredded cheese.

Roasted Potatoes
with Rosemary and Garlic

These potatoes make an elegant accompaniment to grill-roasted meat, steamed seasonal vegetables, and a crusty loaf of bread. Use any wood pellets you have on hand, as there is virtually no smokiness added when cooking at higher temperatures. Enjoy!

YIELD: 4 SERVINGS
RECOMMENDED PELLETS: YOUR CHOICE
MARINATION/SEASONING TIME: NONE
COOKING TIME: ABOUT 50 MINUTES

1½ tablespoons extra virgin olive oil

1½ tablespoons minced garlic

1 tablespoon finely minced fresh rosemary leaves

½ teaspoon sea salt

½ teaspoon coarsely ground black pepper

6–8 red potatoes (about 1½ pounds), scrubbed and quartered

2 tablespoons minced fresh parsley for garnish

1. Start the pellet grill and set the temperature control to 375°F.

2. Combine the olive oil, garlic, rosemary, salt, and pepper in a large bowl. Add the quartered potatoes and toss until they're coated with the oil, herbs, and spices.

3. Arrange the potatoes in a single layer on a baking sheet. When the grill reaches the desired temperature, place the baking sheet on the grate, close the door, and allow the potatoes to roast for 45 to 50 minutes, or until they can be easily pierced with a fork.

4. Transfer the potatoes to a heated serving dish, sprinkle with the parsley, and serve immediately.

Roasted Sweet Potato Slices

Sweet potatoes are a family favorite and are served at every function, regardless of the occasion. Since I began using a wood pellet grill, it's been easier than ever to cook up delicious sweet potato slices. This dish is wonderful with any entrée and makes a delicious accompaniment to a breakfast of scrambled eggs and bacon.

YIELD: 4 SERVINGS
RECOMMENDED PELLETS: YOUR CHOICE
MARINATION/SEASONING TIME: NONE
COOKING TIME: 40 TO 45 MINUTES

$1/_4$ cup melted butter

2 tablespoons extra virgin olive oil

$1/_2$ teaspoon sea salt

$1/_2$ teaspoon coarsely ground pepper

4 large sweet potatoes, scrubbed, peeled, and cut into $1/_4$-inch slices

2 tablespoons chopped parsley for garnish

1. Start the pellet grill and set the temperature control to 375°F.

2. Combine the butter, olive oil, salt, and pepper in a large bowl. Add the potato slices and toss until they're coated with the butter mixture.

3. Arrange the potato slices in a single layer on a perforated grilling pan. When the grill reaches the desired temperature, place the pan on the grate, close the grill door, and roast for 40 to 45 minutes, or until the slices are tender when pierced with a fork and have a slightly crisp exterior.

4. Transfer the potatoes to a heated serving dish, sprinkle with the parsley, and serve immediately.

THE COMPLETE WOOD PELLET BARBEQUE COOKBOOK

Twice-Baked Potatoes with Garlic, Dill, and Cheddar

These delectable potatoes are a taste treat not to be missed, especially when paired with grilled meats. If you're barbequing a meat that requires a lower temperature, just cook the potatoes a little longer. Any wood pellets will work just fine.

YIELD: 8 SERVINGS
RECOMMENDED PELLETS: YOUR CHOICE
MARINATION/SEASONING TIME: NONE
COOKING TIME: 1 1/2 HOURS

4 large russet potatoes, scrubbed

2 tablespoons vegetable oil, divided

3 tablespoons coarse sea salt

3/4 cup milk

1/2 cup sour cream

2 tablespoons finely minced garlic

2 tablespoons dried dill

1/2 teaspoon sea salt

1/4 teaspoon ground black pepper

4 ounces shredded sharp Cheddar cheese (about 1 cup), divided

1. Start the pellet grill and set the temperature control to 375°F.

2. Using a small sharp knife, pierce the potatoes in several places to allow the steam to escape. Brush them with the oil and sprinkle with the salt.

3. When the grill reaches the desired temperature, arrange the potatoes on the grate, close the grill door, and allow the potatoes to cook for 1 hour, or until they give slightly when squeezed on the sides.

4. Place the potatoes on a work surface, and cut each in half lengthwise. Scoop out the flesh, leaving a 1/4-inch-thick shell.

5. Place the scooped-out potato flesh in a large bowl and mash roughly. Add the milk, sour cream, garlic, and dill, and stir to blend. Add salt and pepper to taste.

6. Divide the mashed potato among the shells, filling each shell with an equal amount of the mixture. Sprinkle the cheese over the top.

7. Return the potatoes to the grill, close the door, and cook for 15 to 20 minutes, or until the filling is hot and the cheese has melted. Serve immediately.

Mexican Stuffed Potatoes

Earlier in my life, I traveled extensively in support of the U.S. Navy. I had many opportunities to dine on various cuisines, and one of my favorites was Mexican food. On one trip, I enjoyed a stuffed potato that was truly magnificent. Over the years, I have worked hard to duplicate this culinary masterpiece, and this recipe comes pretty close. Serve it with refried beans and perhaps some sour cream or guacamole, and you'll have a meal to remember.

YIELD: 4 SERVINGS
RECOMMENDED PELLETS: MESQUITE
MARINATION/SEASONING TIME: NONE
COOKING TIME: ABOUT 1½ HOURS

4 large russet potatoes, scrubbed

3 tablespoons vegetable oil, divided

1½ tablespoons coarse sea salt

1 pound lean ground beef

1 cup chopped onion

¼ cup Southwestern Seasoning Blend and Rub (page 27) or 1 package taco seasoning mix (your favorite)

1 or 2 jalapeño peppers, seeded and finely chopped

4-ounce can diced green chilies, undrained

12 ounces shredded Cheddar cheese (about 3 cups), divided

Milk (optional)

½ teaspoon sea salt

½ teaspoon ground black pepper

3 tablespoons chopped fresh chives for garnish

2 tablespoons chopped fresh cilantro for garnish

3 radishes, sliced, for garnish

1 cup sour cream

1. Start the pellet grill and set the temperature control to 375°F.

2. Using a small sharp knife, pierce each potato several times. Coat the skins with 1 tablespoon of the vegetable oil and rub with the coarse salt.

3. When the grill reaches the desired temperature, arrange the potatoes on the grate, close the lid, and cook for approximately 1 hour, or until the flesh gives slightly when you squeeze the sides of the potato.

4. While the potatoes are baking, place the remaining vegetable oil in a large skillet over medium heat. Add the ground beef and onion, and cook, stirring constantly to crumble. Add the seasoning blend and stir to mix evenly with the meat mixture. Stir in the jalapeño pepper, and continue to cook until the meat shows no trace of pink. Stir in the green chilies, and set the mixture aside.

5. Remove the baked potatoes from the grill and reset the temperature control to 180°F or "Smoke."

6. Place the potatoes on a work surface and cut off the upper third of each potato lengthwise, so that each potato resembles a long boat. Scoop the flesh out of each potato, leaving a $1/4$-inch-thick shell. Place the scooped-out flesh in a large bowl, along with the flesh that was removed with the top third of the potato (discard the potato skin top). Add the meat mixture and half of the cheese, and stir to blend well. If the mixture is too thick to stir, add some milk as needed. Stir in salt and pepper to taste.

7. Place about $1/4$ cup of the remaining cheese inside each potato shell. Spoon an equal amount of the meat mixture into each potato, and top with a portion of the remaining Cheddar.

8. Arrange the filled potatoes on the grill, close the lid, and cook for 15 to 20 minutes, just long enough to reheat the potatoes, melt the cheese, and add a little smokiness to the mixture.

9. Transfer the potatoes to a serving platter; garnish with chives, cilantro, and radishes; and serve, passing a bowl of sour cream for those who want it.

Getting the Most Out of America's Favorite Vegetable

Did you know that the average American eats approximately 120 pounds of potatoes a year? After dairy products, potatoes are the country's second most-consumed food. That's why I offer so many ways to prepare this popular vegetable on the wood pellet grill.

To enjoy the very best potato dishes, you'll want to start by purchasing the best produce. Select potatoes that are clean, smooth-skinned, and firm. Avoid those with bruises, cuts, or discolorations. If they are shriveled or sprouting "eyes," which are signs of age, pass them by. Especially avoid potatoes that have a green hue or contain green spots. This discoloration is caused by a natural bitter-tasting toxin called *solanine,* which is produced when a potato (or part of a potato) pokes through the soil and is exposed to sunlight. As a natural defense mechanism, the potato produces solanine at the exposed area to keep away garden pests and fungus. When it is consumed in large quantities, solanine is toxic to humans. If you happen to buy a bag of potatoes and discover that some have green spots, simply cut away and discard these areas before using.

When storing potatoes, it is best to keep them in a cool dark spot. Do not put them in the refrigerator or in a place that is warm and humid, such as near the oven or under the sink. And don't leave them on the countertop where they will be exposed to light.

Grilled Vegetables and Pineapple

The natural sugars of the vegetables in this medley are enhanced by the sweetness of the pineapple, making the dish a real treat. Enjoy it as an elegant accompaniment to any meal, especially grilled meats. When dicing the vegetables, for best results, aim for a large dice in which the pieces are all roughly the same size.

YIELD: 6 SERVINGS
RECOMMENDED PELLETS: OAK
MARINATION/SEASONING TIME: NONE
COOKING TIME: 30 TO 40 MINUTES

1 cup large-diced unpeeled red potatoes

1 cup large-diced mushrooms, any type

1 cup cherry tomatoes

1 medium onion, large-diced

1/2 cup large-diced red bell pepper

1/2 cup large-diced green bell pepper

15-ounce can unsweetened pineapple chunks, undrained and large-diced

2 tablespoons extra virgin olive oil

2 teaspoons minced garlic

2 teaspoons dried dill

1 1/2 teaspoons celery seed

1/2 teaspoon sea salt

1/2 teaspoon cayenne pepper

1/2 teaspoon coarsely ground black pepper

2 tablespoons minced fresh parsley for garnish

1. Start the pellet grill and set the temperature control to 350°F.

2. Place all of the vegetables and the pineapple and its juice in a large bowl, and toss until well mixed. Then drain off and discard the liquids.

3. Add the olive oil, garlic, dill, celery seed, salt, cayenne, and black pepper to the bowl, and toss to coat the vegetable mixture with the oil and seasonings.

4. Arrange the vegetable mixture on a large baking sheet. When the grill reaches the desired temperature, place the sheet on the grate, close the door, and allow the vegetables to roast for 30 to 40 minutes, or until they can be easily pierced with a fork.

5. Transfer the vegetables to a heated serving dish, sprinkle with the parsley, and serve immediately.

10.

Beautiful Breads, Perfect Pizzas, and Satisfying Sandwiches

One of the most alluring aromas in the world is that of baking bread. Years ago, I was known to walk out of my way to pass a fragrant bakery and perhaps buy a loaf or two. Since I began using the pellet grill, though, the farthest I have to travel to enjoy this guilty pleasure is my own backyard.

I love making bread for several reasons. First of all, homemade bread is healthier than most of the loaves I can buy because I use the best ingredients and avoid chemicals and preservatives. Second, I can experiment to my heart's content, using different flours, changing up seeds, and even including herbs on occasion so that my breads are never boring and always complement my menu. Perhaps best of all, this activity has inspired me to recreate breads that I enjoyed as a child,

including my grandmother's incredible cornbread and my mom's unsurpassed pizza dough.

This chapter begins with recipes for my favorite homemade breads: Dill Seed Rye, Grilled French-Style Bread, and Old-Fashioned Cornbread. These are followed with a recipe for pizza crust plus directions for making three tantalizing pizzas—Grill-Smoked Mozzarella and Vegetable, Tomato and Basil, and Smoked Italian Sausage and Pepperoni. While each of these pies is a little piece of heaven, I hope you use them as springboards for creativity and invent pizzas that suit your own tastes and preferences. Also included is my recipe for Pellet Grill Focaccia, which uses pizza crust dough to make a delectable herb- and olive-studded flat bread, and one for buttery Smoked French Garlic Bread.

This chapter ends with a handful of recipes for grilled sandwiches—Smoked Spicy Tuna Melts, Smoky Ham and Swiss, and Italian-Style Turkey Boats. While any of these sandwiches can be prepared on a stovetop skillet or in a conventional oven, you'll find that the wood pellet grill adds another dimension, making fillings and even the bread itself taste better.

All of the following bread recipes were designed for use with a sturdy standing mixer that includes paddle and kneading attachments. This makes it a snap to prepare bread any time you want a fresh-baked loaf. But if you don't own one of these appliances, you can simply mix the ingredients by hand, just as people have done for hundreds of years. You'll find directions for hand mixing and kneading in the inset on page 168.

Any homemade bread or pizza is a real treat. When these same foods are prepared in a pellet grill, they are even better—infused with aromatic wood smoke and baked until the crusts are delightfully crisp and appealing. I hope that you'll enjoy making breads, pizzas, and sandwiches in your versatile wood pellet grill.

Dill Seed Rye Bread

If you are used to deli rye, get ready for a very different kind of bread. This loaf is light and airy and includes molasses, brown sugar, and "the thrill of the dill." It lends itself to great sandwiches, chicken and tuna salad in particular. Toasted, it is delicious spread with melted butter and jelly, jam, or peanut butter. The pellet choice is not important as there is little smoke, but whatever wood you choose will certainly permeate the bread to some degree, enhancing its flavor. Dill Seed Rye Bread is our everyday bread and may very well become a favorite in your home as well.

YIELD: 2 LOAVES
RECOMMENDED PELLETS: YOUR CHOICE
MARINATION/SEASONING TIME: NONE
COOKING TIME: ABOUT 45 MINUTES

1¼ cups water	1 packet active dry yeast
1¼ cups prepared coffee	2 tablespoons vegetable oil
2 teaspoons brown sugar	2 teaspoons salt
2 tablespoons molasses	2 cups sifted rye flour
2 tablespoons caraway or fennel seeds	5 cups sifted unbleached bread flour
2 tablespoons dill seeds	

1. Prepare a heavy-duty mixer with a paddle attachment. (If you're going to mix the dough by hand, follow the directions provided in the inset on page 168.)

2. Place the water and coffee in a saucepan, and heat to about 110°F. (The liquid should feel very warm but not hot on the inside of your wrist.)

3. Pour the coffee mixture into the bowl of the electric mixer, and add the brown sugar, molasses, caraway seeds, dill seeds, and yeast. Stir to uniformly incorporate the yeast. Allow the mixture to sit for 10 to 15 minutes, or until foam appears on the surface.

4. Stir the vegetable oil, salt, and rye flour into the yeast mixture. Turn on the mixer to the "Low" setting and blend until the flour is incorporated with the liquid.

5. Slowly add 2 cups of the bread flour to the mixing bowl. Add additional flour $1/2$ cup at a time until a stiff dough forms. When the mixer paddle is no longer effective, replace it with the kneading attachment or dough hook. When the dough is thick and begins to adhere to the dough hook, stop adding flour. There may be up to 1 cup that is unused, which is fine. Continue to knead the dough for 10 to 12 minutes, adding a little flour only as necessary to make the dough smooth and elastic.

6. Grease a large bowl with butter-flavored shortening or nonstick cooking spray, and transfer the bread dough to the prepared bowl. Turn the dough over so that the shiny side is up, and cover with plastic wrap. Place in a warm area, such as an oven (leave the oven off, but turn the oven light on), and allow the dough to rise until doubled in size, 1 to $1^1/2$ hours.

7. Grease two 9 x 5-inch glass or metal loaf pans with butter-flavored shortening or nonstick cooking spray. Punch the dough down and use a knife to cut it into 2 equal parts. Use your hands to shape each piece of dough into a smooth loaf that will fit into a prepared bread pan. Place each piece in one of the pans and cover with plastic wrap. Place in a warm spot and allow to rise until doubled in size, about 1 hour. When the dough is ready for baking, it should have risen above the top edge of the bread pan and be pushing the plastic wrap above. Remove and discard the plastic.

8. Start the pellet grill and set the temperature control to 375°F. When the grill reaches the desired temperature, place the bread pans on the grill grate, close the door, and bake for 35 to 40 minutes, or until the bread is browned on top. When done, the bread will sound hollow when you turn it out of the pan and rap it on the bottom with your knuckle.

9. Remove the bread from the pans and place right side up on wire racks to cool. Eat warm or at room temperature.

Grilled French-Style Bread

Genuine French bread is unique in texture and flavor. In this recipe, I use unbleached bread flour to make a French-style loaf that has a soft interior and a crisp, chewy crust. Try oak, hickory, or mesquite pellets, as they burn drier and a little hotter than the softer woods. Each of these woods will have some influence on aroma and flavor, so experiment to find the one you like best.

YIELD: 2 STANDARD LOAVES
RECOMMENDED PELLETS: OAK, HICKORY, OR MESQUITE
MARINATION/SEASONING TIME: NONE
COOKING TIME: ABOUT 40 MINUTES

1^1/$_2$ cups water	1 tablespoon sugar
1 packet active dry yeast	1^1/$_2$ teaspoons salt
4–5 cups sifted unbleached bread flour	Cornmeal
	2 egg whites, beaten (optional)

1. Prepare a heavy duty-mixer with a paddle attachment. (If you're going to mix the dough by hand, follow the directions provided in the inset on page 168.)

2. Place the water in a saucepan, and heat to about 110°F. (The liquid should feel very warm but not hot on the inside of your wrist.)

3. Pour the water into the bowl of the electric mixer, add the yeast, and stir to uniformly incorporate it into the liquid. Allow the mixture to sit for 10 to 15 minutes, or until foam appears on the surface.

4. In a medium-sized bowl, combine 2 cups of the flour, the sugar, and the salt. Slowly add the bread flour combination to the liquid in the mixer bowl. Add additional flour ^{1}/$_2$ cup at a time until a stiff dough forms. When the mixer paddle is no longer effective, replace it with the kneading attachment or dough hook. When the dough is thick and begins to adhere to the dough hook, stop adding flour. There may be up to 1 cup that is unused, which is fine. Continue to knead the dough for 10 to 12 minutes, adding a little flour only as necessary to make the dough smooth and elastic.

5. Grease a large bowl with butter-flavored shortening or nonstick cooking spray. Shape the dough into a ball and transfer the dough to the bowl. Turn the dough over so that the shiny side is up, and cover with plastic wrap. Place in a warm area, such as an oven (leave the oven off, but turn the oven light on), and allow the dough to rise until doubled in size, about 1 hour.

THE COMPLETE WOOD PELLET BARBEQUE COOKBOOK

6. Grease a 10 x 14-inch baking sheet and sprinkle it with the cornmeal. Set aside.

7. Punch down the dough and transfer it to a lightly floured surface. Knead the dough by hand for 1 to 2 minutes, or until the dough is smooth and elastic. Cover the dough and allow it to rest for 10 minutes.

8. Cut the dough into 2 equal parts. Using a rolling pin, roll each piece of dough into a rectangle about the length of the prepared baking sheet. Using your hands, tightly roll each rectangle lengthwise to form a long roll of dough. Moisten the edge of the dough and seal, slightly tapering the ends.

9. Transfer the loaves to the prepared baking pan with the seam side down. Using a sharp knife, make a few long $\frac{1}{4}$-inch-deep diagonal slashes in the top of each loaf and cover loosely with plastic wrap or a clean kitchen towel. Place the baking pan in a warm spot and allow the dough to rise until nearly doubled in size, about 1 hour.

10. Start the pellet grill and set the temperature control to 375°F.

11. When the grill reaches the desired temperature, remove the plastic wrap or towel that covers the dough. For a crisper crust, brush the loaves with the egg white.

12. Place the baking sheet on the grill grate, close the grill door, and bake for 35 to 40 minutes, or until the crust is golden brown and crisp. When done, the bread will sound hollow when you rap it on the bottom with your knuckle.

13. Transfer the loaves to wire racks and allow to cool before serving.

For a Change

■ To make smaller rolls for individual sandwiches, in Step 8, cut the bread into 2 halves, and cut each half into 4 equal pieces. Working on a lightly floured surface, use a rolling pin to roll each of the 8 pieces into a rectangle approximately 4 x 8 inches in size. Use your hands to roll each rectangle into a small tapered football shape. Arrange the rolls on a cornmeal-dusted baking sheet seam side down, cover with plastic wrap, and allow to rise in a warm place for about 1 hour. Continue with Step 10, but reduce the baking time to about 20 minutes.

Mixing and Kneading Yeast Dough by Hand

Although modern appliances make it fast and easy to mix and knead bread dough, many people prefer to accomplish these tasks by hand, finding it a relaxing and rewarding process. Whether you mix dough by hand because you don't own specialized kitchen equipment or because you want a truly "hands-on" experience, the following directions will help ensure success.

1. Follow the recipe's directions for activating the yeast by mixing it with liquids, sugar, and possibly other ingredients. Wait until the yeast mixture foams to proceed with the recipe.

2. Start adding the flour and other recipe ingredients according to the directions, stirring them into the yeast mixture with a sturdy wooden spoon. When you've added more than half of the flour, remove the spoon and squeeze the dough with your hands until all of the flour disappears into the mass. If the dough is so wet that you can't pick it up, add a small amount of flour and continue to mix it in by hand, a little bit at a time, until you can pick the dough up. Although the bread dough will be very soft at this point, something like wet clay, it is time to start kneading it so that the loaf acquires the proper texture.

3. Dust a large wooden board or other work surface with flour. Place the dough on the surface and turn it over so that it is entirely coated with flour. Using the heels of your hands, press the dough down and away from your body. After a few strokes, fold the dough over from the back to the front, and knead again, adding more flour to the board as it becomes necessary. At first, the dough will be very sticky and difficult to handle. After a few minutes, though, it will begin to feel smoother.

4. After you have kneaded and folded the dough several times, give the dough a quarter turn and knead again. Continue to knead, fold, and turn the bread dough for about 4 to 10 minutes, or until the dough is elastic and springy and has a smooth, satiny surface. When you are able to form the dough into a ball that holds its shape when you lift it from the work surface and hold it in one hand, it is time for the first rising. Carefully follow the directions in the recipe of your choice to complete your loaves.

THE COMPLETE WOOD PELLET BARBEQUE COOKBOOK

Grandma's Old-Fashioned Cornbread

My grandmother was a magician in the kitchen. She made almost everything we ate from scratch, and turned even the most tedious chores, like peeling potatoes, into fun experiences. I especially liked helping her make bread. This recipe is very close to the way Grandma made it, and is a real treat when spread with butter and drizzled with honey. Use any wood pellet that's in the hopper as the high temperature won't produce very much smoke but will have just a little smoky influence.

YIELD: 8 SERVINGS
RECOMMENDED PELLETS: YOUR CHOICE
MARINATION/SEASONING TIME: NONE
COOKING TIME: ABOUT 1 HOUR

2 cups buttermilk	2 cups cornmeal
1 egg, beaten	2 tablespoons cornstarch
2 tablespoons vegetable oil	1 teaspoon salt
1 tablespoon white Karo syrup	$^3/_4$ teaspoon baking soda

1. Start the pellet grill and set the temperature control to 375°F. Grease a 12-inch cast-iron skillet with nonstick cooking spray or shortening, and set aside.

2. Place the buttermilk, egg, vegetable oil, and Karo syrup in a large bowl, and stir or whisk well to mix. Add all of the remaining ingredients, and stir just until mixed. Pour the batter into the prepared skillet.

3. When the grill reaches the desired temperature, place the skillet on the grate, close the grill door, and bake for 50 to 60 minutes, or until a toothpick inserted in the center comes out clean.

4. Remove the pan from the grill and allow to cool for at least 15 minutes before cutting into 8 wedges and serving with butter and honey.

Smoked French Garlic Bread

My wife and I once visited a "mom and pop" barbeque restaurant in San José, California and enjoyed a phenomenal garlic French bread that was smoked just before it was brought to our table. This is close to what we had in San José—even a little better—and is sure to be a hit when served with any barbeque dinner. Use the French bread you bake yourself or a good-quality store-bought loaf, and for the most spectacular results, choose hickory or mesquite pellets.

YIELD: 1 LOAF
RECOMMENDED PELLETS: HICKORY OR MESQUITE
MARINATION/SEASONING TIME: NONE
COOKING TIME: 15 MINUTES

$^1/_2$ cup butter, softened

6 garlic cloves, minced

1 tablespoon crushed dried oregano

1 teaspoon garlic salt

$^1/_4$ cup grated Parmigiano-Reggiano cheese

1 loaf Grilled French-Style Bread (page 166) or commercial French- or Italian-style bread

---

1. Start the pellet grill and set the temperature control to 180°F or "Smoke."

2. Place the softened butter, garlic, oregano, garlic salt, and cheese in a small bowl, and use a fork to mix together.

3. Place the bread on a work surface, and slice it in half lengthwise. Spread half of the butter mixture evenly over the cut side of each loaf half.

4. When the grill reaches the desired temperature, arrange the bread butter side up on the grate. Close the grill door and allow to smoke for 15 minutes.

5. Remove the bread from the grill, cut into serving-size pieces, and serve immediately while still hot.

Grill-Smoked Mozzarella and Vegetable Pizza

Smoking the pizza on the grill enhances the flavor of the cheese and vegetable toppings, and makes the crust taste as if it were baked in an Italian wood-fired oven. The addition of herbs and olive oil provide authentic Italian flavor and aroma. Ah, the memories of my favorite Napoli pizza parlor return. The only thing missing is a cold Peroni beer.

YIELD: 2 PIZZAS (8 SERVINGS)
RECOMMENDED PELLETS: YOUR CHOICE
MARINATION/SEASONING TIME: NONE
COOKING TIME: 15 TO 20 MINUTES

$1/_2$ cup chopped red bell pepper

$1/_2$ cup chopped green bell pepper

$1/_2$ cup sliced onion

1 recipe Best Pizza Dough (page 172), prepared to point of baking

$1/_4$ cup plus 2 tablespoons extra virgin olive oil

1 teaspoon dried oregano or Italian-style seasoning

$3/_4$ cup chopped fresh basil

1 pound mozzarella, sliced $1/_8$ inch thick

1. Start the pellet grill and set the temperature control to "Smoke" or 180°F.

2. Arrange the bell peppers and onion on a small-holed perforated grilling pan or baking sheet. Place the pan on the grill grate, close the door, and allow to smoke for 15 to 20 minutes.

3. Remove the vegetables from the grill, and increase the grill temperature to 350°F.

4. Coat two rimmed 10 x 14-inch baking sheets or vegetable roasting trays with nonstick cooking spray. Place one rectangle of prepared dough in each pan and brush the crust with olive oil to within 1 inch of the edge. Sprinkle the oregano or Italian seasoning over the dough, and evenly spread the smoked vegetables and fresh basil over all. Finally, arrange the cheese over the vegetables.

5. When the pellet grill reaches the desired temperature, place the pans in the grill, close the grill door, and bake for 15 to 20 minutes, or until the bottom of the crust is brown when gently lifted at the corners.

6. Remove the pizzas from the grill, cut into squares, and serve.

The Best Pizza Dough

This light crust makes a terrific base for any of the pizzas presented in this chapter—or any toppings of your choice. Have the toppings prepared before you roll out the dough, and the pizza will come together quickly. The grill deliciously flavors the entire pizza, just as the wood-fired ovens in Italy make pizza so special. This dough may be made in advance and stored in the refrigerator for a day or two, but is not recommended for freezing as the results can vary greatly.

YIELD: 2 PIZZA CRUSTS (8 SERVINGS)

1¼ cups water	1 teaspoon sea salt
1 packet active dry yeast	3 tablespoons extra virgin olive oil, divided
1 teaspoon sugar	3½ cups sifted unbleached bread flour (more if required)

---

1. Prepare a heavy-duty mixer with a paddle attachment. (If you're going to mix the dough by hand, follow the directions provided in the inset on page 168.)

2. Place the water in a saucepan, and heat to about 110°F. (The liquid should feel very warm but not hot on the inside of your wrist.)

3. Pour the water into the bowl of the electric mixer, and add the yeast and sugar. Stir to dissolve the sugar and incorporate the yeast. Allow the mixture to sit for 10 to 15 minutes, or until foamy.

4. Set the mixer speed to "Low" and add all of the salt and 1½ teaspoons of the olive oil. Slowly add 1 cup of flour at a time just until a smooth, soft dough forms. Do not allow the dough to become too dry. There may be ½ to ¾ cup of flour remaining unused, which is fine. When the paddle is no longer effective, replace it with the kneading attachment or dough hook. Continue to knead the dough for 8 to 10 minutes, or until the dough is smooth and elastic.

5. Lightly coat a large bowl with the remaining oil. Turn the dough onto a lightly floured work surface and knead slightly to make a ball. Transfer the dough to the greased bowl and turn it over so that the shiny side is up. Cover with plastic wrap; place in a warm area, such as an oven (leave the oven off, but turn the oven light on); and allow the dough to rise until doubled in size, 1 to 1½ hours.

6. Punch the dough down. If you have time, cover the dough once more and let it rise until it has again doubled in size, about 1 hour. (The second rising is not a requirement, but the crust will be lighter than if used immediately after the first rising.) If you opt for the second rising, punch the dough down again once it has doubled in size.

7. Start the pellet grill and set the temperature control to 350°F. Coat two rimmed 10 x 14-inch baking sheets or vegetable roasting trays with nonstick cooking spray.

8. Cut the dough in half. Working with one ball of dough at a time, place the ball on a lightly floured surface and use a lightly floured rolling pin to roll it into a rectangle that's 9 x 13 inches in size and ¼ inch thick. Place one rectangle of dough in each of the prepared pans.

9. Top the dough with the fillings of your choice. (See the recipes on pages 171, 173, and 174.) Place the pans in the grill, close the door, and bake for 15 to 20 minutes, or until the bottom of the crust has browned. Cut into squares and serve immediately.

Tomato and Basil Pizza

The heat of the grill plus mild smoke transform this simple pie of cheese, tomatoes, and basil into something special. Serve this light and healthy delight with a slightly sweet Pinot Gris wine.

YIELD: 2 PIZZAS (8 SERVINGS)
RECOMMENDED PELLETS: YOUR CHOICE
MARINATION/SEASONING TIME: NONE
COOKING TIME: 15 TO 20 MINUTES

1 recipe Best Pizza Dough (page 172), prepared to point of baking	8 ounces fresh plum tomatoes, diced (about 1½ cups)
¼ cup extra virgin olive oil	¾ cup chopped fresh basil
1 teaspoon dried oregano or Italian seasoning	1 cup shredded mozzarella cheese, or 8 ounces fresh mozzarella, sliced

1. Start the pellet grill and set the temperature control to 350°F.

2. Coat two rimmed 10 x 14-inch baking sheets or vegetable roasting trays with nonstick cooking spray. Place one rectangle of the prepared dough in each pan and brush the crust with olive oil to within 1 inch of the edge. Sprinkle the oregano or Italian seasoning over the dough, and evenly spread with the chopped tomatoes and basil. Distribute the cheese over the tomatoes.

3. When the pellet grill has reached the desired temperature, place the pans in the grill, close the grill door, and bake for 15 to 20 minutes, or until the bottom of the crust is brown when gently lifted at the corners

4. Remove the pizzas from the grill, cut into squares, and serve.

Smoked Italian Sausage and Pepperoni Pizza

Italian sausage and pepperoni make this pizza hearty, and smoke from the wood pellet grill makes it irresistible. Add a bottle of red wine and a few friends, and you have a memorable dinner.

YIELD: 2 PIZZAS (8 SERVINGS)
RECOMMENDED PELLETS: YOUR CHOICE
MARINATION/SEASONING TIME: NONE
COOKING TIME: 15 TO 20 MINUTES

8 ounces sweet Italian link sausages	1½ cups pizza or pasta sauce
1 tablespoon extra virgin olive oil	1 teaspoon dried oregano or Italian-style seasoning
½ cup diced red bell pepper	
½ cup diced green bell pepper	8 ounces sliced pepperoni
½ cup diced onion	¾ cup chopped fresh basil
1 recipe Best Pizza Dough (page 172), prepared to point of baking	2 cups shredded mozzarella cheese

1. Start the pellet grill and set the temperature control to 180°F or "Smoke."

2. Use a fork to pierce the Italian sausages through the casings in several places on all sides. Arrange the sausages directly on the grill grate, close the door, and allow to smoke for 30 minutes. Increase the grill temperature to 350°F and grill for about 15 minutes, or until no trace of pink remains in the center when you cut the sausage in half with a knife. Slice the sausages into ⅛-inch rounds or chop them into pieces, depending on your preference, and set aside.

3. While the sausages are grilling, warm the olive oil in a skillet over medium-high heat. Add the peppers and onion and sauté just until tender-crisp. Remove from the heat and set aside.

4. Coat two rimmed 10 x 14-inch baking sheets or vegetable roasting trays with nonstick cooking spray. Place one rectangle of prepared dough in each pan and spread the pizza or pasta sauce over the crust to within 1 inch of the edge. Sprinkle the oregano or Italian seasoning over the sauce, and top with the sausage, pepperoni, sautéed vegetables, and basil. Evenly distribute the cheese over the meat and vegetables.

5. Place the pans in the grill, close the grill door, and bake for 15 to 20 minutes, or until the bottom of the crust is brown when gently lifted at the corners.

6. Remove the pizzas from the grill, cut into squares, and serve.

Smoked Spicy Tuna Melts

What happens when you combine tuna with savory ingredients like tomato, scallions, capers, and anchovies, and top the mixture with cheese? You get a filling that's bursting with flavor. Sandwich the mixture between homemade French rolls, and you have the ultimate tuna melt.

YIELD: 4 SERVINGS
RECOMMENDED PELLETS: YOUR CHOICE
MARINATION/SEASONING TIME: NONE
COOKING TIME: 20 TO 25 MINUTES

1 tablespoon olive oil

1 medium tomato, seeded and chopped

$1/_2$ cup chopped scallions

$1^1/_2$ teaspoons capers

2 anchovies, chopped (optional)

1 can (6 ounces) tuna, packed in oil or water, drained

$1^1/_4$ cups shredded Cheddar or Pepper Jack cheese, divided

2 tablespoons honey

2 tablespoons brown deli-style mustard

4 French bread rolls, homemade (see "For a Change" on page 167) or store-bought, sliced in half lengthwise

$1/_2$ teaspoon crushed red pepper

1. Start the pellet grill and set the temperature control to 225°F. Preheat the broiler in your kitchen oven.

2. Heat the oil in a medium-sized skillet over medium heat. Add the tomato and scallions and cook until slightly soft, about 4 minutes. Add the capers and anchovies, if using. Stir in the tuna, breaking the fish up into pieces. Finally add $1/_2$ cup of the cheese and gently cook until heated through. Remove the mixture from the heat and set aside.

3. In a small bowl, combine the honey and mustard, stirring to blend. Set aside.

4. Place the halved rolls cut side up on a baking sheet. Toast lightly under the broiler.

5. Spread the toasted side of each roll half with the honey-mustard mixture. Spoon the tuna mixture on the bottom half of each roll, and top with a portion of the remaining cheese and a little of the crushed red pepper.

6. Arrange the tuna melts on a pan and place the pan on the grill grate. Close the door and heat for 20 minutes, or until the cheese melts.

7. Top each sandwich with a toasted roll top and serve hot.

Pellet Grill Focaccia Bread

This fabulous focaccia bread has a light pizza-crust base made flavorful and aromatic with the addition of olives, rosemary, basil, and gentle smoke. While this bread is delicious on its own, you can also serve it with dipping oils or top it with herbed cheese spread. However you serve this grilled treat, it will be a hit.

YIELD: 8 SERVINGS
RECOMMENDED PELLETS: YOUR CHOICE
MARINATION/SEASONING TIME: NONE
COOKING TIME: 15 TO 18 MINUTES

---

1 recipe Best Pizza Dough (page 172), prepared through Step 6*

4¹/₄-ounce can chopped ripe olives, undrained

¹/₄ cup extra virgin olive oil

¹/₂ teaspoon dried rosemary, coarsely chopped

¹/₂ teaspoon dried basil

¹/₂ teaspoon garlic powder

*Before starting Step 4 of the pizza crust recipe, add the can of chopped olives to the yeast mixture. Then add the flour and continue with the recipe.

1. Start the pellet grill and set the temperature control to 350°F. Grease a large sheet pan, and set aside.

2. Place the dough on a floured work surface, and roll into a 12-inch square that's about ¹/₂-inch-thick. Using a sharp knife, cut the dough into eight 3 x 6-inch rectangles. Arrange the rectangles of dough on the prepared baking sheet, spacing the pieces about 1 inch apart.

3. Combine the olive oil, rosemary, basil, and garlic powder in a small bowl. Brush the olive oil mixture liberally over the tops of the dough pieces, using as much of the flavored oil as possible. Use a fork to prick holes throughout each piece of dough.

4. When the grill reaches the desired temperature, place the baking sheet on the grill grate, close the grill door, and bake for 15 to 18 minutes, or until the tops and bottoms of the bread are browned. The bread should sound hollow when tapped on the top. Remove from the grill, transfer to a wire rack, and serve warm or at room temperature.

For a Change

■ If you prefer to make one large rectangular loaf of focaccia, roll out the dough into a ¹/₂-inch-thick rectangle, top as desired, and bake for 15 to 18 minutes, or until the bread has browned nicely.

■ For a more flavorful bread, when mixing the dough, in addition to adding the chopped olives listed in the main recipe, add 1 teaspoon each of dried oregano, dried thyme, and garlic powder, and ½ teaspoon of dried basil. When the dough has been shaped for baking, brush the top with olive oil and sprinkle it with Parmesan and mozzarella cheese. Then bake as usual.

Smoky Ham and Swiss

Ham and Swiss cheese are a classic pairing. When joined by my smoky Dill Seed Rye Bread and a savory horseradish-and-mustard spread, you have a marriage made in heaven.

YIELD: 6 SERVINGS
RECOMMENDED PELLETS: YOUR CHOICE
MARINATION/SEASONING TIME: NONE
COOKING TIME: 20 TO 25 MINUTES

12 slices Dill Seed Rye Bread (page 164)

12 slices ham

12 slices Swiss cheese

HORSERADISH AND MUSTARD SPREAD

¼ cup plus 2 tablespoons butter, softened

2 teaspoons cream-style prepared horseradish

2 teaspoons brown deli-style mustard

½ cup chopped red onion

1. Start the pellet grill and set the temperature control to 350°F.

2. To make the Horseradish and Mustard Spread, place the butter, horseradish, and mustard in a small bowl, and stir to mix. Fold in the red onion.

3. Arrange the bread slices on a work surface and spread one side of each slice with some of the mustard spread. Top 6 of the slices with 2 ham and cheese slices, folding the fillings as necessary to fit the bread. Top each sandwich with another slice of bread.

4. Wrap each sandwich securely in aluminum foil. When the grill reaches the desired temperature, place the foil-wrapped sandwiches directly on the grate and bake for 20 to 25 minutes, or until the cheese has melted and the sandwiches are hot. Serve immediately.

Italian-Style Turkey Boats

Next Thanksgiving, take the "boring" out of turkey leftovers by serving this Italian-inspired sandwich. Combining turkey with Italian herbs, pepperoni, pizza sauce, and cheese, this dish may fast become an after-Thanksgiving tradition in your home.

YIELD: 4 SERVINGS
RECOMMENDED PELLETS: YOUR CHOICE
MARINATION/SEASONING TIME: NONE
COOKING TIME: 20 TO 25 MINUTES

3 tablespoons butter, softened

2 large garlic cloves, finely minced

4 French bread rolls, homemade (see "For a Change" on page 167) or store-bought, sliced in half lengthwise

$^3/_4$ cup pizza sauce

$2^1/_2$ cups diced cooked turkey, mixed white and dark meat

$^3/_4$ cup diced red bell pepper

1 teaspoon dried oregano

1 teaspoon capers

$^1/_4$ teaspoon sea salt

2 tablespoons olive oil

1 cup shredded mozzarella, divided

16 pepperoni slices

$^1/_2$ cup grated Parmesan cheese

1 teaspoon crushed red pepper

1. Start pellet grill and set the temperature control to 225°F.

2. In a small bowl, combine the butter and garlic, stirring to blend.

3. Arrange the sliced rolls cut side up on a baking sheet. Spread each roll half first with the garlic butter and then with the pizza sauce.

4. When the grill reaches the desired temperature, transfer the baking sheet to the grill grate, close the grill door, and allow the rolls to smoke for 15 minutes.

5. While the rolls are smoking, combine the turkey, bell pepper, oregano, capers, and salt in a medium-sized bowl.

6. Heat the olive oil in a medium-sized skillet over medium heat. Add the turkey mixture and cook until thoroughly heated, just a few minutes. Remove from the heat and stir in $^1/_2$ cup of the mozzarella cheese. Set aside.

7. Remove the rolls from the grill, and increase the grill temperature to 375°F.

8. Spoon a portion of the turkey mixture over each of the roll halves. Top with 2 slices of pepperoni and some of the mozzarella, Parmesan cheese, and crushed red pepper.

9. Return the baking sheet to the grill, close the grill door, and cook just until the cheese has melted, 10 to 12 minutes. Serve hot.

THE COMPLETE WOOD PELLET BARBEQUE COOKBOOK

11.

The Sweet Life

Desserts From the Grill

By now, you know that a wood pellet grill can do so much more than cook a steak or a hot dog. It smokes, grills, roasts, braises, and even bakes! That's why your pellet grill can help you make delicious and unique desserts, from cookies and cakes to luscious grilled fruit.

Why make your dessert on a wood pellet grill? First, because it's so easy and so much fun to prepare desserts in the great outdoors. On hot summer days, you can bake cookies without heating up the kitchen or missing out on backyard family activities. Just as important, many desserts are simply better when made in your pellet grill. Even sweet baked goods are more interesting when exposed to a bit of smoke, and fruit is simply transformed on the grill. You see, grilling caramelizes the fruit's natural sugars and softens the flesh, releasing

luscious juices. And again, the smoke works its magic, enhancing flavors and aromas.

This chapter presents my best wood pellet grill desserts. As promised, you'll find a wide selection of delectable baked treats, including sweet and chewy Campfire Oatmeal Cookies, Grilled Pineapple Upside-Down Cake, and nutty Grilled Apple Squares. You'll also discover a variety of luscious fruit recipes, and whether you choose Baked Apples with Rum Raisins, Grilled Fresh Peaches with Cream Cheese and Walnuts, or any other fruitful possibility, you will be impressed by how easy it is to create an extraordinary dessert on your grill.

Often, desserts are an afterthought at a barbeque. The stars are the grilled meats. The following recipes will ensure that at your next backyard cookout, your desserts are as tempting and imaginative as the rest of your meal.

Campfire Oatmeal Cookies

My mom baked the best oatmeal cookies on the planet. She combined a lot of recipe ideas to make them the way she liked them, and they were our favorite snack during many family camping trips in the Rocky Mountains. Don't worry about the wood pellets—at this temperature, there won't be much smoke—but if you can, use freshly grated nutmeg, which intensifies the flavors. Toss in raisins or leave them out, as you prefer.

YIELD: ABOUT 20 LARGER COOKIES OR 30 MINI-COOKIES
RECOMMENDED PELLETS: YOUR CHOICE
MARINATION/SEASONING TIME: NONE
COOKING TIME: ABOUT 12 MINUTES

---

¹/₂ cup butter, softened	¹/₂ teaspoon salt
¹/₂ cup packed brown sugar	¹/₂ teaspoon baking soda
¹/₄ cup granulated sugar	¹/₂ teaspoon ground cinnamon
1 egg	¹/₂ teaspoon grated nutmeg (freshly grated, if possible)
¹/₂ teaspoon vanilla extract	
1 cup quick-cooking oats	³/₄ cup chopped walnuts
³/₄ cup unbleached flour	¹/₂ cup raisins (optional)

1. Start the pellet grill and set the temperature control to 375°F.

2. In a large mixing bowl, use a fork to cream together the butter, brown sugar, and white sugar until well blended and fluffy. Stir in the egg and vanilla extract, and set aside.

3. In a medium-sized mixing bowl, stir together all the dry ingredients except for the walnuts and raisins.

4. Pour the dry ingredients into the butter mixture, and stir to blend well. Then stir in the walnuts and, if desired, the raisins.

5. For a larger yield, use a teaspoon to drop the cookie mixture onto a greased cookie sheet, spacing the spoonfuls 1 inch apart. Otherwise use a tablespoon and separate the drops by 1¹/₂ inches.

6. Place the cookie sheet on the grill grate, close the cover, and bake for approximately 12 minutes, or until lightly browned. (Note that the baking time is the same for both cookie sizes.) Immediately remove the sheets from the grill and allow the cookies to cool completely before you serve them or transfer them to an airtight container.

Luau-Style Grilled Pineapple with Pound Cake

The Hawaiians make grilled pineapple that is so delicious, it's beyond description. A few years ago, I learned their secret: They dip fresh pineapple slices into unsweetened coconut milk, sprinkle the fruit with allspice and raw sugar, and then grill it for several minutes. To complete this luscious dessert, I add a slice of rich store-bought pound cake and, occasionally, a scoop of ice cream or frozen yogurt. For your next backyard Hawaiian vacation, heat up the grill and prepare this delicacy, just as they do on the Big Island.

YIELD: 8 SERVINGS
RECOMMENDED PELLETS: YOUR CHOICE
MARINATION/SEASONING TIME: NONE
COOKING TIME: ABOUT 16 MINUTES

---

2 ripe golden pineapples

14-ounce can unsweetened coconut milk

1$^{1}/_{2}$ cups turbinado sugar*

$^{3}/_{4}$ teaspoon ground allspice

1 pound cake cut into 8 slices

1 quart vanilla ice cream or frozen yogurt (optional)

Mint sprigs for garnish

* Turbinado sugar is a less-refined granulated sugar that is golden in color and retains some molasses flavor. You can find it in most health food stores.

---

1. Start the pellet grill and set the temperature control to 375°F.

2. Peel and core the pineapples and cut each into eight $^{1}/_{2}$-inch slices. Set aside.

3. Shake the coconut milk well to mix. Pour the milk into a wide, shallow bowl or dish. Set aside.

4. Place the sugar and allspice in another wide dish and stir to mix thoroughly.

5. Dip each pineapple slice first into the coconut milk, shaking any excess off, and then into the sugar mixture to coat. As each slice is done, place it on a plate or platter.

6. Arrange the coated pineapple directly on the grill grate, close the lid, and cook for 3 to 4 minutes. Rotate the pineapple if desired to form a crosshatch pattern, and grill for another 3 to 4 minutes. Turn the pineapple slices over and repeat on the second side side.

7. Place a slice of pound cake on each of 8 individual serving plates, and top with 2 slices of grilled pineapple and, if desired, a small scoop of ice cream or frozen yogurt. Garnish with mint and serve.

Grilled Pineapple Upside-Down Cake

This famous American cake is constructed in reverse order: Fruit is arranged in a design at the bottom of the pan so that when the dish is inverted and the baked cake slides out, the fruit is on the top. My great-grandmother was the master of this dessert, and we had it often at her Sunday dinners. When I started baking in the pellet grill, I wondered if the cake would turn out as I remembered, or if it would be influenced by the smoke. To my surprise, it was remarkably like Grandma's, just missing her love. If you add the love back in, this will become a tradition in your family as well.

YIELD: 9 SERVINGS
RECOMMENDED PELLETS: YOUR CHOICE
MARINATION/SEASONING TIME: NONE
COOKING TIME: ABOUT 1 HOUR

TOPPING	CAKE
2 tablespoons cold butter	3 tablespoons butter, softened
3 tablespoons packed dark brown sugar	$1/2$ cup granulated sugar
1 medium-size ripe pineapple, peeled, cored, and cut into 9 rings, or 9 slices canned pineapple, well drained	2 eggs
	$1/4$ cup plus 2 tablespoons milk
	$1/2$ teaspoon vanilla extract
9 maraschino cherries	$1^1/_2$ cups sifted cake flour
	1 teaspoon baking powder

1. Start the pellet grill and set the temperature control to 350°F. Lightly grease the sides of a 9-inch square cake pan with butter.

2. To make the topping, cut the 2 tablespoons of butter into small pieces, and dot the pieces over the bottom of the baking pan. Then sprinkle brown sugar over the bottom.

3. Arrange the pineapple rings over the brown sugar in a decorative pattern, making 3 rows of 3 rings each. Place a cherry inside each of the pineapple rings. Set the pan aside.

4. To make the cake batter, in a medium-sized mixing bowl, beat the softened butter with a whisk or wooden spoon until soft and creamy. Blend the sugar into the butter and stir until the mixture is light and fluffy.

5. Add the eggs one at a time to the butter and sugar mixture, beating each in until it is thoroughly blended. Stir in the milk and the vanilla extract.

6. Place the flour in a small bowl and stir in the baking powder. Using a large rubber spatula or a wooden spoon, fold the flour into the egg mixture until well blended.

7. Spoon the batter into the prepared baking pan, being careful not to dislodge the cherries or pineapple rings. Smooth down the top of the batter with a spatula or knife.

8. When the grill reaches the desired temperature, place the baking pan in the center of the grate, close the grill door, and bake for 50 to 60 minutes, or until the cake is golden brown and a skewer or toothpick inserted in the middle of the cake comes out clean.

9. Remove the baking pan from the grill, and allow the cake to cool for 5 minutes.

10. Run a knife blade between the cake and the sides of the pan to loosen the cake. Place a serving plate over the pan, and invert the pan so that the platter is sitting on the counter. Lift the pan, and the cake should slip out easily.

11. Serve the cake warm, or cool completely before cutting into squares and serving.

Buying and Preparing Fresh Pineapple

Fresh pineapple is bursting with flavor and especially delectable when used in recipes like Luau-Style Grilled Pineapple with Pound Cake (page 181) and Grilled Pineapple Upside-Down Cake (page 182).

When buying fresh pineapple, choose one that is firm and free of soft spots. It should have skin that is a brightly colored mix of yellow and green and a crown of leaves that are supple and green. Avoid pineapple with completely green skin, as this indicates that it was picked too soon and will not ripen properly. Fresh pineapple should also smell slightly sweet. No scent is an indication that the fruit isn't ripe, while a fermented smell means it is past its prime.

Because of pineapple's inedible core and "spiky" skin, peeling and coring it can be challenging. Following these simple steps will help:

1. Place the pineapple on its side on a cutting board. Using a sturdy serrated knife, cut off the crown and the base.

2. Stand the pineapple up and use a slight sawing motion to cut away the skin, moving from the top of the fruit to the bottom. If any spikes remain on the fruit, remove them with a paring knife or a fruit corer.

3. To make slices, simply cut the edible fruit as desired. Then remove the core from each slice with a sharp knife. To make spears, halve the fruit lengthwise before slicing into the desired shape.

Grandma's Grilled Berry Cobbler

My grandmother started her day early, preparing breakfast for the family. She then packed the lunches and sent us off to school or work. When the house was empty and quiet, she worked her magic preparing the evening meal. We kids especially loved her desserts, and this fruit cobbler was a family favorite. Thank you, Grandma!

YIELD: 8 SERVINGS
RECOMMENDED PELLETS: MAPLE OR APPLE
MARINATION/SEASONING TIME: NONE
COOKING TIME: ABOUT 45 MINUTES

2 quarts vanilla ice cream

FILLING

6 cups fresh blueberries

1 cup $1/2$-inch cubes fresh peaches (1 large or 2 smaller peaches)

$1/2$ cup sugar

$1/4$ cup unbleached all-purpose flour

2 tablespoons fresh lemon juice

1 tablespoon grated lemon zest

CRUMBLE TOPPING

$1^1/2$ cups unbleached all-purpose flour

$1/2$ cup sugar

$1/3$ cup packed brown sugar

$1/2$ teaspoon salt

$3/4$ cup chilled butter, cut into $1^1/2$-inch pieces

1. To make the crumble topping, place the flour, sugars, and salt in a medium-size bowl, and stir to blend. Using a fork or a pastry blender, cut the butter into the flour mixture until you have a coarse crumb-like mixture. Cover and place in the refrigerator for 30 minutes.

2. Start the pellet grill and set the temperature control to 375°F. Grease a 12-inch cast-iron skillet with nonstick cooking spray or butter.

3. To make the filling, place all of the filling ingredients in a large bowl and stir to blend. Pour the mixture into the prepared skillet and spread evenly. Then distribute the chilled crumble topping over the fruit mixture.

4. When the grill reaches the desired temperature, place the skillet on the grate, close the grill door, and bake for 45 minutes or until the top is slightly browned. Do not let it brown too much as it will continue to cook after it is removed from the grill.

5. Remove the skillet from the grill and allow the cobbler to cool for 15 to 20 minutes, or until it is warm, but not hot. Scoop individual servings into dessert bowls, top each with a large scoop of ice cream, and serve.

For a Change

■ To make Grandma's Grilled Peach Cobbler, replace the blueberries with 6 cups of cubed peeled peaches (8 to 10 peaches), and prepare as directed in the recipe.

■ To make Grandma's Grilled Apple Cobbler, use 6 cups of cubed peeled apples (10 to 12 apples) instead of the blueberries and peaches. Also replace the granulated sugar in the filling with packed brown sugar, and add 2 teaspoons of cinnamon to the filling.

Grilled Figs

Baking enhances the fig's natural sweetness, and because figs are not often served as dessert, they provide a unique and elegant end to your meal. In the market, look for unblemished fruit that feels heavy for its size. If you see beads of sugar juice around the stem, you'll know that the figs are fully ripe.

YIELD: 6 SERVINGS
RECOMMENDED PELLETS: MAPLE OR APPLE
MARINATION/SEASONING TIME: NONE
COOKING TIME: 10 TO 20 MINUTES

6 firm but ripe figs, halved lengthwise	2 teaspoons brandy or dark rum
2 tablespoons honey	$1/2$ teaspoon ground cinnamon
	Heavy cream

1. Start the pellet grill and set the temperature control to 350°F.

2. Spray a shallow baking pan with nonstick cooking spray, and arrange the figs on the pan, cut side up. Drizzle the figs with honey and brandy or rum; then sprinkle with a generous pinch of cinnamon.

3. When the grill reaches the desired temperature, transfer the pan to the grill grate and close the door. Bake for 10 minutes, or until the figs are heated through and soft, but still hold their shape. If they are not yet done, return them to the grill. They may require up to 20 minutes of cooking time.

4. Remove the baking pan from the grill and allow the figs to cool. Serve warm or at room temperature accompanied with heavy cream.

Grilled Apple Squares

After a grand meal of pork roast or grilled chicken, nothing satisfies like a warm and spicy dessert. This one fits the bill. A nutty brown sugar crust is covered with a delicious apple mixture, and then baked on the grill. A topping of whipped cream flavored with sugar and fruit liqueur adds a final luxurious touch.

YIELD: 6 SERVINGS
RECOMMENDED PELLETS: YOUR CHOICE
MARINATION/SEASONING TIME: NONE
COOKING TIME: ABOUT 30 MINUTES

CRUST

1 cup flour

¹/₂ cup packed brown sugar

¹/₄ cup chilled butter, cut into ¹/₂-inch pieces

¹/₂ cup chopped pecans

APPLE TOPPING

1 egg, beaten

¹/₂ cup sour cream

1 teaspoon ground cinnamon

¹/₂ teaspoon baking soda

¹/₂ teaspoon vanilla extract

1 large or 2 small Granny Smith apples, peeled and finely chopped (about 1¹/₂ cups)

WHIPPED CREAM TOPPING

1 cup whipping cream

3 tablespoons powdered sugar

2 tablespoons apple or pear liqueur

1 Granny Smith apple, cored and sliced into 12 pieces for garnish

1. Start the pellet grill and set the temperature control to 375°F. Lightly grease a square 8 x 8-inch baking pan with butter, and set aside.

2. To make the crust, in a medium-sized bowl, combine the flour and brown sugar. Using a fork or pastry blender, cut the butter into the flour mixture until you have a coarse crumb-like mixture. Stir in the chopped pecans.

3. Measure out 1¹/₄ cups of the crumb mixture and place it in the prepared baking pan. Press it onto the bottom of the pan to form a crust. Reserve the remaining crust mixture.

4. In a small bowl, stir together the egg, sour cream, cinnamon, baking soda, and vanilla extract. Pour this mixture into the reserved crust mixture, and stir until it is well mixed and has an appearance similar to that of cottage cheese. Then stir in the chopped apples.

5. Spoon the apple mixture over the crust, spreading it as evenly as possible.

6. When the grill reaches the desired temperature, place the baking pan on the grate, close the grill door, and bake for 30 minutes, or until a toothpick inserted in the center comes out clean. Remove the pan from the grill and allow it to cool for 15 to 20 minutes, depending on whether you want to serve the squares warm or at room temperature.

7. While the apple squares are cooling, place the whipping cream in a large mixing bowl and use a hand-held or standing electric mixer to beat the cream until it begins to thicken. Gradually add the sugar and liqueur, beating until the mixture forms soft peaks. Keep the mixture refrigerated until you're ready to serve.

8. Cut the crust into 6 rectangles and place each piece on a serving plate. Add a dollop of whipped cream, garnish with 2 apple slices, and serve.

Baking with Apples

With so many apple varieties available, it can be challenging to know which ones are best for baking. Your favorite eating apple, while crunchy and delicious, may become mealy or mushy when baked. My feeling is that you can't go wrong with a tart, crisp Granny Smith, which is considered a premium all-purpose apple. Delicious raw, the Granny Smith is also a good choice for baking (see the recipe on page 188). When slices or chunks of a Granny Smith are baked in stuffings, pies, crisps, or desserts like my Grilled Apple Squares, they maintain their shape and retain a good apple taste.

There are, however, a number of other good baking apple varieties. In addition to holding up well, the best choices should have a sweet-tart taste. Since most baked goods contain sugar, a very sweet apple will absorb the sugar and likely become too sweet.

After the Granny Smith, here are my runners-up for the best baking apples:

Cortland. Firm textured, good sweet-tart balance, very juicy.

Empire. Firm textured, slightly tart.

Fuji. Firm textured, mildly sweet, juicy.

Jonathan. Fairly tart, juicy.

Rome. Mildly sweet, slightly tart.

Most apples are harvested between September and November, although many varieties store well and are available year-round. When buying apples, choose those that are firm with smooth skin and good color. Avoid fruit that has bruises or soft spots, as well as those that are dried and wrinkled. Store apples in the refrigerator or in a cool dark spot until you're ready to fire up your wood pellet grill and make some magic.

Baked Apples with Rum Raisins

My mom baked apples in a conventional oven, and they were delicious, but since we've moved our "oven" outdoors, we have added a bit of smoky intrigue to this delight. If you want only a hint of smoky flavor, use apple or alder pellets. For a more pronounced flavor, opt for maple. Serve with a dollop of vanilla bean or cinnamon ice cream to raise this simple dessert to the next level.

YIELD: 6 SERVINGS
RECOMMENDED PELLETS: APPLE, ALDER, OR MAPLE
MARINATION/SEASONING TIME: NONE
COOKING TIME: ABOUT 1 HOUR

$1/4$ **cup raisins**

Rum

6 large baking apples, such as Rome, Cortland, or Granny Smith

$1/2$ **lemon**

$1/4$ **cup brown sugar**

$1/4$ **cup plus 2 tablespoons graham cracker crumbs**

$1/4$ **cup chopped walnuts**

$1/4$ **teaspoon ground cinnamon**

1 quart vanilla or cinnamon ice cream, or half-and-half (optional)

---

1. Place the raisins in a small bowl and add enough rum to cover. Allow the raisins to soak in the rum for 30 minutes or until plump.

2. Start the pellet grill and set the temperature control to 180°F or "Smoke."

3. Cut a thin slice off the bottom of each apple so it will sit flat in a baking dish. Using an apple corer or a sharp paring knife, core each apple to within about $1/2$ inch of the bottom. To prevent browning, rub the bottom and top of each apple with the lemon and squeeze a few drops of juice into the center cavity. Set aside.

4. In a small bowl, prepare the filling by combining the brown sugar, graham cracker crumbs, walnuts, and cinnamon. When the raisins are plump, drain off any excess rum and gently fold the raisins into the mixture, being careful not to break them.

5. Using a small spoon, fill the cavity of each apple about half full with the filling mixture. Divide any remaining mixture evenly among the apples.

6. Arrange the apples in a metal baking pan large enough to allow smoke to circulate between the apples. Place the pan in the grill, close the cover, and allow the apples to smoke for 25 minutes.

7. Increase the grill temperature to 350° F. Allow the apples to bake for approximately 30 to 40 minutes, or until they are tender, but not mushy, when pierced with a fork or a sharp knife.

8. Serve the apples hot from the grill or chill before serving. If desired, accompany each portion with a scoop of ice cream or some half-and-half.

Uncle Bob's Grilled Pears

In our family, it's a given that when Uncle Bob adds something new to the menu, it is going to be spectacular, and this dessert is over the top. Pears are soaked in a mixture of pear liqueur and spices, and then grilled with maple or apple pellets until they are tender, sweet, and downright irresistible. Serve them with half-and-half, with ice cream, or with nothing at all. And make plenty, because one is simply not enough.

YIELD: 4 SERVINGS
RECOMMENDED PELLETS: MAPLE OR APPLE
MARINATION/SEASONING TIME: 20 MINUTES
COOKING TIME: ABOUT 40 MINUTES

4 large ripe pears	**MARINADE**
Mint sprigs for garnish	1/4 cup pear liqueur
1 quart vanilla ice cream or half-and-half	1/8 teaspoon ground cinnamon
	1/8 teaspoon ground cloves
	Pinch allspice

1. Make the marinade by stirring together all of the marinade ingredients in a small bowl. Set aside.

2. Cut a thin slice off the bottom of each pear so it will sit flat in the baking dish. Using an apple corer or a sharp paring knife, core each pear to within 1/2 inch of the bottom.

3. Spray a metal baking dish with nonstick cooking spray and arrange the pears upright in the pan. Brush the marinade over both the exterior and interior of the fruit so that it has maximum contact with the marinade. Allow the pears to soak up the marinade for 20 minutes, brushing on additional marinade as it is absorbed into the fruit until you have used up all of the liquid.

4. Start the pellet grill and set the temperature control to 350°F. As the grill is heating up, place the baking dish on the grill grate and close the door so that the smoke will interact with the marinade. Roast the pears for about 40 minutes, or until they are easily pierced with a fork or sharp knife.

5. Serve the pears hot from the grill or cool slightly before you garnish with mint and serve with vanilla ice cream or half-and-half.

Grilled Fresh Peaches
with Cream Cheese and Walnuts

Juicy in-season fruit makes a great start for any dessert. In this recipe, ripe peaches are roasted on the grill, filled with a mixture of cream cheese and walnuts, and drizzled with honey. Simple yet elegant, these peaches will have your guests asking for more

YIELD: 4 SERVINGS
RECOMMENDED PELLETS: YOUR CHOICE
MARINATION/SEASONING TIME: NONE
COOKING TIME: ABOUT 25 MINUTES

2 freestone peaches, peeled, halved, and pitted (see the inset below for peeling directions)

2 tablespoons softened cream cheese

2 tablespoons coarsely chopped walnuts

2 teaspoons honey

1. Spray the grill grate with nonstick cooking spray. Start the pellet grill and set the temperature control to 350°F.

2. When the grill reaches the desired temperature, arrange the peaches, cut side down, directly on the grate. Close the grill door and allow the peaches to roast for about 20 minutes or until easily pierced with a skewer or toothpick. If desired, rotate the peaches after the first 10 minutes or so to create crosshatch grill marks.

How to Peel a Peach

Peeling peaches for a grilled dessert can be time-consuming and even a little frustrating—unless you know a few tricks. Follow these steps to peel your peaches quickly and easily.

1. Wash the peaches thoroughly in cold running water. Then set them aside.

2. In a saucepan, bring water to a boil; then remove it from the heat. Fill a bowl with ice and water, and set it aside.

3. Submerge the peaches in the hot water for about 45 seconds. Then use a slotted spoon to transfer the peaches to the ice water, and allow to sit for 20 seconds.

4. Remove the peaches from the ice bath and use a paring knife to gently cut the peel at the end of each peach. Using your fingers, carefully remove the peel. It should be easy to separate the peel from the fruit. If not, repeat the hot bath followed by the ice water.

THE COMPLETE WOOD PELLET BARBEQUE COOKBOOK

3. While the peaches are roasting, place the cream cheese and walnuts in a small bowl, and mix to form a soft paste.

4. Turn the peaches over so that the pit side is on top. Spoon a fourth of the cream cheese mixture into the hollow of each peach half, and drizzle with a little honey. Close the grill cover and roast for approximately 5 additional minutes.

5. Remove the peaches from the grill and serve immediately.

The Best Dessert Wines

All dessert wines have one thing in common: They are sweet and deliciously complex in flavor. This means that they can either be sipped along with dessert or enjoyed on their own after a satisfying grilled or barbequed meal. The following wines—which are some of my personal favorites—can each be paired with one or more of the desserts featured in this chapter or savored in lieu of dessert.

Port. Originating in Portugal, Port-style wine is now produced all over the world. This rich red wine is generally sweet, but can also be dry or semi-dry. It is usually made from late-harvest grapes which, after fermentation, are fortified with a neutral grape brandy to result in alcohol levels between 18 and 21 percent. Port is great with grilled pears and figs. It can also be enjoyed with dark chocolate desserts and Stilton cheese.

Madeira. Made in Portugal, this red wine is similar to Port in that it is fortified with brandy. Madeira can be created in many styles, one of which is a sweet wine that beautifully complements desserts. The taste of this wine is toffee caramel-like because of the heat used during the winemaking process, and highly complex due to long aging in wood casks. Enjoy it with baked apples or grilled apple squares. It also complements desserts that feature milk chocolate, mocha, nuts, or caramel.

Late Harvest Riesling. After the first harvest, when wine grapes are normally picked, some fruit is left on the vines to continue to ripen and develop additional sugars. Just before the grapes become raisins, they are harvested and processed like a Port wine, but without fortification. The magnificent result—a sweet white wine with intense fruit flavors—is a perfect match with grilled figs, pears, or pineapple, and also complements any cake that includes fruit.

Sauternes and Barsacs. These sweet white wines are made from Sémillon and Sauvignon Blanc late-harvest grapes that develop a fungus—a "noble rot"—that works magic with the fruit. Sweet, with apricot-like flavors, Sauternes and Barsacs are generally well-balanced and luscious, with high residual sugar and nearly 13 percent alcohol. Serve them with grilled pineapple or pears, baked apples, or apple squares, as well as with fruit tarts, crème brûlée, and caramel and hazelnut desserts.

Muscat. Made of one of the oldest varieties of grapes, this white wine is generally sweet with vibrant floral and citrus flavors, and aromatics of orange, tangerine, and musk. It is a great match with berry and peach cobblers.

Resources

When cooking on your wood pellet grill, high-quality herbs and spices are needed to create distinctive rubs, seasoning blends, and barbeque sauces. Many of these products can be found at your local supermarket, but an even wider range is available through the companies listed below. Also included below are a number of sources for grilling tools and accessories. All of the following companies can be contacted by phone or through their websites.

HERBS, SPICES, AND FLAVORINGS

McCormick and Company
18 Loveton Circle
Sparks, MD 21152
Phone: 800-632-5847
Website: www.mccormick.com

Founded in 1889, McCormick is a great resource for herbs, spices, spice blends, barbeque spice blends, recipes, and information on seasonings.

My Spice Sage, Inc.
5774 Mosholu Avenue
Bronx, NY 10471
Phone: 877-890-5244
Website: www.myspicesage.com

This company offers over 400 spices, herbs, and seasoning blends at wholesale prices. The website fills you in on each product's country of origin and other helpful information.

Spice Barn
762 Carle Avenue
Lewis Center, OH 43035
Phone: 866-670-9040
Website: www.spicebarn.com

Spice barn provides high-quality herbs, spices, and seasoning blends, including unusual ingredients such as Worcestershire powder. Spice jars and labels are also available.

GRILLING COOKWARE AND ACCESSORIES

Chefs
5070 Centennial Boulevard
Colorado Springs, CO 80919
Phone: 800-338-3232
Website: www.chefs catalog.com

At Chefs, you'll find a huge selection of kitchen tools, grilling pans and baskets, and other items designed for use on the grill.

Cooking.com

4086 Del Rey Avenue
Marina Del Rey, CA 90292
Phone: 310-450-3270
Website: www.cooking.com

In addition to a long list of kitchen items, Cooking.com offers a good selection of grilling tools and cookware.

Kitchen Fantasy

27576 Ynez Road, Suite H1
Temecula, CA 92591
Phone: 951-693-4264
Website: www.kitchenfantasy.com

A small business offering high-quality goods at reasonable prices, Kitchen Fantasy sells cookware, kitchen gadgets, cutlery, and cooking utensils and tools.

Sur La Table

P.O. Box 840
Brownsburg, IN 46112
Phone: 800-243-0852
Website: www.surlatable.com

Sur la Table offers a wide range of grilling pans and accessories, including grill baskets, woks, and pans; basting pots and brushes; rib racks; vertical roasters; grill tongs; and more.

Williams-Sonoma

Phone: 877-812-6235
Website: www.williams-sonoma.com

This company sells a full-line of grill-related products, including skewer sets, tongs and other grilling tools, thermometers, and grilling cookware.

METRIC CONVERSION TABLES

COMMON LIQUID CONVERSIONS

Measurement	=	Milliliters
1/4 teaspoon	=	1.25 milliliters
1/2 teaspoon	=	2.50 milliliters
3/4 teaspoon	=	3.75 milliliters
1 teaspoon	=	5.00 milliliters
1 1/4 teaspoons	=	6.25 milliliters
1 1/2 teaspoons	=	7.50 milliliters
1 3/4 teaspoons	=	8.75 milliliters
2 teaspoons	=	10.0 milliliters
1 tablespoon	=	15.0 milliliters
2 tablespoons	=	30.0 milliliters

Measurement	=	Liters
1/4 cup	=	0.06 liters
1/2 cup	=	0.12 liters
3/4 cup	=	0.18 liters
1 cup	=	0.24 liters
1 1/4 cups	=	0.30 liters
1 1/2 cups	=	0.36 liters
2 cups	=	0.48 liters
2 1/2 cups	=	0.60 liters
3 cups	=	0.72 liters
3 1/2 cups	=	0.84 liters
4 cups	=	0.96 liters
4 1/2 cups	=	1.08 liters
5 cups	=	1.20 liters
5 1/2 cups	=	1.32 liters

CONVERTING FAHRENHEIT TO CELSIUS

Fahrenheit	=	Celsius
200–205	=	95
220–225	=	105
245–250	=	120
275	=	135
300–305	=	150
325–330	=	165
345–350	=	175
370–375	=	190
400–405	=	205
425–430	=	220
445–450	=	230
470–475	=	245
500	=	260

CONVERSION FORMULAS

LIQUID

When You Know	Multiply By	To Determine
teaspoons	5.0	milliliters
tablespoons	15.0	milliliters
fluid ounces	30.0	milliliters
cups	0.24	liters
pints	0.47	liters
quarts	0.95	liters

WEIGHT

When You Know	Multiply By	To Determine
ounces	28.0	grams
pounds	0.45	kilograms

Index

THE COMPLETE WOOD PELLET BARBEQUE COOKBOOK

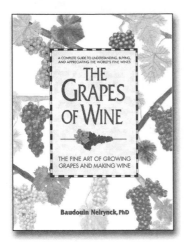